Sport in the Global Society

General Editor: J.A. Mangan

ITALIAN FASCISM AND THE FEMALE BODY

SPORT IN THE GLOBAL SOCIETY
General Editor: J.A. Mangan

The interest in sports studies around the world is growing and will continue to do so. This unique series combines aspects of the expanding study of *sport in the global society*, providing comprehensiveness and comparison under one editorial umbrella. It is particularly timely, with studies in the political, cultural, anthropological, ethnographic, social, economic, geographical and aesthetic elements of sport proliferating in institutions of higher education.

Eric Hobsbawm once called sport one of the most significant practices of the late nineteenth century. Its significance was even more marked in the late twentieth century and will continue to grow in importance into the new millennium as the world develops into a 'global village' sharing the English language, technology and sport.

Other Titles in the Series

Italian Fascism and the Female Body

Sport, Submissive Women and Strong Mothers

GIGLIOLA GORI

University of Urbino

R Routledge
Taylor & Francis Group

LONDON AND NEW YORK

First published 2004
by Routledge
2 Park Square, Milton Park, Abingdon, Oxfordshire OX14 4RN

Simultaneously published in the USA and Canada

by Routledge
29 West 35th Street, New York, NY 10001

Routledge is an imprint of the Taylor & Francis Group

© 2004 Gigliola Gori

British Library Cataloguing in Publication Data

ISBN 0 415 345995 (hbk)
ISBN 0 415 346002 (pbk)
ISSN 1368-9789

Library of Congress Cataloging-in-Publication Data

A catalog record for this book has been requested

Typeset in 10.75pt on 12.5pt Times New Roman by Cambridge Photosetting Services, Cambridge
Printed in Great Britain by MPG Books Ltd, Victoria Square, Bodmin, Cornwall

Dedication

To my father Lino and my mother Elsa, who spent their early youth and jointly founded a new family under Fascism

Contents

Contents

List of Illustrations

Foreword

The theory and the practice of sports in the Soviet Union and in Nazi Germany have been studied by hundreds of scholars who have produced thousands of books and articles, many of which have been translated into English. There have also been, in recent years, a number of important books on the sports of Communist China. The sports of Fascist Italy, however, have received much less attention. Italian historians have, of course, described the ideological foundations, the institutions, and the achievements of sports during the Fascist era, but very little of their work has appeared in English. Victoria De Grazia's *The Culture of Consent* (1981) remains a good introduction to the organisation of leisure by the Fascist regime, but there is no translation of Felice Fabrizio's *Sport e Fascismo* (1976) or of the valuable documents collected in *Atleti in Camicia Nera* (1983).

Publishing a revised and expanded translation of Gigliola Gori's *L'Atleta e la Nazione* (1996) seems, at first glance, an odd way to remedy the deficit (in English) of available work on Fascist sports. Her focus is on *female* athletes rather than on their far more numerous and athletically successful male counterparts. In fact, although it is indeed regrettable that we lack more general studies of Fascist sports, J. A. Mangan is right to include a translation of *Italian Fascism and the Female Body* in his grandly inclusive series on the social history of sport. Gori's book seeks – successfully in my opinion – to answer the most intriguing of the many questions asked about Fascist sports. Some of these questions are concerned with theory. How did the Fascist regime, which made the promotion of athleticism a central aspect of its ideology, deal with Italy's traditional relegation of women to the restrictive roles of wife and mother? Specifically, how did the *Fascisti* who proclaimed that Mussolini wanted female athletes ('*Il Duce le volle sportive*') square that bold slogan with the Roman Catholic Church's adamant conviction that Italian women were divinely destined to produce *bambini* rather than Olympic medals? Some of the questions concern practice. Did the regime's promotion of female athleticism actually motivate significant numbers of Italian women to participate in sports? Was female participation emancipatory, as many have claimed, then and now, or was it merely another instance of the state's instrumentalisation of 'docile' female bodies, as followers of Michel Foucault have insisted?

After discussing the 'cult of virility' and its literal embodiment in Italy's sport-addicted *Duce*, Gori takes us back to nineteenth-century debates over physical education and the role of sports in women's emancipation from the constricting bonds of traditional femininity. When she returns to a treatment of the Fascist era, she discusses not only the regime's oftentimes contradictory models of femininity but also the institutional networks established within the educational system and outside of it. (Like Nazi Germany, like the USSR in its Stalinist phase, Fascist Italy was prolific in the creation of 'after work' ['*dopolavoro*'] organisations.) It seems absolutely right, in a study that includes a number of brief biographical sketches that the book's climax is a lively discussion of – and a fascinating interview with – Ondina Valla, the Olympic champion (1936) who may well still be Italy's most famous female athlete.

In her concluding chapter, Gori asks two important questions: 'First, did physical and sporting activity really increase among Italian women during the Fascist era? Second, did the consciousness of possessing an athletic body, well-trained within Fascist organisations, really promote the emancipation of at least some Italian women, in spite of the masculine hegemony of the time?' Gori answers cautiously but clearly: 'The answers to both questions cannot but be positive.' Readers of this meticulously researched and carefully argued study will agree.

If Gori's excellent work is a harbinger of work yet to be written (and translated into English), by her and her colleagues, the complaints about a paucity of research with which I began this foreword will – happily – become passé.

ALLEN GUTTMANN
Amherst College

Series Editor's Foreword

'The study of history', A.L. Rowse once famously declared, 'leads straight to an informed and responsible concern with politics'.[1] The statement will serve as an apt description of *Italian Fascism and the Female Body: Sport, Submissive Women and Strong Mothers*.

Le coeur a ses raisons and perceptive readers will appreciate that at the heart of *Italian Fascism and the Female body* is a concern,implicit and explicit, with the historic misogyny of patriachy. Woman, claimed Nietzche, in *The Anti Christ* was God's second mistake. Something of this attitude pervaded Italian Fascism and its calculated use of women as instruments of political purpose. Fascism turned Orwellian words into action. In Orwell's nightmare world of *1984*, it will be remembered, '… the Party slogan was "who controls the past controls the future: who controls the present controls the past". The result is a continuing changeless present. "History has stopped. Nothing exists except an endless present in which the Party is always right"'.[2]

Gori has written a fascinating study of righteous authoritarian female conditioning.

Antonio Salandra, the pre-fascist Italian prime minister, was of the view that 'active minorities … in every great country carry along with them the inert majority'.[3] However, at the centre of the Italian fascist totalitarian effort there was a paradox. Even the most constrained, subdued and regulated, on occasion, due to the resiliance, complexity and contrariness of the human psyche, can turn disadvantage to advantage. Furthermore, sometimes the dilemnas of dictatorial regimes can assist this. Gori makes this quite clear.

In recent considerations of imperial sport and its relationship to politics, concern has centred on the gap between the intentions of imperial actors and actual imperial outcomes.[4] The same concern with avowed intentions and unexpected consequences, is apparent, in an European setting (the source of so much recent global imperialism), in *Italian Fascism and the Female Body*. Human obduracy can be a real force in history.

Three remarkable *Tours de l'Horizens* of women, sport and totalitarianism now grace the series Sport in the Global Society. All three authors are to be congratulated on their seminal contributions, in equal measure, to gender studies,women's studies and sports studies.

J.A. MANGAN
Series Editor, Sport in the Global Society.
March, 2004.

NOTES

1. A.L. Rowse, *The Use of History* (London: The English Universities Press, 1963), revised edition, p.53.

2. See Jonathan Clarke, *Our Shadowed Present* M*odernism, Postmodernism and History* (London: Atlantic Press, 2003), p.257.

3. Quoted in Richard F. Hamilton and Holger H. Herwig, 'Italy' in Richard F. Hamilton and Holger H. Herwig (eds.), *The Origins of World War 1* (Cambridge: CUP, 2003), p.386.

4. See, for example, Boria Majumdar and J.A. Mangan (eds.) *Sport in South Asian Society; Past and Present* (London: Routledge, 2004), passim.

5. The two earlier volumes, of course, are Fan Hong, *Footbinding, Feminism and Freedom: the Liberation of Women's Bodies in Modern China* (London: Frank Cass. 1997) and Dong Jinxia, *Women, Sport and Society in Modern China: Holding Up More Than Half The Sky* (London: Frank Cass, 2003).

Preface

This book is the result of research that started a long time ago. It aims to examine the extent to which Fascism opened the way to female physical education and sport in Italy. By using all manner of available media Fascist propaganda spread throughout the country and the world the image of a strong nation of healthy sportspeople, including women, yet we do not know much about the gender issues raised by this propaganda.

The problem is that, while the phenomenon of mass sport during the Fascist era has been studied by scholars of Fascism in general, and also analysed in specific books on sport, the emphasis has generally been on the more prominent male sector of sport. In contrast, the female sector, which was underrepresented in Fascist times, has not been studied deeply and constitutes an interesting field for further investigation. Attention will also be paid to the previous development of female physical culture, starting with the pioneering efforts made in the nineteenth century, in order to better qualify and quantify the impact of Fascism on Italian women's sport. This book is thus broadly dedicated to the specific theme of female 'athleticisation', but will also examine the possible effect of this process on women's emancipation in a country founded on traditional paternalistic values and hegemony.

During the Fascist era there were several different moral and even aesthetic models for women, owing to the ambiguity of Fascist policy, which stressed maternity and, at the same time, demanded female engagement in society. Women had to move strictly within an old-fashioned framework structured by medicine and eugenics, religion and traditional education, while, on the other hand, the country aspired to modernity and made sport into a national myth. It was difficult for general female emancipation, which had been promised by the Fascist revolution and was actually occurring in other industrialised nations, to advance under the regime because of the Italian tradition of male hegemony. However, the very engagement of women in some sporting activities promoted and supported gender emancipation, as will be demonstrated in the present work.

General framework

The late nineteenth century, the period of the formation and strengthening of the newly constituted Italian nation state, was open to initiatives in favour of gymnastics in the name of patriotism and 'hygiene', influenced both by positivism and by scientific studies. Women were also involved in these new programmes, although in a peculiar and restricted way. The culture of the female body introduced a new lifestyle, and gave at least some women a certain consciousness of their identity and rights, promoting their acceptance within Italian society.

However, in the tumultuous first decades of the twentieth century, the growth of nationalism, and the advent of new and revolutionary ideologies, supported Italian participation in the First World War, and led to the subsequent rise of the Fascist movement. In these years a few women were made more aware of their identity and rights by feminist movements. These 'new women', opposing the traditional model inherited from the patriarchal culture of the nineteenth century, were more involved in work, politics and society.

Nevertheless, under the subsequent Fascist regime the mass of women were forced to retreat from public life and return to being submissive to men, even though at the same time they were increasingly expected to strengthen their bodies and their willpower within Fascist organisations, adapting as best they could to the contradictory female models imposed by the *Duce* (Leader) Benito Mussolini and other members of the Fascist hierarchy. The Fascist 'new woman' had to stress and combine antithetical values in different ways: respect for tradition came to mean spirituality and tenderness, while modernity meant physicality and ruthlessness.

However, women's collective engagement in physical education and suitable sports contributed to renewing the traditional feminine image. Women became self-assertive, ready to leave their homes and families, and to fight for ideological beliefs, in spite of the hegemony of masculine identities and misogynous feelings during the Fascist era.

Mussolini's government undertook a number of initiatives in relation to physical education and sport. These were considered to be the regime's main means for enhancing the health, fighting spirit, devotion and dedication of Italian society, with the aim of making it possible for Italians to accept even martyrdom in the Fascist cause. Mussolini's aim was to forge 'new men', drawing on a myth, partly of Nietzschean origin, that had found supporters among intellectuals in Italy at the beginning of the twentieth century, preparing the way for the advent of Fascism.

Fascism intended to achieve full control of Italian society by reorganising the lives of citizens of both sexes, including, of course, the education of the body and leisure activities. The opening up of numerous different activities by both the Ministry for Education and the National Fascist Party induced the great mass of Italians to practise all kinds of sport and other recreational activities, with the assistance and under the guardianship of the regime.

Although the regime deprived the people of any autonomy by organising all their time, it gave them rationalised and assisted leisure, financed by the 'social state', in order to obtain the widest possible consensus concerning the political choices made by Fascism. In gymnasiums, stadiums and sports grounds alike, politics was banished in favour of a sort of 'activism' that attracted the masses if only because, for the first time in Italian history, people could have a free choice, at no cost, among activities that had previously been reserved for the highest classes alone. The common people could start to practise many kinds of sports, and could also visit beautiful Italian cities and the most fashionable tourist sites, travelling on the cheap 'popular' trains made available by the state. They could also send their children to the numerous holiday resorts owned by the state. Not surprisingly, many people enjoyed the very pleasant sensation of perceiving themselves to be at the centre of the regime's attention. As for Fascism itself, the extensive services offered for the development of physical education and sport had to accomplish some well-defined educational tasks, regenerating the supposedly weak character of Italians by transforming them into a race of strong-willed, courageous 'new men', and removing citizens from excessively private ways of life into a more social and collective lifestyle.

Although Mussolini himself was not a racist, he undoubtedly believed in the notion of an 'Italian race', simply meaning the Italian people, as the concrete and material expression of 'the Nation', and aimed at forging authentic Italians. In a speech delivered to the Chamber of Deputies on 26 May 1934 the *Duce* affirmed that 'Fascism will devote itself more deeply to the character of the Italian people, instead of furnishing their brains too sumptuously.'[1] This task was carried out by the schools and other educational institutions, as well as by social organisations, through a complete overhaul of the pre-existing institutions and the unceasing spread of propaganda through the press, radio and newsreels.

In fact, having very quickly abolished those sporting societies that were independent and therefore beyond the reach of Fascist ideology – notably Boy Scout associations, and groups imbued with Catholicism or socialism – the National Fascist Party framed sporting activities strictly within the terms of the *Carta dello Sport* (Sports Charter) of 1928, which proclaimed the values to be instilled through physical education and sport practised in the numerous Fascist youth organisations. Young people were also urged to develop a competitive spirit through periodic cultural and sporting competitions, such as the *Ludi Juveniles*, the *Agonali* and the *Littoriali*, which involved spectacular displays aimed at impressing spectators.

In the 1920s the involvement of women in sporting activities was encouraged by the Fascist movement, in line with the revolutionary spirit of the first period of Fascism, which exalted the body and its activity. However, during the first half of the 1930s, when the regime had become fully established, the campaign launched to promote the regime's demographic policy urged women to remain in their homes, and to become submissive wives and strong mothers of numerous children. Physical activities for women were reduced to basic gymnastics and a few suitable sports, which were to be practised within Fascist organisations such as the *Opera Nazionale Balilla* (ONB), under the supervision of physicians specialising in sports medicine. Despite this change of emphasis, the Catholic Church remained opposed to the 'athleticisation' of women. The resulting opposition, as well as other forms of opposition to a number of Fascist policies for sport, came to be subsumed within the wider debate on youth education in which the Church and the state took up antithetical positions.

The hegemonic Fascist ideology thus had to compromise with the dominant role of the Church in Italy, not only in relation to religion in the strict sense, but also in relation to those political issues and youth activities that concerned the Vatican. The power and prestige of the Catholic Church among Italians had to be taken seriously by Mussolini, who found a solution to his potential problem by securing consensus through the Concordat between his regime and the Vatican. The Concordat (also known as the Lateran Pacts) was negotiated over a long period, entirely in secret, and then formally signed on 11 February 1929. This historic document, presented as securing the 'restitution of God to Italy and of Italy to God', stated that the Italian government accepted the authority of the Church over the country, thereby conciliating powers that had been enemies ever since Italy was unified in 1870. Pope Pius XI enthusiastically affirmed that the *Duce* was a man sent by Providence. The Concordat provided for the exemption of the Church from taxes and for financial support for its activities. It also guaranteed that Catholic doctrine would be taught in primary schools; that religious marriages, which now also had civil recognition, would remain entirely under the Church's control; and that Catholic lay associations could continue their activities. However, the latter point, which obviously affected sporting and recreational activities, was controversial and was not respected by the Fascist regime for long. Although the Pope fought for their survival, all the Catholic youth associations involved in sport were abolished in the early 1930s, so that they could not compete with the Fascist youth institutions, whose paramount task was to forge a new Fascist generation.

Other controversies between Fascism and the Church arose in regard to the racial laws of 1938. Through these laws the regime once again disregarded the terms of the Concordat by prohibiting marriages between Catholics, on the one hand, and Jews or people of 'mixed race' on the other. In addition, the continuing opposition to Fascism of individual priests, whether the Church authorities were in consensus with the regime or not, indicates that there were problems between the Church and Fascism throughout the Mussolini era.

Following the transformation of the Kingdom of Italy into an empire, with colonies in Africa, and then the forging of an alliance with Nazi Germany, male and female role models were redefined in the second half of the 1930s. In order to transform Italy into a nation in arms it was decided that the physical and moral education of Italians should be enhanced through a new, militarised body, the *Gioventù Italiana del Littorio* (GIL). By absorbing all the pre-existing institutions GIL was made capable of controlling any and every citizen, women included. Female membership of GIL was strongly encouraged by the regime, which was aware of the fact that physically and morally stronger mothers and daughters were more and more needed to support the conscription of their husbands and brothers as soldiers of the 'Fatherland'. Women's participation, even in competitive mixed displays wearing Fascist uniforms, became quite usual in these years. However, massive involvement in social activities allowed more women to achieve a degree of social emancipation, which was an unexpected and undesired result of the new policy.

During the Second World War women were not enrolled in the army, but they were expected to support the enrolment of men and to take up the jobs made vacant as men became more involved in the conflict. In 1943, after Mussolini, having been deposed, escaped from his enemies to create the *Repubblica Sociale Italiana* (RSI) in part of northern Italy, volunteer female soldiers were accepted within the RSI's army. At the same time a number of women fought side by side with male partisans and participated actively in the 'liberation' of Italy, combating both Nazi and Fascist soldiers up to the conclusion of the war.

State of research

The history of physical education and sport has been largely neglected in Italy, where mainstream historians have shown little interest in the subject and even social historians have not explored it to any great extent. Only recently has it found a certain acceptance within the academic world, thanks to the research of a few scholars operating in the fields of contemporary history, sociology and education, and within the country's higher institutes of physical education, which were recently transformed into university faculties or departments of 'motor sciences'. A number of contributions have been made by journalists and amateur historians as well.

Within the history of Italian culture of the body, physical education and/or sports in general, several books and essays, and a number of articles from a few specialised magazines, have been published in Italy during the past three decades. The most notable works in this field have been P. Andreoli's *La donna e lo sport nella società industriale* (1974), a general study of women and sport; R. Bassetti's *Storia e storie dello sport in Italia. Dall'Unità ad oggi* (1999), an essay on the history of sport in Italy, including a number of biographical profiles; G. Bonetta's magistral book, *Il corpo e la nazione. L'educazione ginnastica igienica e sessuale nell'Italia liberale* (1990); P. Cambone's book on team sports, *Storia culturale dei moderni giochi sportivi di squadra.* (1996); M. Di Donato's *Storia dell'educazione fisica e sportiva. Indirizzi fondamentali* (1984), a general history of physical education; P. Ferrara's *L'Italia in palestra. Storia, documenti e immagini della ginnastica dal 1833 al 1973* (1992), a well-documented book on the history of gymnastics; F. Fabrizio's *Storia dello sport in Italia. Dalle società ginnastiche all'associazionismo di massa* (1977), a history of sporting associations; S. Jacomuzzi's *Gli sport* (1964–65), a three-volume study of the most widely practised sports; S. Giuntini's *Sport scuola e caserma dal Risorgimento al primo conflitto mondiale* (1989), a book on physical education and sport during the past 200 years; G. Gori's *Educazione fisica, sport e giornalismo in Italia. Dall'Unità alla prima Olimpiade dell'era moderna* (1989), a study of the advent of sport and sports journalism, and a collection of essays on physical education and sport in the Kingdom of Italy, *L'atleta e la nazione. Saggi di storia dello sport* (1996); M. Martini's *Correre per essere. Origini dello sport femminile in Italia* (1996), a book on the origins of women's sporting activity; A. Papa and G. Panico's *Storia sociale del calcio in Italia. Dai club dei pionieri alla nazione sportiva* (1993), a book on the social history of Italian football; S. Pivato's *I terzini della borghesia. Il gioco del pallone nell'Italia dell'ottocento* (1990), on traditional sports in the nineteenth century, as well as three books on sports and ideologies of the twentieth century (*La bicicletta e il sol dell'avvenire. Sport e tempo libero nel socialismo della Belle époque* [1992]; *Sia lodato Bartali. Ideologia, cultura e miti dello sport cattolico* [1985]; and *L'era dello sport* [1994]); N. Porro's books on sport, sociology and policy, *L'imperfetta epopea* (1989), *Identità, nazione, cittadinanza. Sport, società e sistema politico nell'Italia contemporanea* (1996) and *Lineamenti di sociologia dello sport* (2001); F. Ravaglioli's *Filosofia dello sport* (1990), a detailed examination of the phenomenon of sport from a philosophical point of view; A. Teja's *Educazione fisica al femminile. Dai primi corsi di Torino di Ginnastica educativa per le maestre (1867) alla ginnastica moderna di Andreina Gotta-Sacco (1904–1988)* (1995), a book about physical education for women; G. Triani's *Pelle di luna pelle di sole. Nascita e storia della civiltà balneare* (1988), based on research on the advent of summer seaside bathing; and M.P. Ulzega and A. Teja's book about sport in the army, *L'addestramento ginnico-militare nell'esercito italiano 1861–1945* (1993).

There have also been a few collections of papers in this field, among them AA.VV. (eds), *Itinerari di storia dell'educazione fisica e dello sport* (1987); R. Grozio (ed.), *Catenaccio & contropiede* (1990); P. Lanfranchi, (ed.), *Il calcio e il suo pubblico* (1992); A. Noto, and L. Rossi, (eds), *Coroginnica. Saggi sulla ginnastica, lo sport e la cultura del corpo 1961–1991* (1992); and A. Roversi, (ed.), *Calcio e violenza in Europa* (1990).

As far as contemporary history journals are concerned, P. Lanfranchi has edited a special issue of *Ricerche storiche*, entitled *Sport, storia, ideologia* (1989), and both Italian and foreign historians published essays in *Storia contemporanea* (1989 and 1990). Among Italian specialist magazines we should mention *Lancillotto e Nausica–Critica e storia dello sport*; *Ludica*; and *Ludus–Sport and loisir* – now simply *Sport and loisir*. These magazines contain articles and essays on physical education, traditional games and sport.

However, little has been published on the specific topic of sport and Fascism. Just two books should be mentioned: R. Bianda, G. Leone, G. Rossi, and A. Urso, *Atleti in camicia nera. Lo sport nell'Italia di Mussolini* (1987); and F. Fabrizio, *Sport e Fascismo. La politica sportiva del regime 1924–1936* (1976).

On the more specific theme of women's sports and Fascism there are just a few articles in academic journals, such as M. Addis-Saba, and R. Isidori-Frasca, 'L'angelo della palestra. Esercizi muliebri per il regime', in *Lancillotto e Nausica*, Volume I (1986); and some contributions in book form such as M. De Giorgio, *Le italiane dall'Unità ad oggi* (1993); V. De Grazia, *Le donne nel regime Fascista* (1993); S. Giuntini's paper in N. Torcellan, and A. Gigli Marchetti, (eds), *Donna lombarda 1860–1945* (1992); and G. Gori, *L'atleta e la nazione. saggi di storia dello sport* (1996).

Finally, Rosella Isidori-Frasca published the very first book on Italian women and sport in the Fascist era, entitled *... E il duce le volle sportive* (1983); more recently, Lucia Miotti and Marilena Rossi-Caponeri edited *Accademiste a Orvieto. Donne ed educazione fisica nell'Italia Fascista 1937–1943* (1996), and Alberto Brambilla, *Donne nello sport a Busto Arsizio* (1999).

Methodology

Following Antonio Gramsci's theories on hegemony,[2] we shall assume that during the Fascist era what took place in physical culture and in gender relations had an impact on the struggle over hegemony, not only at the time but on into contemporary Italy. In this respect the research presented in this book starts where Victoria De Grazia left off,[3] looking in more detail at how the culture of consent worked in terms of women's physical activity. In a wider perspective, we shall also look at women's physical activity as a possible means to support the phenomenon of gender emancipation that was occurring during the Fascist years, namely, the battle of Italian women against prejudice and discrimination, and for the achievement of equal rights and opportunities.

The first part of this book explores both the culture of the male body under Fascism and that of the traditional nineteenth-century woman, with reference to contemporary documents and images, as well as more recent publications that present a general picture of the situation of Italian society at the time. There is a significant lack of research concerning the bodily culture of the 'new woman' living at the beginning of the twentieth century, but it is possible to study the ideal model of this 'new woman' *a contrario*, through the defamatory readings of nationalists and Futurists, regarding the traditional and romantic woman of the past.

It should be emphasised that recent years have seen a process of historical review taking place in Italy on the phenomenon of 'Fascism'. This process aims at verifying whether the interpretation of Fascism that became widely accepted after the fall of the regime is accurate. Many Italian historians now argue that Fascism was for too long investigated in a hasty and univocal manner. The monumental historical research of Renzo De Felice, who is generally regarded as the greatest Italian expert on Fascism, will therefore be taken into account here.[4]

The research on the physical and sporting culture of women during the Fascist era presented in this book is essentially based on material produced during the Fascist era itself. This material consists of legislative acts, books, daily newspapers, journals, the specialist sporting press, photographs, films and works of art. Given the standardisation of the news selected by the Fascist censors, the picture that appears is mostly factious and hagiographic, perfectly in line with the intentions of the regime.

In this book some attention will also be paid to biographies and oral testimonies taken from former female athletes, such as Ondina Valla, the first Italian woman to win an Olympic gold medal, as well as other women practising sporting activities. The opinions of former physical education teachers trained at the Academy of Orvieto, who were young and active during the Fascist era, will also be included. It should be noted that these testimonies, although meaningful, display the effects both of a certain nostalgia for the good times that these women experienced in their youth, and of their advanced ages when they were interviewed. Clearly, they do not offer objective observations or critical elaboration, but they do express the subjective way in which these individuals experienced their sporting activity under the Fascism regime and, more generally, how they felt at that time.

Fascism as a cult of virility and the *Duce* as its political athlete

If one considers Fascism to be a political movement of the right aiming at totalitarianism, undoubtedly it was established in Italy by Benito Mussolini. Founded in Milan on 23 March 1919, his movement took the name of the *Fasci Italiani di Combattimento*. Within a few years the Fascist movement had gained power, as a consequence of the March on Rome of 28 October 1922, and very soon it took complete control of society under the government of the *Duce* (Leader) Mussolini.

In those years the rampant nationalism on which Italian Fascist ideology was based found fertile ground in every European country where the wounds of the First World War were still open, and especially in Germany, through Hitler's Nazi ideology. All the regimes and movements of the right that arose in Europe between the two world wars may be seen as tributaries of Fascist Italy. Italy had initiated the first experiment since the French Revolution of 1789 in the institutionalisation of a new 'secular' religion in Europe,[1] and had already expressed all the leading ideas of subsequent versions of fascism, from the 'nationalisation' of the masses to the 'religiosity' of the symbols. The Italian Fascist plan included defence of the 'race', in which a massive cult of the body had an important part, as it contributed to forging the 'new Italian' on the basis of Fascist aesthetics and style. This new man had to coincide with the model embodied by the leader, Mussolini, with whom Italians were induced to identify, with more or less success.

As will be seen, in Italy the predominant ideologies came together in the Fascist revolution. Once power had been obtained Fascism built a mighty pyramidal organisation, structured by the *Partito Nazionale Fascista* (PNF). The intention was to mobilise the masses according to the requirements of the regime, with an ideology based on a kind of civic religiosity. It very soon became a political religion, in which belief in myths, rites and symbols was linked to faith in Mussolini, the 'man of destiny'. People were asked to 'believe, obey, fight' in the name of the *Duce*.

Care was taken to spread the ideology in order to obtain popular consensus on every political decision. In truth, of course, consensus was discontinued over the years. It reached its apex in 1936, as a consequence of Italy's victory in its war with Ethiopia, when the myth of imperial Italy became a reality, but it was very soon reduced because of the excessive intrusiveness of the regime, increasingly becoming little more than a background for the regime's self-celebration. The final blows to the maintenance of consensus came with Mussolini's disastrous decisions on foreign policy, from Italy's military failure in Spain to the tightening of the regime's bonds with Nazi Germany, which entailed the imposition of racial laws on Italy and, finally, participation in Hitler's war.[2]

The main aim of the Fascist educational plan was *fascistizzare* (to 'fascistise'), that is, to transform Italians – traditionally perceived as individualistic and indolent – into a chosen race of strong 'new men'. They had to be mindful of the glorious past of the Roman empire and be ready to imitate its grandeur, in order to found a new civilisation that was destined to last forever. Such a plan, which accompanied Fascism from its advent, deeply involved schools, employment, spare time, culture and the arts. The task was to forge the character of citizens in order to give birth to the 'new Italian', a virile, dynamic, bellicose individual. This plan was even a source of inspiration for Hitler, whose reorganisation of German people's lives was inspired by the Italian model with the *Duce*, or *Führer*, as its spiritual guide.

Historical and ideological premises

The term 'Fascism' had its roots in Italian culture. It derives from the Latin *fascis*, a symbol comprising an axe and a bundle of rods that was linked to the cult of the 'sacred fire'.[3] Even before the constitution of the *Fasci Italiani di Combattimento* in 1919 the symbol had already been used by the interventionist movement known as the *Fasci di Azione Rivoluzionaria*, promoted by Mussolini in 1915 after he had left the Socialist Party.[4] The symbol was also used by those members of the Futurist movement who formed the *Fasci Futuristi*. However, the fate of the symbol remained tied to Mussolini and the Fascist movement, which became the PNF in 1921, down to the fall of the regime in 1943.[5]

Within the *Fasci Italiani di Combattimento* there were dissatisfied veterans of the First World War – *Arditi* soldiers, irredentists, Futurists and *Dannunziani*, followers of Gabriele D'Annunzio[6] – from a wide range of social backgrounds. They believed in the comradeship born of the war, in an ardent nationalistic spirit and in the need for radical change in society. As exponents of the Fascist truth they were firmly directed by their charismatic leader Mussolini, and were ready to engage in revolutionary adventure and impose their creed by force. The conquest of power in 1922 was a kind of *coup d'état* which neither the government nor King Victor Emmanuel III could oppose; it was then widely considered as a temporary and necessary step to re-establish order in a nation in crisis. In fact, it was the first step towards the foundation of a dictatorial regime that lasted two decades.

The success of the Fascists, who considered themselves defenders of the country and regenerators of its morals, could be attributed mainly to their repetition of the theme of the 'sacred Fatherland' on which the civil and moral unity of Italians was built. This had been a successful ideological theme since the nineteenth century. From 1861, when the Kingdom of Italy had been established and had begun controlling most of the country (with such notable exceptions as Rome and Venetia), the problem of how to accomplish the moral regeneration of Italians had become fundamental. Italians had suffered domination and division, losing their identity as a people, for at least 14 centuries, since the fall of the western Roman empire. The Fatherland was seen as the 'supreme corporate body' and as the 'first educator', to which a 'religious' devotion, up to and including the sacrifice of one's life, had to be given. It found its ideologist[7] in Giuseppe Mazzini, and its convincing advocates among liberal businessmen and officials. Up to about the end of the nineteenth century the liberal government, having rejected the revolutionary and republican aspects of Mazzini's creed, had endeavoured to educate citizens in the cult of the Fatherland and the formal ideal of liberty, overhauling the schools and military education,[8] and emphasising the monarchic institution, the traditions of the Fatherland and the heroism of the fallen.

The 'nationalisation' of the masses by means of the exaltation of the cult of the Fatherland, by now diffused to a large extent throughout Europe, brought meagre results in Italy. The common people's atavistic distrust of the aristocratic governing class worked against it. Rarely did any of the common people become involved in patriotic demonstrations, as the leading liberals feared not being able to control their strength. There was opposition from the Catholic Church, which, having been deprived of its remaining temporal powers in Italy after the seizure of Rome by Italian forces in 1870, opposed the new civic religion by any means available. The Church's main purpose was to maintain at least its spiritual supremacy over the consciences of Italians.[9]

By the beginning of the twentieth century the twin themes of civil religion and moral regeneration of citizens had ceased to form a primary objective for the government, but they remained matters for further study and debate among intellectuals. As for the Church, it now had to face the new danger of socialist ideology, which was largely atheistic and materialist, as well as the threat of the nationalistic 'pagan' movement of Enrico Corradini, who drew inspiration from Japan.[10] When the clearly anti-Bolshevik Fascist ideology gained power, the Church did not oppose it, considering Mussolini's anti-clericalism to be less dangerous than Marxist ideology.

The end of the First World War, in which Italy, though victorious, had sacrificed thousands of lives, left the fate of the city of Fiume and the region of Dalmatia unresolved. The Italian irredentists' claims on these territories, as well as the diffuse state of effervescence caused by participation in the First World War, gave a new impulse both to the theme of civil religion – which was celebrated by means of the cult of martyrdom and heroes – and to the theme of revolutionary nationalism. These themes found authoritative voices in intellectuals of the time, such as Filippo Tommaso Marinetti, the founder of Futurism, and the celebrated poet D'Annunzio.

The Futurist movement had been founded by Marinetti in 1909. It promoted such values as instinct, strength, courage, war, youth, sport, dynamism and speed, as exemplified in bicycles, motorcycles, cars and aeroplanes. In his *Fondazione e Manifesto del Futurismo* (Foundation and Manifesto of Futurism) Marinetti affirmed:

> Up until now literature has exalted thoughtful immobility, ecstasy and sleep. We want to exalt aggressive movement, feverish insomnia, running footsteps, mortal jumping, slapping and fisticuffs.[11]

Initially, Futurism was presented as a total ideology that incorporated art, customs, morals and politics in a revolutionary and nonconformist vision of life. It supported the Fascist movement, although after 1920 many Futurists detached themselves from Mussolini because they disagreed with the rightwing shift of Fascism. Futurism then abandoned any totalitarian intentions and survived as a literary and artistic school, finding followers and supporters in several European countries. Nevertheless, Futurism bequeathed a number of values to Fascism, such as the cult of anti-intellectualism, antagonism, virility, youth, speed and sport, and an innovative use of language in political propaganda. Other values, such as dynamism and individualism, were soon damped down in favour of the new Fascist order. Despite the declared friendship between Mussolini and Marinetti, the only intellectual Futurist who obtained a position in the government was Giuseppe Bottai.

Gabriele D'Annunzio, man of letters, poet, aesthete of great charm, military commander and sportsman,[12] placed his very refined art at the service of the religious myth of the Fatherland, proclaiming himself its *Vate* (high priest). He sought to restore the past greatness of ancient Rome, by that time forgotten, and to breathe new life into the political and religious ideologies of the preceding centuries. Through his attempt to seize Fiume for Italy by force, in 1919, D'Annunzio realised a fusion between oratorical art, patriotic mysticism and political activism.[13] Together with his followers in the Fiume adventure, whom he called 'legionaries' in remembrance of ancient Rome, the *Vate* established an Italian government in Fiume, the Regency of Carnaro, and inspired the founding of the utopian League of Fiume, which aimed to galvanise all oppressed populations to revolt.[14] The brief experience at Fiume ended with the abandonment of the city by order of the Italian government, but it notably enhanced the myth of D'Annunzio as the proto-type of the 'new man', victorious in every enterprise and therefore capable of founding the new Italy.

Mussolini, who had rhetorically supported the occupation of Fiume, was considered a traitor by D'Annunzio's followers for failing to participate in it. Nevertheless, the Fiume adventure in effect constituted the first step in a wider revolutionary plan agreed by Mussolini, which was to end with the March on Rome – an idea suggested by D'Annunzio – and the subsequent conquest of Italy.

In 1924 Fascism was tarnished by the assassination of the opposition deputy Giacomo Matteotti. Italy was deeply shaken and even the survival of Fascism itself was in grave danger. The scorn of many coagulated around the figure of D'Annunzio, who, with his charisma, seemed the only man capable of driving Italians on to the realisation of the new Italy. However, the initiative failed to find practical realisation and the poet decided to retire to his resi-dence at Vittoriale near Lake Garda. There he withdrew into himself and became a disenchanted observer of subsequent events.[15] The *Duce* wanted to maintain a certain friendly relationship with D'Annunzio, but this was always polluted by ambivalence and jealousy: Mussolini felt both admiration for the genial man of letters and a certain hostility towards the man himself, thus undermining the myth that fluttered about him. This passionate relationship, somewhere between love and hate, lasted until the poet's death in 1938.

In conclusion, then, the ideologies of the first two decades of the twentieth century, having been interwoven with revolutionary appeals, nationalistic claims, youthful dynamism and political mysticism, favoured the Fascist movement, which appropriated them. Despite the numerous 'punishment expeditions' and the consequent violence committed by members of Fascist squads, Mussolini seized power after the March on Rome without shedding any blood. In Italy the climate of uncertainty and disorder, which seemed to have brought the country almost to the brink of civil war, suggested a prudent acquiescence by most people in the *coup d'état*. This had been arranged by Mussolini, who had been careful to secure the connivance, or at least the neutrality, of a number of powerful people. Indeed, the *coup* was a 'telephone revolution', as the irascible Fascist Italo Balbo called it when he realised that the March on Rome had been little more than a parade.[16]

The myth of the 'new man'

In the years of the Fascist regime most Italians experienced the personal charm of Mussolini, fed by a conscious propaganda directed by himself. A man of the people, and therefore able to understand the people's demands, the *Duce* created a myth of himself by adapting the image of the Nietzschean 'superman' to Italian mentalities. According to Nietzsche (or, at least, the interpretation of his highly ambiguous writings that was then dominant), once human beings had eliminated laws that separated good from evil, and recognised the death of God, they could become gods themselves, as omniscient and almighty supermen relying on their own will and intelligence. This ideology became the basis of the European totalitarian systems of the twentieth century, as forms of absolute hegemony over life and death, good and evil.[17]

The superman cult had already made its appearance in Italy at the beginning of the twentieth century. The superman, who had willpower, power of thought and intensity of life, would not allow himself to be suffocated by current ethics, but would overcome them in order to give birth to a new man and a new Italy. In 1915 the nationalistic writer Giovanni Papini, influenced by Nietzsche, had written the essay *Maschilità* (Manliness), arguing that the 'new man' had to be more brutal, bestial and barbarous, having abandoned the romantic spirit inherited from the past.[18] Above all, the biography of the mythical master of life Gabriele D'Annunzio exemplified the aspiration to 'supermanism', which he pursued by following a lifestyle completely apart from the usual pattern, indeed beyond good and evil.

Benito Mussolini aimed at becoming a superman even as a young journalist and modest man of letters. In 1908, in a short essay entitled 'Philosophy of Strength', he underlined how Nietzsche, one of his favourite authors, had advocated the return of idealism by saying:

> a new kind of free spirit will come, strengthened by the war, ...
> a spirit equipped with a kind of sublime perversity, ... a new,
> free spirit will triumph over God and over Nothing.[19]

Among intellectual currents, it was principally the Futurist movement that absorbed the mysticism of the superman, accepting, as Marinetti did in his romance *Mafarka le futuriste*, the Nietzschean *leitmotiv* of 'will, superman, flight'. For the Futurists the 'new man' was not an isolated individual, even if he could make his choices freely: he was 'the expression of an elite of supermen, for their own decisions gained by the same attitude towards life, by discipline and by the aspiration to guide the nation.'[20]

The new Futurist man, in his disdain for death and bookish culture, and his love for virile action and violence, the dynamism of mechanics and war – considered by the Futurists to be a party[21] – found followers among young people who had grown up in the shadow of the First World War. In an excited vision of the Italian spirit, Marinetti maintained that there were people particularly endowed with 'creative genius, elasticity in improvisation, strength, agility and physical resistance, impetus, violence and fury in the fight.'[22] According to Marinetti, these qualities made the Italian people the noblest of all peoples. This utopian and racist vision was a theme repeatedly used by Mussolini, inciting the glorious Italian 'race' to become the protagonist of the great enterprises of the regime.

The Duce, symbol of the 'new Italian'

The Futurist idea of the 'new man' was not originally a nationalistic one,[23] and it was also closely associated with individualism. As a consequence, it had to be transformed by Fascism before it could generate the idea of the 'new Italian', a purely national model that best suited the Fascists' plans for the socialisation and standardisation of the masses. Such an idea was thought to be admirably personified by the *Duce*. With incessant propaganda, using all available means, Mussolini, a great communicator and an expert in the psychology of the masses,[24] built his myth and superimposed it onto the myth of Fascism, so much so that in the following years Fascism increasingly coincided with 'Mussolinism'. Once the declared anti-Fascists had been eliminated by violence or imprisonment the first objective of Mussolini was to achieve the 'sacralisation' of political ideology. It was a central theme around which the consent of the totality of individuals had to join, without distinction of any kind, just as was expected for religious creeds.

From 1923 to 1932 the regime placed new Fascist holidays side by side with the public holidays of the previous civil religion. These public holidays celebrated previously consolidated myths, such as the nation, the monarchy, the First World War and those who had fallen in battle, but celebrations were also held to commemorate the March on Rome, the foundation of the Fascist movement and the birth of ancient Rome.[25] To the pre-existing national symbols the new Fascist religion added new ones: the *fascio littorio*, the black shirt, the pennants, the skull and crossbones, the cudgel, the club, the dagger, the Roman salute, the anthem *Giovinezza* [Youth] and a new calendar for the Fascist era. Manipulating history in its favour, Fascism attributed to itself the greatest merit for most of the events that were celebrated, and eliminated those that could be evoked in opposition to its politics.[26]

Finally, in the last decade of the regime, when political 'sacralisation' was complete, Fascism dilated its myths, particularly emphasising the idea of *Stirpe Italica* ('Italic descent'), meaning the body of Italian-speaking people proudly conscious of their roots in the glories of ancient Rome, as heirs to the Roman spirit and empire. Meanwhile, the burst of youthful energy that had supported the advent and the affirmation of Fascism suffered a process of sclerosis and repeated self-representation.[27] Ceremonies, parades, sporting spectacles and the *Duce*'s speeches to 'oceanic crowds' united in delirium increasingly imitated those of Hitler's Germany.

Like any other religion, the Fascist religion needed its own idol, incarnated in Mussolini, whose fame had already been consolidated before the advent of the regime. Of modest origins, with a history of interrupted studies and a difficult youth, and cultivating a rebellious and nonconformist persona, Mussolini was endowed with great intuition and ambition. The determination that he put into each of his decisions brought him followers from the beginning of his political career. As a child of the common people, he initially joined the Socialist Party, but he later detached himself from it because he rejected its neutralism. From 1914, as founder and editor of the daily newspaper *Il Popolo d'Italia*, he promoted Italian participation in the First World War, in which he fought with honour and was also wounded. After the war he used his newspaper as the voice of the Fascist movement. His personal charisma and the strength of his ideas were amplified by the press, and he set himself at the head of the movement. With the support of business leaders and the middle classes, he conquered the *piazze* (squares) of Italy and thus seized power.

The myth of Mussolini as statesman saved Fascism from the crisis that followed the murder of Matteotti in 1924. Mussolini's myth also allowed him to charge himself with the moral responsibility for that tragic event. From 1926, having abolished all liberties and centralised all powers, the *Duce* devoted equal care to the consolidation of the regime. He was well aware that he had to cohabit with the realities of monarchy and papacy, and also make allowances for the persistence of individualism in the Italian people.

Mussolini presented himself as the perfect prototype of the 'new Italian', 'the living and working model of the ethical and political individuality' to which Italians had to aspire.[28] His relative youth (he was 39 when he came to power), his unscrupulousness in politics, his dynamism in action, and his well-publicised passion for speed, movement and sport all corresponded to the values that were already being exploited by the Futurists. These values differentiated Mussolini totally from the politicians who had preceded him, and helped him to present himself as a modern and efficient head of state, able to achieve peace, order and progress in Italy. He lived in an era that had discovered the effectiveness of radio, photography and cinematography, as compared to writing, thanks to the simplicity with which such media were able to address the masses even if they were illiterate. Films, photography and radio were mobilised to exalt the omnipresent *Duce*, the 'envoy of destiny' who could save Italy.

The 'extraordinary' qualities of the *Duce* were visually displayed in the perfected Fascist style. These qualities were shown by means of theatrical gestures, which were rough but effective. Hands on hips, legs wide apart, with set jaw and rolling eyes, the orator Mussolini spoke to the crowd in a virile, stentorian voice. The spectators, when appropriately solicited, had to answer the *Duce coram populo,* shouting their assent in unison.[29] This frequent display was usually recorded by photographers and cameramen. They portrayed Mussolini from below in order to increase the apparent height of his actually rather stumpy figure. His speeches were immediately diffused by radio, and then publicised all over Italy by means of newsreels and photographic services.

During the 1930s notable contributions to the growth of the Mussolini myth were made by the school of *Mistica Fascista* (Fascist mystics), focusing on the cult of the *Duce*,[30] and by innumerable hagiographic biographies.[31] These emphasised Mussolini the self-made man, the difficult years of his infancy, his heroism in war, his care for the humble, his sobriety, and his tireless ability in work and in sport. By describing his parents as 'saints', some of these biographies even celebrated his 'holy' birth.

The rest was done by censorship, which suppressed any news that might darken the image of the *Duce*. Every day the press received *veline*, sheets of instructions from the central Press Office in Rome that detailed what could and could not be published, and with what emphasis. It was forbidden to alter the perfect image of the new Italian prototype, Mussolini: for example, his name could not be associated with the negativity of illness or death. Emblematic in this sense was the *velina* that ordered: 'Do not say that the accident to Agnelli's child occurred along the Mussolini Pier in Genoa, but just say that it occurred in the bay of Genoa.'[32]

In the 1930s the myth of the *Duce* led to 'Mussolinism', the almost total identification of Fascism with Mussolini. He was isolated like a god on Mount Olympus. Distrusting everyone and everything, he became the one and only person in command, and doggedly managed to adhere almost completely to the granite self-image that he had built. This phenomenon was fatal both to him, because the ideology he embodied in his person became petrified, and to the development of Italian civic consciousness. Italians, already accustomed to obsequiousness and political passivity because of their unfortunate past, put their destinies in the hands of this new and powerful *deus ex machina*. The hazardous political choices that Mussolini made in the second half of the 1930s – the colonial empire, the alliance with Hitler, the wars – might also be interpreted as attempts to revitalise Fascism and Mussolini's image, by then ageing, in the eyes of Italians and the world.

In spite of this the propaganda induced many Italians, spellbound by the myth of the *Duce*, to believe that, by means of the strength of his ideas, his willpower and the sturdiness of his 'always young' body, finally Mussolini would rescue them from the past and drive the country to a glorious future. The price to be paid seemed to many Italians (though of course not all) to be quite reasonable: to allow the transformation urgently required, and to give birth to the 'new Italian'.

The aesthetics of virility and Fascist institutions

The 'new Italian' was to be the product of conversion to the new religion of the state. By not detracting from orthodoxy, the regime devoted maximum effort to the 'Fascistisation' of Italians, seeking to mould character and habits of life to the Fascist style, which represented a new aesthetic model incarnated by Mussolini.

Unlike the liberal politicians who had preceded him, the *Duce* did not fear the masses and was not overtly opposed to them, but he claimed nonetheless that the masses could not govern themselves. A popular leader and a strong government were necessary. In order to transform the masses it was necessary to convince them to follow the new Fascist aesthetics and life style. This task had to be realised through the suggestion of abstract symbols and the living symbol of the *Duce*, which could act efficaciously on the irrationality of popular feeling. In Fascist aesthetics the cult of physical beauty had a significant place alongside the cult of 'choral beauty' expressed by the masses celebrating the liturgies of the regime. The upper and middle classes had already been aware of this myth for a long time, and many of their members were fascinated by D'Annunzio's sophisticated aesthetic model and, more generally, by the paradigm of classical beauty.

The idea that a well-structured mind should correspond to an adequate bodily structure had been circulating in Europe since the early eighteenth century. A beautiful body would represent the coalescence of the aspiration for order and the aspiration for progress, through the clear harmony of forms modelled on the aesthetic canons of classical statuary.[33] Fascism exalted the cult of classical masculine beauty, as it fitted very well into the plan to make Italian men virile by means of special attention to physical sturdiness and to eugenics. The virility of the masculine body was essential to the representation, in a modern key, of the ancient and bellicose Italian 'race' as the new model, first for the nation, then for the rest of Europe and, finally, for the whole world. The beauty of virile and sturdy Fascist men, eternally young and powerful, was contrasted to the ugliness of non-Fascist men – such as the aged liberal bourgeois, with his flabby body, the Ethiopian, or the stereotype of the Jewish profiteer with his prominent nose – who were to be destroyed and replaced.[34]

The 'new Italian' was induced to assume the Fascist style, which was based on supporting the canons of beauty advocated by the regime and like the ancient Romans, putting *mens sana in corpore sano* at the service of the cause. Having installed a colossal hierarchical organisation, the regime inserted all citizens into it from birth, assuming that the youngest bodies and minds would accept the new creed more easily and thus assure the faithful perpetuation of the regime.

The Fascist institutions for early childhood included the *Opera Nazionale Maternità ed Infanzia* (ONMI), established in 1925, which provided sanitary, hygienic and preventive assistance to mothers and to children up to three years old. The aim of ONMI was the defence and physical and moral improvement of the 'race'.[35] Its statute declared that: 'to educate Italian youth "Fascistically", that is manfully … is one of the fundamental aims of the regime, whose urgency and beauty are felt by everyone.'[36]

In this way the regime intimately insinuated itself into the Italian social tissue, endeavouring to 'Fascistise' the worlds of the school, the workplace and spare time. The regime especially promoted the education of young people at school. In 1921, 35.8 per cent of the population was illiterate, but by 1931 this had decreased to 21 per cent, a concrete sign of the modernisation of society. Obviously the school was also an essential means for bringing children to the Fascist creed and subjecting them to efficient pre-military training.[37] School pupils were enlisted in the *Opera Nazionale Balilla* (ONB), which had been founded in 1926 to support the schools in the physical and moral improvement of young people. Boys and girls between eight and 14 years old were compelled to wear uniforms and were enrolled in groups whose names evoked values linked to the Roman spirit, the Fatherland and the War. Depending on their age, boys were enrolled as *Balilla* or *Avanguardisti*, and girls were enrolled as *Piccole Italiane* or *Giovani Italiane*. In addition, younger children of both sexes were enrolled as *Figli della Lupa* (Children of the She-Wolf'). One of the most famous slogans of the ONB was 'Book and musket, *Balilla* perfect', as if to underline the soldierly character of the organisation.

Whoever did not continue studies at a higher level was enlisted, from 1923 onwards, in the *Milizia Volontaria per la Sicurezza Nazionale* (MVSN) and, from 1930 onwards, in the *Fasci Giovanili di Combattimento* (FGC), institutions with a purely military character that prepared their members for conscription. *Gruppi Universitari Fascisti* (GUF) operated in the universities, and from 1927 they came under the direct control of the Fascist Party: they combined sporting activity with pre-military training.

Adults were warmly invited to enrol in the party and to wear the *camicia nera* (black shirt), at least for the assemblies of the *Sabato Fascista* (the Fascist Saturday). By the end of 1942, when the party reached its maximum membership, the party and the other Fascist organisations together had 27,376,571 members out of a population of about 46 million.[38]

As far as spare time was concerned, in 1925 the *Opera Nazionale Dopolavoro* (OND) was founded for workers, without overt political pressure. By 1935 the OND boasted cinemas, theatres, companies of amateur actors, orchestras, bands, professional and cultural associations, libraries, and choir schools.[39] Among the activities offered by the OND both modern sporting activities and the more traditional games gained widespread support.[40]

By the middle of the 1930s the expansionist aims of the *Duce* had accelerated and therefore the main purposes of the nation had to be defined again. The model of a generically militarised nation was replaced by that of an armed and aggressive nation. In each of the Fascist bodies the military character of indoctrination and physical training was emphasised, with a view to preparation for possible future wars. After the victorious war against Ethiopia, which led to the foundation of the Italian Empire in 1936, the various bodies already mentioned were absorbed into the *Gioventù Italiana del Littorio* (GIL), which lasted from 1937 until the fall of the regime six years later.

All these Fascist organisations improved their representation across the country, and therefore that of the Fascist creed, by means of spectacular mass assemblies, which included not only the usual ceremonies, with their rites and symbols, but also numerous gymnastic and sporting contests promoting activism and physical fitness. Among these displays the *Littoriali*, the *Agonali*, the *Ludi Juveniles*, the *Campi Dux* and the OND contests should be mentioned. In the presence of the *Duce* and members of his hierarchy, crowds of spectators enthusiastically followed the athletic performances. The athletes embodied the uniformity and order of Fascist aesthetics in the geometric perfection of their choreographic execution.

As far as the sporting education of conscripted soldiers was concerned, it should be emphasised that ever since 1921, even before the Fascists took power, the Central Military School of Physical Education in Rome had been equipped with ultramodern laboratories and facilities. This school trained officers in ways of teaching discipline in the barracks. Physical activities for soldiers, with a rich and varied programme, had to be executed by barechested pupils in the open air, although sweaters were permitted in winter. These pupils were trained daily for about 90 minutes at a time. Regimental contests were organised regularly in order to test the standard of the soldiers' physical preparation. As the years went by the training programme for officers became ever more onerous. From 1934 onwards officers and non-commissioned officers in the reserve were forced into post-military training, which had to be repeated every ten years. Finally, a sort of general military training was decreed for common people between the ages of 18 and 55.

Fascism, as we have seen, had absorbed a number of themes from pre-existing cultural currents. It had fully accepted the central position of physical education and sporting activities in the military training of the masses. In particular, it was inspired by the Futurist movement, which, aiming at a 'virile' education of the people, supported the pre-eminence of gymnastics over books.[41] Marinetti wrote:

> Male children, in our view, should be trained far away from female children, because their early games are clearly masculine, that

is, without any affective morbidity or womanish sensibility, but lively, bellicose, muscular and violently dynamic.[42]

The 'ideal' Futurist state, of course, had to take care of physical, moral, intellectual and patriotic education, including daily gymnastics at school, and had to found many physical education institutes for the training of future teachers.[43] The publicity that the Futurists wanted to give to the diffusion of sporting habits can be exemplified by Marinetti's screenplay for a film entitled *Vita Futurista*, in which scenes of 'morning gymnastics, fencing, boxing, sword fighting (between Marinetti and the Futurist Remo Chiti) and boxing matches (between Marinetti and a Mr Ungaro)' were to be shown.[44]

From the very beginning of the regime the practice of physical education and sport was considered by the Fascists to be an efficacious way of matching aggressiveness, violence, and the state of collective effervescence that had been inspired by the First World War, through the moulding of well-disciplined and efficient new people. The country was equipped with many new stadiums,[45] gymnasiums and sports fields,[46] as well as academies to train both male and female teachers of physical education.[47] The intention was to transform Italy into a sporting nation that would gain the admiration of other peoples. The result of these policies was quite remarkable. In 1928 there were about 502 sporting facilities in the country, but by 1935 the number had increased to 5,198. In the same year, 1935, the number of students involved in physical education at school was 470,000 in total, as compared to 180,000 in 1928.[48]

The sporting sector was well controlled, by either eliminating leftwing sporting associations or strongly delimiting the field of action of Catholic groups.[49] In addition, from 1926 onwards the regime ensured that the leaders of the *Comitato Olimpico Nazionale Italiano* (CONI) were men of reliable political faith.[50] In December 1928 the *Carta dello Sport* (Sports Charter) was issued. It officially endorsed the importance of physical and sporting education, which had to be practised by the organisations of the regime, such as the ONB, the MVSN, the OND, and the GUF. By putting the CONI at the head of all sporting federations, the *Carta dello Sport* added to its institutional task of connecting Italy to the International Olympic Committee (IOC) the task of being the only body responsible for Italian sport as a whole.[51]

The result of this political decision was good as far as Italy's sporting image was concerned. At the international level the CONI worked quite well, as the results of the Olympic Games and other world competitions demonstrated abundantly. Italy gained second place among participant nations at the Los Angeles Olympics in 1932 and third place at the Berlin Olympics in 1936;[52] it also won the football World Cup in 1934 and 1938. In addition, a number of Italian boxers, cyclists, aviators and racing drivers gained records and victories in international contests.[53]

During the 1930s the regime not only drew in new participants through popular physical activities, but also successfully forged champions by selecting the most talented individuals, who were trained as sports professionals. Stimulated by financial support, honours and prizes,[54] and excited by the Fascist propaganda that defined them as superheroes, these athletes, known in the United States as 'Mussolini's boys', had the task of increasing national pride and enhancing the new image of Italy by fighting successfully, with a virile and dynamic spirit, against the athletes of the major powers. In a speech to athletes on 28 October 1934 Mussolini instructed them as follows:

> You must be tenacious, chivalrous, daring, [you must] remember
> that when you fight outside the country, at that very moment the
> honour and the sporting prestige of the nation are entrusted to
> your muscles and above all to your spirit.[55]

As sporting displays created consensus by involving huge masses of spectators, they flourished throughout the 1930s. The press reported that in 1936 there were about 30,000 sporting displays, attended by about 40 million spectators.[56] There was, of course, some exaggeration inherent in the incessant propaganda, and the data are probably not wholly reliable, but these numbers are indicative of a very popular phenomenon, on which the regime counted as a way to encourage spectators to be more active by fully adhering to the new Fascist style.

The *Duce* as sportsman

The exaltation of the virile body as a metaphor for the fascist creed was common to all fascist movements, but its materialisation in the body of the *Duce* was a peculiar Italian phenomenon. Mussolini was elevated to become a symbol of virility itself, not only by the power of his ideas and the sexual escapades that were attributed to him, with some reason,[57] but by the strength of his muscles and the versatile talent that – it was claimed – allowed him to practise every type of sport with success. Above all, the *Duce* loved motor cars and therefore motor-racing as well as aeronautics, having surely been influenced by the Futurists whose art – according to the harsh judgement of the anti-Fascist Gobetti – was merely 'the art of a travelling salesman of sporting goods'.[58]

Mussolini also exhibited himself as experienced in horse-riding, fencing, swimming, gymnastics, tennis, skiing and boxing.[59] He had himself photographed running with soldiers, skiing down the Terminillo Mountains, swimming in the Adriatic Sea and harvesting grapes or reaping corn together with farmers. He also displayed his bare chest without embarrassment. These sporting and agricultural displays aroused the admiration of many people because in Italy, a poor country with a predominantly rural economy, they represented the *Duce* both as a kind of Nietzschean super-sportsman and as a man of the people.

Flattering words were often devoted to the sporting abilities of Mussolini,[60] but there was a great deal of mystification involved, since the *Duce* was not pre-eminently a man of sport. As a young man he had done some fencing, which was a popular activity in Italy, especially over questions of love and politics, and his passion as a spectator at boxing bouts was well-known. With regard to other sports, however, far from realising Marinetti's model of the 'new man' he was still very much an intellectual of the nineteenth century.[61] Mussolini, a sickly person for most of his life, considered basic physical education important for health, and considered sport as (in Dennis Mack-Smith's words) 'an effective means to inculcate discipline and team spirit in a society he judged too anarchic and individualist'.[62] Having assumed the importance of sport in modern society – and being, above all, an exhibitionist – he wanted his image to coincide with that of the sportsman *par excellence*, and therefore he perpetuated this myth both in Italy and abroad.

Since the *Duce* was not a real athlete in the first place, his myth did not need to change much over the years, nor was any compromise with ageing required. He continued to invite foreign journalists to his residence, the Villa Torlonia, to witness him riding, fencing and playing tennis against very complaisant sports teachers.[63] He also had his presence pointed out on beaches as a swimmer, on the snow as a skier and in the skies as a pilot, in order to enchant people through portrayals in photographs and newsreels. The *Duce* was not handsome: he was short, with a large, bald head, and had prominent features characterised by a lantern jaw. However, he embodied the aesthetic model of virile beauty in the eyes of many Italian men, who, spellbound by his magnetic charm, wanted to imitate his physical appearance and lifestyle.

This phenomenon was particularly evident among the leading circles of the regime, the *gerarchi* (members of the hierarchy), among whom the censor Achille Starace stands out. He was widely disliked as an imitator, even a caricature, of Mussolini, but was a loyal defender of the Fascist style and practised all kinds of sporting exercises. In 1938 Starace forced his already aged colleagues to perform physical exercises that were difficult even for younger men. In a notorious *velina* of 1938 he insisted that, on the occasion of a meeting in Rome, the aged employees of the National Directory and the federal secretaries had to show off by diving from a springboard, taking part in horse-jumping and swimming 50 metres.[64] This ridiculous show was not repeated.

In these varied and often fictitious ways the *Duce*'s athletic body – the living symbol of Fascist virility – became the main source of inspiration for many Italian men, overshadowing any alternatives. It was also celebrated in literature, the figurative arts and films, as will be shown in the next section.[65]

1.1 Achille Starace, Head of GIL, engaged in a 'soldierly' vault

The cult of the body in literature and the arts

During the early years of the regime Mussolini's ideology was the object of a cultural debate that culminated in 1925, when intellectuals openly took sides and signed two opposing documents: the *Manifesto* of the Fascist intellectuals, compiled by the philosopher Giovanni Gentile;[66] and the *Manifesto* of the anti-Fascist intellectuals, compiled by the philosopher Benedetto Croce.[67] By this point, however, the regime had eliminated the more dangerous anti-Fascists, and, while it still wished to control the rest of its enemies, it saw little need to intervene too much in the field of elite culture. In any case, even those intellectuals who had signed Croce's document were to be acquiescent or disengaged in regard to the Fascist regime.

Thus, at least at its highest levels, the cultural world – especially literature – cannot be said to have been at the service of the current ideology. Equally, however, it was neither vital enough nor creative enough to offer any significant opposition.[68] Mussolini himself considered the past not as a barrier to the new, but as a point of departure for a glorious future. He was therefore eclectic and open to innovation, all the more so because he did not have precise cultural preferences.[69] In the field of popular culture, meanwhile, the regime was omnipresent. Daily newspapers, periodicals and scholarly texts, as well as the whole range of popular literary production – from romances to biographies – were rigorously controlled by the regime because of their broad dissemination in society.

Among those intellectuals who actively supported Fascism with more or less conviction, many were seduced primarily by the charm of the *Duce*. The playwright Luigi Pirandello, who won the Nobel Prize for Literature in 1934, used to say of Mussolini: 'He, you see, makes Italy, and makes the world, he makes all of us as he wants: he creates us from time to time according to his whim.'[70] The anti-conformist writer Curzio Malaparte composed a poem for the *Duce*, which sketched an effectively synthetic portrait of him.[71] In 1929 the aggressive physical image of the *Duce*, a metaphor for his political aggressiveness, inspired Marinetti to write an essay, *Ritratto di Mussolini* (Portrait of Mussolini), in which he declared that:

> Physically he is built in the Italian way, outlined by inspired and brutal hands, forged and engraved according to the model of the masterly rock of our peninsula. [His] imposing, square jaw and prominent disdainful lips … spit boldness and aggression onto everything that is slow, pedantic and meticulous.[72]

The journalist Indro Montanelli was critical of Fascist ideology, yet in his youth he wrote an article entitled *Mussolini e noi* (Mussolini and Us) that offers one interpretation of the feelings that average Italians may have had about the *Duce*:

> When Mussolini looks at you, you cannot but be naked in front of him. But he is naked in front of us as well. There are people who, to be considered somebody, need to wear a uniform or a badge, but not Mussolini. His face and his 'torso of bronze' rebel against draperies and harnesses. Anxious and impatient, we snatch them from his back, contemplating only the inimitable essentiality of this man, whose shaking, vibrating and thumping are formidably human. The rest is not important.[73]

All the arts were appropriated to the physical image of Mussolini, notably his muscular 'torso of bronze'. The theme of the athletic body of the *Duce* was already present in the 1920s, but at the beginning of the 1930s it received an additional impulse when it was set at the centre of a new propaganda cam-

1.2 A fashionable t-shirt with
Mussolini's image

paign to spread the Fascist style among Italians.[74] At a relatively low artistic level we can find Mussolini in book illustrations, posters, medals and postage stamps, in the showrooms of amateur artists and in handicrafts. Some of the common people, having received the message, exalted in their turn the effigy of the *Duce*, making portraits of him even out of such materials as flowers or grains of corn.[75] These portraits could be found hanging on cardboard mounts in many people's homes. It has been calculated that between eight million and 30 million postcard portraits of Mussolini were circulated during the Fascist era. The successful cult of the virile male seems to have satisfied the well-solidified feelings of mainstream Italian society, which was still deeply sexist and patriarchal.[76]

At an intermediate artistic level, and in order to promote 'popular universal art' as a culture without any class distinction, large-scale pictorial and mosaic decorations were created in public buildings. This was an easier way to display Italian art to large numbers of people than restricting it to museums would have been, since many common people felt uncomfortable about going into such places of elite culture. This situation had already been denounced by the Futurists, who accused museums of being mere symbols of 'obsession with culture'.[77]

As for 'militant art' – art that was openly placed in the service of the regime's political ideology – it was viewed as a 'perfect means of spiritual government'.[78] 'Militant art' was broadly encouraged by means of exhibitions, such as those held by the official labour unions, as well as contests and prizes, such as the annual *Littoriali* ('lictoral contests') of Art or the Cremona Prize. Such works presented idealised images of the virile bodies of the *Duce* and other athletic Fascist men, often in the form of pseudophotographic portraits. The aesthetic value of these pictures was mainly based on the choice of beautiful models, in a tedious representation of the healthiness of people of 'Italic Descent'.[79]

Even figurative art at the highest level, which in the Fascist years was mostly expressed through Futurism, Modernism and *Novecentismo*, stuck – with some exceptions – to the themes laid down by Fascism in both sculptures and paintings. Once again the principal theme was the athletic body of the *Duce*, who was portrayed standing, on horseback, dressed as a Roman commander[80] or a Renaissance prince,[81] or in such guises as revolutionary hero,[82] sacred icon[83] or hero of fanciful allegories.[84] In 1932, on the occasion of the tenth anniversary of the Fascists' seizure of power, an Exhibition of the Fascist Revolution was held in Rome. It included works by some of the best figurative artists of the country, who gave special attention to the human figure as an inspiring model for their art. Above all, the figure of Mussolini was the omnipresent subject in every gallery at the Exhibition, as the synthesis of the Italian people and Fascism itself.[85]

The architecture of the Fascist regime was monumental, following the Roman architectural style, but at the same time it was simplified along the geometric, rationalistic lines favoured by Modernism. Architects, like artists, broadly used the themes of the virile *Duce*'s body and the ideal Fascist athlete in decorating their buildings. The *Stadio dei Marmi* (Stadium of the Marbles), located inside the Mussolini Forum (now known as the *Foro Italico*), an architectural complex designed by Enrico del Debbio and opened in 1927, was one of the best examples of architecture in the 'Fascist style'. The upper perimeter of the Stadium was decorated with 60 colossal statues in white marble, representing naked athletes as symbols of the eternal youth and virility of the 'new Italian'. The intention behind these four-metre-high colossuses was to evoke ancient Roman greatness, although they actually echoed both Michelangelo's *David* and the nude figures painted by Ingres. The statues stimulated not only malicious comments from Italian women and homosexual *voyeurs*,[86] but also the irritation of the Church and of 'respectable people' unaccustomed to seeing nudity exhibited so openly.[87] The Mussolini Forum also contained a gigantic marble obelisk weighing 300 tons that was dedicated to the *Duce* as the craftsman of every rebirth and the animator of every enterprise. By evoking the granite image of the *Duce*, the obelisk somehow represented a phallic metaphor for him and thus perfectly suited the 'virile' context of the Forum.[88] There were also plans to provide the Forum with a colossal bronze statue, 80 metres in height, symbolising the strength and virility of the new Italy. This half-naked Hercules should have had Mussolini's features, but, after the *Duce*'s head and foot had been moulded in bronze, it was realised that the statue would be technically impossible to complete. The plan was quietly set aside, in great haste, and Mussolini was said to be very disappointed.[89]

As for cinematography, although it had been institutionalised by the regime it did not constitute a real state cinema enterprise, since only a few films were openly propagandist. Among these were Blasetti's *Vecchia guardia*, Forzano's *Camicie nere*, Perilli's *Ragazzo*, Genina's *L'assedio di Alcazar* and Alessandrini's *Luciano Serra pilota*.[90] A few other films, such as Blasetti's *Sole e terra madre*, focused on agriculture, while others, such as Camerini's *Rotaie*, focused on the industrialisation of the country: both these themes were particularly closely linked to Fascist policies. However, of about 700 films produced in Italy under Fascism most had no close reference to political reality. The greatest public acclaim accrued to historical costume dramas, such as Gallone's *Scipione l' africano*, and to the series of films known as *telefoni bianchi* (white telephones), which adapted the style of Hollywood to present the amusing lives of the absentminded and optimistic lower and middle bourgeoisie. However, if one takes a closer look, one can see that the disengaged objectives of the protagonists of these films – love affairs, family, money – and their pride in their own social condition, however modest, perfectly complied with the aims of Fascism, which considered indifference to politics as functional to the stability of the regime. In the *telefoni bianchi* films the Italian way of life was embodied in the male protagonist, generally a young and successful man, who resolved the most tangled situations by giving his enemy 'four slaps'. The actor most often used to embody this prototype of the Italian male, virile and slow of speech, was Amedeo Nazzari. Ironically, however, due to his tall and elegant figure Nazzari reflected the American ideal of the handsome Latin man, not the Italian masculine beauty then incarnated by the *Duce*.[91]

The duty of indoctrinating society was entrusted, not to such feature films, but to documentaries and to the newsreels of *L'Unione Cinematografica Educativa* (LUCE), a body founded in 1924. These documentaries took the form of lessons on agriculture, history and geography, or propaganda about industrial achievements, land reclamation and archaeological discoveries. Particular attention was devoted to documentaries on the perceived need to increase the population of Italy, presenting images of happy and multiple maternity. These documentaries involved themes linked to eugenics and the defence of the 'race', showing struggles against illness, and the strong and methodical 'new Italians' involved in gymnastics and other sporting performances.

It was mainly left to the compulsory projection of newsreels in schools, communes and cinemas to ensure the maximum diffusion of the news, obviously filtered in advance by Mussolini's Press Office. The declared aim of the newsreels was the civic and moral education of citizens, but in reality they were pompous and resonant packages of Fascist parades and celebrations. Particular emphasis was placed on choreographic and paramilitary displays by Fascist youth, and to the image of Mussolini, shown in his public life, and sometimes in his private life too. All Italians, including those who lived in remote regions, could thus see the *Duce* in person, and, if they wished to, admire the magnetism of his looks and his unrestrained gestures.[92]

Mussolini was fully aware of the extraordinary effect of such images, which he wanted to see reverberating all over the world. For instance, in 1933 he agreed to be the protagonist of an American film entitled *Mussolini Speaks*, in which he behaves with the boldness of a movie star. In the final scene of the movie the *Duce* appears in the Roman Forum, as if to underline his ideal connection with the great figure of Julius Caesar. His body language in this film is made up of agitated gestures combined with hard, statuary postures, to great effect. In fact, most of the scenes displaying the *Duce* among crowds were selected from footage shot for Italian newsreels.[93] *Mussolini Speaks* was mainly circulated abroad, where it presented a positive image of the self-made man Mussolini, the new politician, the athletic leader of Italy.

Thus, Italian culture as a whole was manipulated from above so that artists would join in the regime's project of making Italians into a 'virile' people, notably by applying the figurative and cinematic arts to the task of transforming the *Duce* into a myth. Nevertheless, Italian culture really functioned more as spectator than as actor in the tragicomedy played out time after time by Fascist politicians on the colossal stage of the nation. It should not be forgotten that there were many individuals among the cultural elite who were more free-spirited: they were blamed for being too cool towards Fascist ideology and were scornfully called 'defeatists'.

Racism and the politics of the body: Fascist style and 'Aryan' aesthetics

With the coming to power of Hitler in Germany in 1933, Italian Fascism had to compete with another rightwing totalitarian regime. Mussolini immediately and enthusiastically underlined through the press his belief that the birth of a new Fascist regime in Europe had been inspired by the Italian example,[94] but in the following years the *Duce* had to deal with a dictator whom he considered dangerous, and with a nation historically regarded as an enemy of Italy since at least the previous century.

Hitler had always declared himself a fervent admirer of Mussolini and the Italian Fascist government, from which he had taken inspiration in many fields,[95] but nobody could be indifferent to the sinister spell that he exerted on the German people, nor to the fanatical anti-Semitism of his creed. In exalting the superiority of the German 'race' above all others, Hitler's ideology also impugned the 'Latin races', creating further difficulties for Mussolini. In the early years of the Nazi regime the *Duce* conducted a policy that was certainly not favourable to Germany, but following his war against Ethiopia (1936), which was condemned by the League of Nations, Mussolini moved closer to Hitler's policies as the 1930s went on.

In 1938 their alliance brought about the promulgation of racial and anti-Semitic laws in Italy.[96] Both the Fascist Grand Council (the effective centre of state power) and Mussolini himself tried to justify the new policies by explaining to the people that Fascism was not subject to the Nazi dictatorship at all, but was pursuing a coherent strategy, for the defence of the Italian 'race', that had already been planned for a long time.[97] While this was a falsehood, it was true that racism towards the black people of Africa – especially during and after the conquest of Ethiopia – had already generated the imposition in Italy's new empire of severe penalties for fraternisation between the Italian colonisers and the natives in Libya, Eritrea, Somalia and Ethiopia alike.[98]

The turn towards overt official racism in 1938 cost the regime a great deal. The consensus that it had manufactured up till then was disrupted by opposition from the Church and, it appears, from most Italians too. Italy's long history of foreign domination had created a melting-pot of cultures and ethnicities, and Italians tended to be much less anti-Semitic than anti-Germanic. After all, while there had long been a Jewish community living largely unmolested on Italian territory, the Italian people had suffered under Austrian rule for centuries, and had gained their independence only after battles against the Austrians that were still within living memory. As a consequence Italian public opinion did not make a refined distinction between Germans and Austrians, since they both spoke the detested stentorian German language. In addition, the chilly and at the same time imperious image of Hitler, displayed in newsreels, seems to have frightened many Italians.

The campaign against Italian Jews was indeed the result of a conscious political choice by Mussolini himself. Even though he was not ideologically anti-Semitic,[99] the *Duce* probably wanted to teach the international Jewish community a lesson, in the belief that they had opposed his war against Ethiopia. At the same time he may well have thought that Italian Fascists needed a new and exciting objective. The campaign against the Jews offered those young militants who were disappointed by the results of the 'Fascist revolution' a new cause through which to dissipate their frustrations, and also an ideal reason for fighting.[100] The question was debated at various levels in Italy, and the shift to anti-Semitic policies was supported by some intellectuals, who issued publications and declarations in an attempt to explain its supposed scientific validity, and its philosophical and ethical rationale.[101]

The new policy also gave renewed emphasis to the myth of the 'Italic Descent'. On the occasion of the Anti-Hebrew Congress of 1938 Rome was baptised as the 'Capital of the Aryan Empire'. Indeed, the regime proposed to take the myth even further: the plans for the Roman Exhibition E 42 – which did not take place due to the war – used the threatening expression 'Italic Race' instead of 'Italic Descent'.[102]

In any case, there were important differences between Mussolini's worldview and Hitler's: while the worldwide supremacy of the 'Aryan race' was a central aim of Hitler's policies, Mussolini's aims were substantially focused on the transformation of the character and lifestyle of the Italian people within the Italian empire. The ideological theme of the supremacy of 'Aryans' referred to the past, which made the actions of fallen modern heroes and of ancient Germanic heroes into a myth. In contrast, the 'new Italians', although they were heirs to the ancient 'Italic Descent', were expected to throw themselves forward into an indefinite glorious future. It was understood that this would induce those of other 'races' to admire and imitate them, in a utopian plan for a worldwide process of 'Fascistisation', but this was not the same as the racially defined hierarchy of nations envisaged by the Nazis.

Subsequent events demonstrated that the Italian laws inspired by Hitler did not have the devastating effects that might have been expected. Only a few Italians really believed in the correctness of the new laws, and as a consequence the laws were applied only sporadically and with difficulty.[103] Germany was to gain power over much of Italy at a late stage in the war, but it can hardly be said to have gained hegemony anywhere in Italy.

By the end of the 1930s Mussolini still assumed that the prospect of a major war lay far in the future. Nevertheless, the example offered by the mobilisation of the German people also served to deepen the impact of militarism on Italian life, acting on the supposed heritage of the ancient Roman spirit. Under the direction of the pro-German Achille Starace, Secretary of the PNF, and in the name of the 'glorious Italian race', all Italians had to address each other with the polite second person *voi* (you). They also had to greet each other in a more 'virile' way by stretching out their right arms in the *saluto romano* (Roman salute), while soldiers had to march on parade using the *passo romano* (Roman step), the Italian version of the Teutonic goose step. Anything that could be considered alien to the 'Roman spirit', from regional dialects to foreign words, was officially banished, in order to keep the people 'purely European', and to preserve the physical and psychological characteristics of the 'race'. Yet, unlike in Germany, these bans had hardly any effect.

In order to imitate Nazi Germany even more closely, the mobilisation of the masses received the highest impetus under the GIL from 1937 onwards. Physical education and collective pre-military drill predictably became more prominent. The main aim of Italian physical training was still focused on the 'Fascist style' – popular health, strength, discipline and will, without any aesthetic satisfaction – while the extreme cult of the male body as a symbol of 'Aryan' beauty, which in Germany had been expressed as the search for a fine physical form satisfying ancient Greek canons, found little resonance in Italy.[104]

Hitler's blond athletes, whose bodies appeared to be sculpted like those of ancient Greek ephebes, were rather different from 'Mussolini's boys', who incarnated a more modest physical model. In Italy the 'virile' ideal was principally expressed, not by athletes' perfect bodies, but by the strength of their moral will, which had to be trained not only for physical activities but also for daily life. With their bare but undefined torsos, and their short, brown Mediterranean legs engaged in the difficult task of marching in 'Roman step', young Italian men could be seen as dull, uninteresting imitations of the Hitler *Jugend* (Hitler Youth), who were chilling in their uniform beauty and their spectacular, perfect execution of the goose step during Nazi parades.

It is therefore all the more ironic that ever since the middle of the 1920s, when Nazism was still very far from attaining power, Italian Fascism had worked hard to mount perfectly synchronised displays by semi-nude young men as a vital sign of their discipline and cohesion. On this there is early evidence in the words of Lando Ferretti – prominent both in sport and in the ruling party – who had commented on athletic displays by soldiers in 1928:

> To watch thousands and thousands of statuesque soldiers, naked under their martial helmets, immediately obey orders as a single soldier, means watching a powerful and disciplined sight, which is irresistible.[105]

Conclusion

The Italian people did not attain a perfect homogeneity and did not become totally transformed into 'new Italians', even after 20 years of indoctrination. The biggest obstacle to the homogeneous transformation of society was probably the individualism of most Italians, which was coupled with a certain critical attitude towards politics, the product of the longstanding geographical, historical and cultural divisions within the country. In a more general way, in spite of the insistent propaganda urging the common people to adopt a new 'Fascist style', their tastes were never effectively homogenised and, outside the ambit of politics, the cultural debate continued largely undisturbed. In contrast, the Nazis campaigned against 'degenerate art', and even burned books and works of art in order to affirm the value of what they regarded as 'pure art'.[106]

The two Leaders, Hitler and Mussolini, both had strong personal charisma and self-awareness as 'men of destiny', but they were incomparably different. Hitler played his part with terrifying conviction, while Mussolini was less determined and more accustomed to taking advantage of events as they occurred, relying on a cynical opportunism that, as time went by, even damaged himself.[107] Hitler's image, taken from Nordic mythology and the supposedly Nietzschean idea of the 'superman', was chilly and detached, while Mussolini's image, with its deep roots in the rural and patriarchal tradition of the Romagna region, was openly displayed to the crowd. Italians were informed about his frugal meals, his extraordinary ability to work without sleep, the lapidary brevity of his thoughts, which were written everywhere on walls in large letters, and his 'ever young' and athletic virility. Mussolini, an extrovert who was used to exploiting all possible means of communication, did not fail to show the world a modernistic image of himself as an eminent political athlete engaged in the making of history.[108]

Nazism, which made the beauty of the male body into one of its principal symbols, could not avail itself of Hitler's image to promote this symbol to the world. Germany had acquired a leader with little or no interest in or aptitude for sport, and his regime therefore had no easy way of embodying the ideal type of the 'Aryan race' in the person of the *Führer*. Mussolini's 'athletic' body was unhealthy but was widely displayed nonetheless as the prototype for men of 'Italic Descent'. Unfortunately for him, the repeated public displays of his bronzed torso were judged to be undignified, if not ridiculous, especially – and perhaps not surprisingly – by his ally Adolf Hitler.[109]

Model women and physical training before the Fascist era

The political development of Italy over the one hundred years that preceded the advent of Fascism may be characterised by reference to the patriotic and nationalistic ideals derived from Romanticism. The dream of unifying Italy under the House of Savoy, after years of wars and negotiations, was realised in 1861 and completed after the siege of Rome in 1870. The new Kingdom of Italy gave itself the objective of forming an Italian nation by unifying very different cultures, mentalities and traditions inherited under the secular rule of foreign princes and the Church. This objective actively engaged the politicians and officials of the young state, who sought to affirm its identity and power in line with other nations.

As part of the process of forging a national identity, civilian gymnastic societies arose in Italy on the crest of a wave of enthusiasm for German military gymnastics. The latter had been practised in Piedmont by the army of Savoy since 1833, under the guidance of Rudolf Obermann (1812–69), who went on to develop gymnastics in the Kingdom of Italy as a whole.[1] Initially, the new societies attracted members of the aristocracy and the upper bourgeoisie, whose longstanding devotion to the body, and its training as a protagonist of the destiny of individuals alongside spirit and mind, had been reinforced by Enlightenment thought.[2] However, from the mid-nineteenth century onwards this idea was increasingly transformed into a social aspiration as the government engaged in a project for the general physical regeneration of the population, aimed principally at involving workers, who were regarded as ill-prepared to cope with the effects of industrialisation and modernisation.

Meanwhile, the various Italian gymnastic societies had joined together and founded the *Federazione Ginnastica Italiana*, which, while weathering various changes in fortune and in leadership, directed Italian physical culture as a whole.[3] In the last part of the century associations for sailing, rowing and cycling appeared, while the English games of cricket, lawn tennis and football also began to be played. Some of these sporting associations initially relied upon the Federazione, but later freed themselves from its tutelage by organising their own competitions and founding new, specialised national federations.[4]

All these organisations contributed a great deal to the popularising of English games, especially football. In an attempt to absorb and domesticate football some even claimed that it was of Italian origin on the grounds that it resembled an old Florentine game called *calcio*. By the start of the twentieth century football had replaced the *giochi ginnici*, gymnastic games mainly deriving from the Renaissance, as well as the traditional games of *pallone al bracciale* and *tamburello*, which had been dominant in the nineteenth century.[5] Football thus became the Italian national game *par excellence*.

The *Federazione Ginnastica* gave expression to the gymnastic and patriotic ethics of Italians by organising colossal rallies at which great gymnastic exploits served as metaphors for the greatness of the Fatherland. Being closely allied to the liberal government, the *Federazione* displayed flags, distributed medals and encouraged the singing of national anthems, all in the name of a radiant patriotism at the national and international competitions that it held regularly in the principal Italian cities.[6] These displays were reminiscent of German gymnastics festivals, and not surprisingly, since Italian gymnastics followed the ideals that had been transferred and adapted from the German *Turnen* movement by Obermann and others.

As in other European countries, in Italy the process of mass 'nationalisation' used grandiose gymnastic and patriotic parades as effective symbols through which to transmit to the people the sense of their belonging to the nation, entailing a kind of 'nationalisation' of the body. The theme of the pedagogical value of gymnastics in schools was taken up by the new state, from the beginning, as the main way of affirming the ethical and social role of physical culture in Italy.[7] Gymnastics was added to the curriculum under laws and decrees that made it compulsory and periodically updated the schools' programmes.[8] In the nineteenth century physical activity in schools was aimed at making young men stronger, preparing them for compulsory military service and forging character, as well as more generally regenerating Italian physiques by improving the health of the people. The practice of gymnastics within schools and in society at large was not, however, limited to boys and young men, since schools also worked hard to promote gymnastics for girls, especially with a view to inculcating hygienic and healthy habits.

Following the associative model of male gymnastics, a new interest in social and competitive activity developed over the years among women who had experienced physical education at school. A few women succeeded in overcoming the obstacles interposed by a mainly patriarchal and masculinist mentality, and succeeded in being accepted as members by some important gymnastic societies. This new outlet for women's socialisation and the first displays by female gymnasts in public aroused not only the indignation of 'respectable people' but also the admiration of more open-minded men.

Around the turn of the nineteenth and twentieth centuries strong nationalistic and colonialist impulses increasingly cancelled out the positivist optimism and the political 'myth of peace' that had characterised the previous years.[9] Attention to manly bodies was given a new emphasis. The body was considered to be the living and ideal gymnasium, to be trained for future military enterprises. During the same period, however, the female body remained firmly tied to the medical sciences, which made it into an instrument for improving health and providing a growing population, and nothing more. The small number of daring female athletes who, challenging convention, competed in sports, sometimes even against men, were considered to be an interesting phenomenon, but were certainly not regarded as presenting an acceptable model of femininity.

In these years many women, whether among the highly educated or among the working class, were seeking ways to take their places in the political and social life of the nation. A small number of determined female intellectuals started fighting for their own rights and those of other women, thus opening up a process of gender emancipation, under the influence of the feminist movements active elsewhere in Europe. The nineteenth-century model of physically and morally fragile women, modest in their demeanour and dedi-cated solely to domestic work, was now outflanked by a new model of women who would be more open to employment opportunities, and to participation in political and social decision-making. They were obstructed, however, by strong new nationalistic and anti-feminist movements that were imbued with the assumption of women's inferiority.

Specifically in relation to the culture of the body, while the government urged the male population to make themselves stronger it still asked the 'weaker sex' only to adhere to physical and hygienic practices that could help in procreation and in the growth of healthy children for the Fatherland. Elsewhere Charles Darwin's theory of evolution was misappropriated to create an ideology of 'social Darwinism', emphasising the strengthening of the body without any gender discrimination, but this did not find much support in Italy. Both traditional Italian culture and the Church considered Darwin's theory itself, let alone its misuse in social theories, a revolutionary attempt to undermine the Scriptures. Texts by foreigners that supported the notion of women's mental and biological inferiority circulated freely in Italy from the beginning of the new century. Many Italian intellectuals were convinced that women were unavoidably subject to limitations, and that the only 'natural' destiny for them was not the public realm of society, but the private realm of the family. Others, meanwhile, blamed traditional-minded women for blackmailing men sexually.

During the First World War, in which Italy participated from 1915, physi-cal education and sport, as well as all other activities that were not strictly linked to the war effort, were predictably put aside. All able-bodied men were sent to the Front, while huge numbers of women entered the field of paid work, most of them for the first time. This new experience, which most of the women concerned coped with successfully, signalled the first concrete step towards their political, economic and social emancipation.

After the war, when Italy succumbed to grave social disorder, an elite of conscious and active women either joined avant-garde movements or gave their support to the pre-existing liberal, Catholic or socialist organisations. These women sought to contribute to the Italian cause and at the same time to obtain the rights that were traditionally denied to them. However, the advent of Fascism restructured the dimensions of their aspirations.

Girls and educational gymnastics in the nineteenth century

In the nineteenth century the accepted model for women was dictated by the Catholic Church, which wanted women to be modest, reserved, religious and charitable, and to remain housewives. Being anchored in tradition, the Church, through the authority of the Pope, opposed any form of women's emancipation by underlining their family duties as being fundamental.[10] In addition, Romantic verse and other forms of literature emphasised either women's fragility and sensitivity in general, and their silent heroism or, in contrast, the languid and sinful sexuality of the 'vamp', a new model of femininity that appeared at the turn of the nineteenth and twentieth centuries but drew on older stereotypes of women as sinful. Italian law treated women as eternal minors, almost incapable of taking part in legal proceedings and therefore deprived them of economic and political rights. Under Italian family law, as consolidated in 1865 in the Pisanelli Code, women were subject to the authority of the male head of the family, and once women had married they were excluded from taking responsibility for their children and could not act in commercial or legal matters without their husbands' consent.[11]

Notwithstanding this conservative trend, Italian women found a measure of emancipation by entering the worlds of schooling and work, although their progress was tardy compared with what was being achieved, with some help from feminist movements, in other countries. Women working in factories, offices and educational institutions fought hard for their rights in society. The scale of the problems they faced may be indicated by the fact that in 1871 only 24.2 per cent of women were literate (as compared to 38.2 per cent of men).[12]

A further incentive to emancipation came from the growing affirmation of bodily culture, following the new positivist creed of respect for science. This culture, which propagated the healthiness of the body as an absolute social value with no regard for gender, stirred the stagnant waters of the age-old masculine and paternalistic tradition by offering the female body a certain degree of attention.

Even before Italy was unified innovative ideas about the culture of the body for women were circulating in Lombardy under the influence of the Enlightenment. These ideas were taken from, among other sources, Clias's text *Callistenia o ginnastica per le giovani*, which had been translated into

Italian by Eugenio Young in 1829,[13] as well as experiments conducted in Cremona by the priests Ferrante Aporti and Alessandro Gallina, who favoured the practice of gymnastics by children of both sexes for at least one hour every day.[14] The main impulse, however, came from Rudolf Obermann, who intervened on several occasions in favour of female gymnastics. In texts published in the periodical *Letture di famiglia* he proposed dancing classes, as well as a wide range of physical exercises and games, to help girls become more generous, stronger and prouder, so that they could better perform their future roles as women and mothers. It was taken for granted that girls had to be trained apart from boys, and should follow a suitable programme of exercises avoiding over-strenuous activities, but the target for both sexes was quite similar: to forge people capable of facing any and every kind of battle, throughout their lives, with strong and virile spirits. Obermann emphasised his belief that by believing in and practising gymnastics future parents, and especially the future mothers who were particularly important in the training of the young, would improve their ability to shape their children's physical and moral education, and 'that simpering, those affections, those affected demonstrations of fine feelings, those excesses of irritability would be banished, those faints forgotten.'[15]

Obermann's programme of gymnastics was not original, but was based on German and Swiss precedents, notably the work of Guts-Muths, Pestalozzi, Jahn and Spiess. Obermann's proposal for the strengthening of Italian men was widely accepted, but his advocacy of feminine gymnastics was considered with a certain mistrust, both by the middle class, because of its 'virility', and by the lower class, because it was thought to be a danger to physical safety.[16]

Under Casati's Law of 1859 (named after the Minister of Education, Gabrio Casati) educational gymnastics became a compulsory element in the curriculum of schools, without regard for gender, although in practice the general tendency was still for boys to practise it exclusively. Then, in 1861 all *Reali educandati femminili* (royal educational institutes for girls) in the former Kingdom of Naples were required by law to start compulsory courses in dance and gymnastics.[17]

This exceptional initiative reflected the previous cultural and political history of the Kingdom of Naples. In the last decades of the eighteenth century the Enlightenment had found important followers in Naples, who believed in gymnastics as a pedagogical value for all citizens. In 1786 Gaetano Filangieri had even published a book, *Scienza della legislazione*, supporting physical exercise for both sexes. Naples had undergone an exciting but brief revolutionary experience as the Parthenopean Republic in 1799, and later, under the successive reigns of Joseph Bonaparte and Joachim Murat (1806–15), Naples had somehow breathed again the air of liberty, equality and fraternity emanating from the French Revolution.

Under Casati's Law male teachers in primary schools were enabled to attend special training courses from 1861 onwards. These courses were held in the new teacher-training School of Gymnastics headed by Obermann and in the gymnasiums of the first Italian gymnastic society, in Turin. Statistics show that in the school year 1863–64 there were 17,923 male pupils but only 57 female pupils involved in gymnastic classes in 255 Italian schools.[18] It should be added that among these schools only 41 had gymnasiums and equipment, and that most teachers were not trained as such but had been soldiers, professional acrobats, dancers or horsemen. In particular, the paucity of female pupils can be explained by the common belief that gymnastics was somehow a dangerous discipline for women's health and modesty, especially when the teachers were men.

Finally, from 1867 onwards the Ministry of Education decided that specific courses for female teachers were to be organised in the School of Gymnastics in Turin, to train teachers who would work with female pupils. In the meantime all the provincial governments and educational authorities of the newly established Kingdom of Italy were urged by the government to encourage the diffusion of educational gymnastics for both sexes in primary schools across the country.

The region of Venetia, which was annexed to Italy in 1866, was particularly favourable to female gymnastics. The Venetians had been ruled by the Austrians since 1797, learning from them the habit of practising gymnastics in Fröbel's kindergartens. Pietro Gallo started a course for 48 female primary school teachers in Venetia in 1868 and by the following year 466 girls were taking courses in educational gymnastics.[19] By 1872, 2,561 of the 6,939 pupils taking gymnastics courses in the city of Venice were girls.[20]

During the 1870s gymnastics classes for girls were also successfully introduced in primary schools in Bologna, Genoa, Padua and Verona. By 1872, 51,012 boys and 16,285 girls were engaged in gymnastics in Italy: in other words, in just eight years the number of girls taking part had increased by a factor of 300. However, their distribution across the country was uneven. Only 48 of the 70 provinces had gymnastics classes for girls in their schools, and the majority were concentrated in Turin, Milan, Venice, Verona and Naples.

In the school year 1874–75 the Normal Gymnastics School for secondary school teachers was opened within the Gymnastics Society of Turin. Then, in 1877, Dr Emilio Baumann founded a new teacher-training school within the *Virtus* Society of Gymnastics in Bologna, to help the Turin establishment in training gymnastics teachers of both sexes. Baumann pointed out that only 249 female teachers had gained the gymnastics degree in Turin in the previous three years and that, while 183 of these women were already teaching in schools in the area, in Bologna there were no female gymnastics teachers at all. He obtained support for his school from the municipality of Bologna by insisting that 'female teachers especially could find new jobs and start brilliant careers.'[21]

Baumann's rational gymnastics was inspired by both Obermann's military model and Ling's scientific methodology, but it was adapted to take account of Italy's basic needs and scarce resources. Baumann was opposed to what he called 'artificial exercises', such as those using the gymnastics equipment prescribed both by Obermann and by Ling; he was in favour of 'natural exercises', such as walking, marching, climbing, jumping and so on. In his view, gymnastics had to help to prepare people to undergo any difficulty in their social lives or at work by strengthening their bodies and wills.

Baumann's method was not widely applied in Italy. In 1884, for example, only 24 Italian cities or towns had gymnasiums, and only 11 had outdoor gymnastic facilities.[22] This suggests that even those teachers who had attended the school in Bologna could not teach much of Baumann's 'natural exercises', as there was a grave shortage of facilities in the schools of the time. Most gymnastics teachers trained children in ordinary class-rooms, thus practising the 'gymnastics in the midst of school benches' that Emilio Baumann had proposed as an effective if inadequate alternative. Other innovators in the field of physical education, such as Pietro Gallo and Costantino Reyer Castagna, co-operated in organising Baumann's school in Bologna, which was considered relatively modern in comparison with its older rival in Turin.

By the late 1870s the Minister of Education, Francesco De Sanctis, had won his parliamentary battle against the still pervasive opposition to gym-nastics in schools, and especially to female gymnastics, using his consider-able moral power and cultural weight. De Sanctis's policy was inspired by the practices of the most advanced nations, such as Britain, Germany and Switzerland, where gymnastics was considered a fundamental means of education, and of physical and moral regeneration, for young people. Casati's Law had not been applied consistently or completely: now, however, the role of educational gymnastics was reasserted as a compulsory discipline in De Sanctis's Law of 1878, and Article 3 laid down that: 'In female schools at every level gymnastics will have an exclusively educational character and will be regulated by special rules.'[23]

In order to increase the numbers of qualified gymnastics teachers the government launched a campaign, lasting from 1879 to 1882, to bring primary and secondary school teachers up to date throughout the country. In 1879 biannual schools were opened in nine Italian cities, taking set numbers of teachers for retraining. In the first year of these courses 364 teachers attended these schools. In addition, about 933 intensive courses were provided in the various Italian provinces, among which 416 courses were attended by women.

The school authorities did not totally agree with De Sanctis, predictably enough, and they did not always operate in strict accordance with the law that bears his name. The female programmes of educational gymnastics inspired by the school in Turin appeared to be poor imitations of the programmes for male teachers, which prescribed stiff movements, German-style gymnastic equipment and military exercises, all of which were far removed from the prevailing image of womanly softness and grace. In 1879, for example, the director of education for the province of Florence, a certain Cammarota, expressed his 'disgust that women aged 25, 30 or 35 have participated in jumping, turning around and so on'.[24] A number of female teachers successfully sought exemption from teaching gymnastics at school, presumably responding to pressures from public opinion and the press.

This reluctance to train young girls in gymnastics, which was mainly due to the influence of the prevailing Romantic model of weak women, hindered the realisation of the government's optimistic plans to give all Italian women energy and health through physical education. One problem was that almost all girls hid their dirty hair and faces under thick layers of powder: it was reported that in 1871, for example, 500 of the 600 girls practising gymnastics in schools did so.[25] Their gymnastics teachers, who also had the task of teaching them elementary norms of hygiene, therefore had to face resistance from their own pupils, as well as from parents and local authorities.

In addition, the recruitment of teachers was ill-organised and inadequate. By 1886 there were still only 756 fully qualified female gymnastics teachers in Italy.[26] On the other hand, judging from the complaints published in the sporting press, these teachers achieved deeds of real heroism and self-denial, despite receiving little more than 'starvation wages' in local government-owned schools. In a letter published in the specialist magazine *Il Ginnasiarca* one young teacher compared her wages of 46.70 lire a month to the wages and extras given other teachers: 600 lire a month, accommodation and a supply of firewood.[27]

By the last decade of the nineteenth century educational gymnastics had become frozen into intellectual formulas and, like other disciplines, was taught in a heavy and boring way. Pupils of both sexes had to learn long routines of physical exercises by heart, to be repeated until each group could achieve perfect and simultaneous execution. This trend was widely debated within the cultural world, which was divided between supporters of traditional physical education in gymnasiums and those who favoured newer sports and games in the open, on the British model.

One writer, Edmondo De Amicis, who in general strongly advocated traditional gymnastics, stigmatised the pretentious and overstated manner in which physical education was discussed in this period. De Amicis was opposed to all excess in female bodily culture, criticising the obtuseness of the government, which demanded gymnastics courses even for 'old mothers with grey hair, young pregnant women or women breastfeeding their babies, [and] nuns serving as schoolteachers: a real Heaven-sent scourge.'[28] De Amicis's novel *Amore e ginnastica* (Love and Gymnastics, 1892) is emblematic of the prevailing outlook concerning modern women who were fond of gymnastics. The novel concerns a sturdy gymnastics teacher, Miss Pedani, who is beautifully shaped, but dresses very simply and modestly, and is free from any tendencies to coquetry. De Amicis presents Miss Pedani as a new model of womanhood, a kind of apostle of gymnastics on behalf of Italian health. She accurately describes how good female pupils were at difficult gymnastic exercises in Italian schools:

> I have a dozen pupils ... who could perform in theatres, true acrobats who can turn around a fixed bar, jump over a board about 1.5 metres wide, [and] vault, ... their arms and legs are made of steel.[29]

Miss Pedani is depicted as decidedly masculine: the character was probably inspired by two well-known gymnastics teachers in Turin, Rosa Giordana and Teresa Bertotti. She is admired for her strength but feared as a possible wife and mother. She has such faith in her work that she is opposed to marriage, and tells a hopeless suitor who asks for her hand that she is not tender, her heart is manlike and she cannot become a good mother.

The arguments over educational gymnastics and/or games involved not only intellectuals in general, but also scholars from the scientific and technical fields. The physiologist and university teacher Angelo Mosso supported athletics and sports in contact with nature, after the British fashion, affirming that the educational gymnastics practised in the Italian school was too difficult to be learned and at the same time too modest in its motor achievements. Mosso was aware of the economic and social problems linked to the modernisation and industrialisation of the country, and recognised that both public and private schools were attended mostly by children from wealthier families, while the children of the poor tended to stay away. In 1881 61.03 per cent of Italian men and 73.51 per cent of Italian women were illiterate.[30] Mosso called for sports and games for all, and especially for the delicate children of the working class, as the best means to fight illness and pollution in the cities. He was also aware of the feminine condition, and proposed suitable activities, including Swedish ladders, for improving women's strength and health, as well as men's.[31] Mosso's goal was to lead male and female pupils alike towards the practice of modern sports, as these were, in his view, healthy, sociable and recreative activities in the open.[32]

Most medical scholars did not agree with Mosso. As we have seen above, Dr Emilio Baumann tried to improve Italians' health and willpower through his 'rational gymnastics'. He was not against sport and games in general, but, more realistically, he was aware of the poor conditions of pupils and schools, and criticised British sports as appropriate only for wealthy people. Another physician, Dr Angelo Gamba, from the teachers-training school in Turin, doubted that any games or sports were suitable for girls, although he did concede that they had a certain value. In his opinion, sports were right for strong boys, but Italian girls were too weak and delicate to undertake sport without danger. He concluded that girls should first be required to train their upper bodies by hanging by their arms.[33]

These discussions led in 1893 to the introduction by Martini, another Minister of Education, of new guidelines for physical education in schools. These combined military and nationalist traditions, the new British sports and scientific bodily culture.[34] Gymnastics was renamed physical education, training in marching and military drill was considerably reduced, and modern, 'rational' exercises, like those suggested by Baumann, were added to the curriculum. Some forms of athletics and some British games, such as lawn tennis and football, were also addded, following Mosso's advice and the practices of advanced nations such as Germany. Finally, in the name of national pride and identity the *giochi ginnici* (gymnastic games) of the Italian Renaissance were also added, together with a long list of children's popular games from different parts of the country.[35]

Even in this reform programme, however, physical education for girls was still intended to inspire soundness, energy and courage, in order to prepare them to become good mothers and educators. Competitive games were still generally considered unsuitable for their delicate constitutions and were not recommended, with the exceptions of lawn tennis and swimming, although the latter had to be practised with regard for the conventions on female morality and decency.[36] Nevertheless, the door to greater participation by women in sport had at last been officially opened.

In any case, the fall of the government and the appointment of a new Minister of Education, Baccelli, marked the setting aside of the reform of 1893, which was never implemented. The new government, led by Francesco Crispi, showed a determination to create a strong military nation, capable of repressing internal disorder and carrying out colonial ventures. Crispi directed Baccelli towards projects of pre-military conscription for boys aged 16 to 19, and encouraged the popular gymnastic societies, which were regarded as suitable for the making of future soldiers. The problem of female bodily culture was left to one side. Girls continued practising educational gymnastics at school under the terms of De Sanctis's Law.

After Crispi's government left office, however, some more democratic initiatives were undertaken, such as the foundation of the *Istituto Nazionale per l'Educazione Fisica e i Giuochi Ginnici nelle Scuole e nel Popolo* (National Institute for Physical Education and for Gymnastic Games in Schools and for the People) in 1897. This body aimed at diffusing a variety of physical activities to benefit young and old, men and women, rich and poor. In the optimistic programmes of the Institute all women were encouraged to practise sports through national and local committees consisting, it was claimed, of bright and realistic women determined to organise physical activity among women. The intentions were noble, but many problems made the life of the Institute precarious. Having strongly supported the diffusion of sports and games in Italy, and of course the innovative Institute, Mosso later bitterly affirmed that all such projects were deflated, little by little, by inaction.[37]

Female pioneers and early sporting enterprises

By the end of the nineteenth century women's route to achievement in sport did not pass through educational institutions but through the gymnastic societies (as will be shown below). The prevailing patriarchal culture of the country, which exalted women's role within the family and was confirmed by Pope Leo XIII's encyclical *Arcanum* (1880); the moralistic vision of the female body, which emphasised womanly decency; the pseudobiological view of the female population mainly as producers of future members of the 'race': none of these did anything to encourage women to take up competitive physical activities. Modern sport was still a masculine preserve.

However, there were some exceptions, as can be found by reference to the newspapers of the time. These depict the occasional sporting enterprises of women as amazing and unusual phenomena, deserving of special attention. Not surprisingly, a number of sportswomen were aristocrats, following the habits of their class like their counterparts in other European countries, but there were also students and workers from the middle and even the lower classes who enjoyed taking part in sporting events, defying conventional opinion.

For example, at a national gymnastics and fencing contest held in Naples in 1881, male and female gymnastics teams put on joint displays. A special women's regatta had been scheduled, but insistent rain did not allow this particular event to proceed.[38]

Next, in 1889 a magazine reported that the first 100-metre race for women had been held on 8 September in Arona, a small town in Lombardy, as part of the *Ludi Aronesi* (Games of Arona). The winner of the race, which was organised by the local Pro Patria Society, was a certain Miss Colombo, who competed against the Misses Radice and Zaccheo.[39] In the following year, 1890, a group of girls clad in 'decent' bathing costumes ran a race in front of about 10,000 spectators in Verona. There is also evidence that two working-class women from Lombardy, Anna Pozzi and Maria Tamburini, challenged each other to run a long-distance race, for about three kilometres, in Milan 1898. This race, from the city's Garibaldi Gate to its Venice Gate, was followed by most citizens with astonishment.[40]

From local newspapers we also learn that a female fencer, Giulia De Luca, performed marvellously against a man during a meeting at the Exhibition Palace in Rome on 21 November 1889. In 1891 she fenced with men in Rome and Catania, and then, together with her pupil Siena Rocchetti, competed against other men in the Politeama Theatre in Naples.[41] Target-shooting societies enrolled women from 1895: the first was Margherita Magagnini, who competed in a contest in Rome that September, but the rest became members of societies in the North of the country.[42]

Mountaineering was a passion of Margherita of Savoy, the Queen of Italy, who started climbing the Piedmontese Alps in 1885. Her example encouraged other women to try this difficult activity. In 1894 a group of men, and, pre-sumably for the first time, women, climbed the Monte Rosa together.[43]

On 6 April 1893 the Lawn Tennis Club of Rome organised its first contest for women. The participants were exclusively aristocratic. The first tennis contest for women in Milan was held in 1896. It was reported that in the same year Franca Florio competed in a doubles match with three men.[44]

A number of aristocratic ladies, such as Princess Agnese Hercolani and Countess Clementina Bastogi, tried to popularise cycling for Italian women, following the lead of Queen Margherita, who enjoyed cycling as well as walking and mountaineering.[45] A famous cycling race was held in 1893 around the Piazza Doria in Milan, between the florist Adelina Vigo and the actress and singer Lina Cavalieri.[46] In 1893 and 1894 a number of cycle races for both men and women were organised in Milan, Genoa and Lugo (in Romagna), and the female cyclist Alessandrina Maffi won many races against men.[47] These women cyclists provoked scandal and malicious com-ments, and in 1894 the *Unione Velocipedista Italiana* (Italian Cycling Union) decided to ban competitive cycling for women. Nevertheless, the prestigious Audax Prize, instituted in 1897 for cyclists who covered 18 kilometres in no more than 18 hours, was awarded to Alessandrina Maffi in 1898.[48]

It was also in 1897 that female dancers at La Scala in Milan had to learn how to ride bicycles to perform in an original ballet, *Sport*, choreographed by Luigi Manzotti. This ballet, which presented sports such as horse-riding, fencing, tennis, target-shooting, rowing, football and gymnastics, involved not only dancers and acrobats, but also members of the *Pro Patria* and *Forza e Coraggio* gymnastic societies.[49]

Such Italian women were sporting pioneers not only in relation to Italy but in relation to the whole world. Their extraordinary enterprises should be placed beside those of celebrated British women who, despite being labelled eccentric, competed in athletics, archery and boxing at about the same time. Yet in many sports, such as the future national game of football, women began taking part much later in Italy than in many other countries.

Emancipated sportswomen at the start of the twentieth century

At the beginning of the twentieth century Italian politics was characterised by a progressive democratisation of the liberal state. Some liberal politicians had a positivistic faith and championed the rights of the lower classes, but they insisted that social change had to take place without any disorder, in line with a strategy that did not 'dramatise' ideological conflict but allowed for smooth evolution. This was now the era of Giovanni Giolitti, an eminent positivist statesman who encouraged, but also carefully controlled, the industrial transformation of Italian society over a number of years. Women were also involved in this process, since they constituted half of all the workers engaged in industry: employers welcomed them because they would work for lower wages.[50]

In the first years of the new century the process of democratisation culminated in a new law reducing the length of the working day. From 1902 onwards workers were encouraged by the government to take up physical education in their spare time. This trend helped some women to begin early emancipation from the more traditional womanly roles, and also encouraged a kind of emancipation in the field of sport. Working side by side with men, female workers had become aware not only of their duties but also of their right to have a social life and to enjoy themselves. However, in the years preceding the First World War a strong nationalistic and anti-feminist current opposed women's emancipation, and worked to push them back into the home.

The first, emblematic example of a progressive man who helped women to affirm their rights through competitive gymnastics and modern sport was probably the gymnastics teacher Leopoldo Nomi-Pesciolini. He opened a female section of the Sienese Society of Gymnastics in 1881 and encouraged his own daughter, Ida, to join it.[51] This section did not last long, but in 1890 the Roman Gymnastics Society started physical education classes for girls from wealthy families who were aged between five and 14. This society, which had been founded with help from the National Federation of Gymnastics, also supported the creation of a Roman committee of aristocratic ladies, supervised by Fortunato Ballerini, on behalf of the Federation. In 1891 this committee organised ballroom dancing courses and elegant carnival parties that testified to the aristocratic tone of these first initiatives. In 1897, Article 1 of the society's statutes was revised to state that the women's committee was to spread female physical education among the citizens of Rome through gymnastics, dance, and games. In that year a special display by British ladies living in Rome was organised by the committee: it included a women's cycle race.[52]

At about the same time the *Federazione Ginnastica*, meeting in Florence, set up a central committee for women, led by ladies of the aristocracy, to spread physical education among women through conferences, exercise programmes, gymnastics and sports. Sub-committees of at least three ladies were to be organised by the new committee in every province. In practice the committee did not urge women to take up modern sporting activities, but promoted a peculiar kind of 'feminine' physical activity. Strength and energy of the body were banished, but plasticity, smartness and flexibility of movements were recommended, in order to emphasise women's effortless grace.[53] The committee achieved little else. The aristocratic ladies were mainly absorbed in their own private lives and their relationship to the National Federation was characterised by submission to the influential men who had promised so much on paper but did not adequately support women's sport.

In the industrialised cities of the North the rising movement among women in favour of modern sport was more aggressive and more determined. Women's sections were founded within the biggest sporting societies, but at the beginning they had difficulty in being accepted and in being allowed to work with full autonomy. The sporting societies were strongholds of male chauvinism, still anchored to the martial and 'virile' ideology of the past that claimed sport as a male preserve, forbidden to the 'fairer sex'.

Northern women pushed open the doors of the gymnastic societies with the help of enlightened men, such as Angelo Radaelli, and emancipated ladies such as Dr Amelia Cavallero Mazzucchetti of Milan. The Female *Mediolanum* was founded in Milan in 1897 as part of the *Mediolanum* Society, with the support of a group of middle-class ladies, mostly school-teachers, who were determined to have a committee of women only, acting autonomously. They started their own programme by organising Alpine excursions, as well as dancing and swimming courses. Again in Milan, the Female *Insubria* Society, founded in 1898, aimed especially at organising interscholastic gymnastic contests among girls, with such prizes as the *Clementina Arcari* Cup for primary school girls, and the *Vis et Elegantia* Cup for women students and female members of sporting societies.[54] In Turin the Gymnastics Society first opened a women's tennis section in 1898, then admitted girls to its gymnastics courses.

By the beginning of the twentieth century only about 100,000 people, in a country of 34 million, were engaged in physical activity within the gymnastic associations. The increasing number of women's sections in these associations was most notable in northern cities such as Alba, Asti, Brescia, Genoa and Modena, and in Rome. Not only upper-class or middle-class ladies were involved, but also women from more modest backgrounds. In Turin, for instance, the 'posh' Gymnastics Society of Turin enrolled 22 female gymnasts in 1900, 68 in 1901 and about 400 in 1907, while in 1901 the lower-status Gymnastics Society and the Free School for Workers had 39 and 47 female members respectively. In Milan, *Insubria* had 50 female members in 1898 and 130 in 1903, while the *Mediolanum* reached 200 subscriptions in the same year.[55]

This relative popularisation of female gymnastics within the societies led to the first Italian women's contest, hosted by Milan in 1902 as a spectacular sideshow to the most important male gymnastics contest. This public display was judged unsuitable for women by most of the spectators. Public opinion was not against women's indoor gymnastics but disapproved of displays of their well-trained bodies in public, since they could excite men's sexual desires. Even eminent individuals such as the politician Gregorio Valle boycotted the initiative, denouncing the performances by young girls, who unbecomingly showed emotion and strain while competing for victory, as well as the shorts worn under their very long skirts, which rose just a little when they attempted the high jump. Valle wrote: 'It was such an indecent performance that, on behalf of decency and respect for feminine dignity, I am sure that this female gymnastics competition in Milan will not be repeated in the future.'[56]

In spite of the traditional morality that still defended the modesty of women's bodies as sacred temples, in the following years this kind of mixed show became much more common. In 1904 the sixth national gymnastics contest in Florence hosted 94 female athletes from societies in Milan, Messina, Modena, Pistoia and Rome.[57] In 1905 the municipality of Vercelli organised a special national gymnastics contest in which 59 male and six female teams took part, and in 1907 about 4,500 women participated in the national gymnastics meeting in Venice.[58] Separate trains, hotels and timetables were organised in Venice to safeguard the decency and morality of the female teams, under the strict control of a committee of Venetian ladies. The female gymnasts who went to Venice were members of societies in northern and central Italy: in the south women of every social class were still generally barred from physical exercise.[59]

The first national contest for women only was held in Milan in 1908. The 18 teams taking part mostly came from the industrialised towns of Italy, where paid work was helping women to become emancipated from traditional patterns of life. These women, who had found it hard to join sporting associations, finally succeeded. The second national contest for women was held in Turin in 1911. By 1913 about one third of the 200 Italian gymnastic societies had female sections.

Women still had to fight to obtain more power, technical autonomy and specific programmes within these associations. On the other hand, female competitive gymnastic displays were at last accepted as public exhibitions of an educational discipline previously performed in school. They could be justified in the name of moral and physical strength, and the improvement of 'racial' health.

From the first decade of the century onwards female athleticism grew within the gymnastic societies. In 1911 special individual contests for women were organised on the occasion of the national gymnastics contest in Turin.

Athletes had to throw an iron ball weighing about five kilograms, take part in the long jump and run 80 metres in 15 seconds. In 1912 female athletes also competed in the high jump in Vicenza.[60] Tennis, widely considered to be a suitable sport for women, was taken up by upper-class children in such cities as Florence, Genoa, Milan and Turin. The female tennis star of the time was Rosetta Gagliardi.[61]

A number of daring women of different social classes thus challenged the conventional view that sporting activities were inherently masculine. People gossiped, and the press reported their achievements with mingled admiration and astonishment, presenting these aggressive, strong, muscular modern women as models in total contrast to the bashful, weak and delicate femininity inherited from the previous century. In 1914 Luigina Serponi ran 100 metres in just over 16 seconds, but she wore a very long and heavy skirt for the sake of feminine decency.[62] In 1910 the cyclist Miss Maffi and another woman, Maria Forzani, both competed energetically in Milan, and their cycle race was filmed by Luca Comerio for his documentary *Corsa ciclistica femminile* (Female Cycle Race).[63] It was reported that Rosina Ferrario was the first woman to obtain the prestigious licence of Caproni's aviation school, in 1913. In 1914 the motorcyclist Vittorina Sambri, a 'tomboyish' girl, achieved the fastest average speed among competitors in the Italian championship in Turin.[64] The tennis player Rosetta Gagliardi, already mentioned, also took part in fencing and swimming, and became well-known as a roller-skater in 1911, when she won the first national championship for women in that sport. Another all-round athlete, Dina Mancio, did well in ice-skating in 1915.[65]

In 1902 the *Rari Nantes* Society in La Spezia organised the first championship for female swimmers, who covered 200 metres. In the following years female swimming contests were held in coastal cities such as Genoa, Bari and Naples. Very few women were involved in these competitions, which required them to swim at least 100 or 150 metres.[66]

Women also became more involved in downhill skiing and mountaineering. Women participated in skiing, bobsleigh and sledging contests in 1909 and 1914, and founded the *Unione Sportiva Studentesse Italiane* (Italian Female Students Sporting Union) in Turin in 1918, thus helping courageous women to learn to climb mountains without any aid from men.[67]

Although cycling was popular among women, it was still considered morally and physically dangerous for them, not only by public opinion and the Church but also some eminent physicians. One of them, Paolo Mantegazza, in his book *L'igiene della bellezza* (published in Milan in 1912), supported ball games and foot races for girls, but objected to cycling: 'Eve's daughters should not get on a bicycle if they wish to combine hygiene and morality.'

By the beginning of the twentieth century the most pressing problem was still the issue of enhancing physical education by including sport in the basic curriculum for schools. This problem had still not been resolved after many years of debate. Government campaigns to encourage parents to send their children to school had helped to reduce illiteracy among women from 73.51 per cent in 1881 to 60.82 per cent in 1901. Primary schools were also the only places in which children, especially those from the poorest families, could learn to properly train their bodies and acquire hygienic habits for life. Yet in 1904 about 50 per cent of pupils, of both sexes, obtained exemption from physical education classes in a number of Italian schools. This could be explained by the fact that most schools lacked running water and that many school gymnasiums were former churches or were even in basements, where dust, humidity and cold undermined the teachers' efforts.[68]

These problems were partially addressed by Daneo's Law of 1909, which was inspired by the work of a commission, chaired by Angelo Mosso, which had reported in 1904. Daneo's Law promoted official recognition of physical education teachers (but did not provide higher salaries), regulated exemptions from physical education classes, increased the number of hours devoted to the discipline, and added games and sporting activities to the programme. It also initiated compulsory university courses in physical education, intended to train future teachers of any discipline; this was clearly intended as a way of compensating for the lack of qualified physical education specialists. Daneo's Law was relatively ineffective, however, for a number of reasons. The continuing lack of gymnasiums and other facilities, the failure to provide financial support, and the unpreparedness of teachers all told against it, while the government preferred to spend money on improving the army.

Anti-feminism and emancipation in the 1910s

At the start of the twentieth century an increasing number of initiatives were undertaken in pursuit of general female emancipation, as groups of women linked to socialist, Catholic and bourgeois movements fought for civil rights. However, after about 1910 new paternalist policies slowed down female emancipation and therefore hampered their social life, including their sporting activities. Women's emancipation suffered from the gradual abandonment of the positivist faith in linear human progress regardless of gender, as well as from the rise of nationalistic ideologies whose advocates wanted strong women for the betterment of the Italian 'race', but also wanted them to stay at home, far away from physical activities, in order to produce numerous children.

This new trend was also supported by theories about female biological inferiority imported from other countries, such as Otto Weininger's views on the female sex and character, and Paul Julius Moebius's ideas about women's mental inferiority. Moebius claimed that women could realise their 'nature' only through maternity and childhood, while any 'unnatural' attempt at emancipation would cause 'masculinisation' of women and the decline of the human species.[69]

Times had changed. The irrational 'myth of war' replaced the positivist 'myth of peace'. The government undertook a general militarisation that brought about the outbreak of war against Libya in 1911. This policy was aimed at training young men through military gymnastics at school and within civil society, in order to increase the number of soldiers, and instil sentiments of dutifulness and obedience to the law. The government ordered the *Federazione Ginnastica Italiana* to organise special courses for military preparation from 1907 onwards.

In contrast, only the most basic physical training was provided to girls at school, in the name of 'race hygiene', and nothing else was done to promote women's sporting activities. Maternity was to be the only way in which women could prove themselves true patriots.[70] As a consequence it was not until the 1920s that the *Federazione Ginnastica Italiana* established a new and more powerful national women's committee, with its own statutes, programmes and contests.

The strong current of nationalism and anti-feminism in Italy was supported by many intellectuals. Among them was the journalist Giovanni Papini, who believed in women's biological inferiority,[71] and the poet Gabriele D'Annunzio (discussed in Chapter 1). D'Annunzio promoted a negative image of women by portraying them mainly as sensual, 'vampish' creatures to be loved to perdition.[72]

Even the most modernist movement, Futurism, founded by Marinetti in 1909 (and also already discussed in Chapter 1), demonstrated a low opinion of Italian women. Futurism exalted virility and war in the name of male pride, and celebrated speed, machinery and flight. These values centred around bodily culture, which was greatly encouraged as the discipline best able to bring down the traditional intellectual culture. Having, in their own view, established the 'supremacy of gymnastics over books',[73] the Futurists demanded the foundation of special institutes for training physical education teachers, but women were left out of their proposals, and they also assumed that boys had to be trained apart from girls in schools.[74] In general, the Futurists regarded traditional-minded women as dangerous because of their romantic and weak spirits, but they also feared the modern 'vamps', who, they believed, blackmailed men sexually. The impulse given by Futurism to the practice of physical activities, even through the invention of new, 'simultaneous' sports,[75] did not really influence the conservative masculine trend of the time. In fact, only female dancers were involved in Futurist performances, symbolising machinery and flight by means of dynamic 'air dances that expressed the Futurists' *fisicofollia*' (physical madness).[76]

However, Futurism cannot be considered as a movement totally opposed to women. The Futurists did not believe in an inherent female inferiority, but attributed women's lower status to the effects of different spiritual and bodily cultures.[77] They supported the movements for women's suffrage and liberation, believing that women should have the same opportunities and rights as men. For example, in 1919 the Futurist writer Alberto Vianello beseeched women not to be 'females – meaning *sheep*', but to become true women, taking part in action side by side with the most daring Italian men.[78] Several women artists and intellectuals joined the Futurist movement.

The First World War was especially favourable to female emancipation in general. The home front needed women's moral support and strength to help the men fighting and dying on other fronts, who were tended by volunteer nurses in military hospitals. As in other countries, Italy also required women workers in industry, agriculture and public services. The government encouraged and exalted women's heroism and their spirit of sacrifice, and public opinion started to look at women with a new respect. It was even claimed that Italian women had obtained much more in the years of war than in the previous decades.

However, even by the end of the war the Italian feminist movement was not very strong. Since 1910 the movement had been ideologically and politically divided among nationalist, interventionist, Catholic, proletarian and pacifist tendencies. Futurist women and female supporters of D'Annunzio had also started contributing to the feminist cause, but their extremely avant-garde ideals only increased the general confusion.[79] The war had emphasised the already significant differences between, on the one hand upper-class and middle-class women, who tended to participate as volunteers, – and working-class women, whose right to go on working in factories and offices would have to be defended after the war. Women could find common ground only by promoting a kind of 'female social action', mainly focusing on the right to vote.

The idea of allowing women to continue in paid work was not popular, because it was thought that their jobs should go to men returning from the war.[80] Consequently, the law on women's legal capacities, approved by Parliament in 1919, was considered as a kind of 'demobilisation prize' given to working women before they were sent home once again.[81] Nevertheless, the rights of some working women were promoted by Sacchi's Law, also enacted in 1919, which provided that women could compete on equal terms with men for posts in the civil service. The most important bill concerning women – the one granting them the right to vote – was passed by the Chamber of Deputies in 1919, but after the fall of the government that sponsored it the Senate set it aside in 1920. The feminist movements stressed the importance of women's physical culture, which was also encouraged by D'Annunzio. Under his Regency of Carnaro, the shortlived republic he established in Fiume (see Chapter 1), men and women had equal rights and duties, including military service. D'Annunzio stated that 'bodily education should be practised by both sexes in well-equipped outdoor gymnasiums'.[82] However, the problem of increasing support for women's sport was not really faced in Italy, with a few exceptions such as that offered by the new periodical *Almanacco della donna italiana*, which included a section specially dedicated to sportswomen from its first issue, in 1920, onwards.[83] This section, written by Giuseppe Monti, was considered quite innovative, if not transgressive.

By the beginning of the 1920s Italian women were finding it hard to exercise the rights that they had gained during the war. The Fascist movement attracted people of different creeds and classes, including some combative women, who believed that Fascism's revolutionary power could help their cause.

Fascist models of femininity

During the two decades of Fascism, the ideal image of manhood was embodied by the 'virile' Mussolini (as discussed in Chapter 1). Italian women, on the other hand, were expected to embody different models of femininity, derived from a policy that sought to combine aspirations for modernity, secularisation and imperialism with aspirations to safeguard traditionalism, religion and stability. Although all Italians suffered as the regime worked out these contradictions, women in particular, the weaker half of the population, were compelled to put aside most of their expectations, whatever their particular class background. Fascinated by the *Duce*, many, perhaps most, Italian women adapted themselves to Mussolini's will by attempting to model themselves on his plans, in the name of the Fascist cause. The wind of female emancipation that had been blowing from the beginning of the twentieth century was increasingly moderated by a newly re-emphasised 'masculinism' that asserted that women were different from men and inferior to them.

At the beginning this traditionalism was not really supported by Fascism, which in its pioneering years appeared to be one of the most modern, innovative and revolutionary movements in Italy, and to be far removed from any commitment to gender-based discrimination. Many women became convinced that Fascism could also fight for their rights. However, once the regime had been firmly established, the question of female emancipation was set aside in favour of a manly hegemony based on traditional paternalism. Under pressure from the Catholic Church, which had always supported female modesty and maternity, as well as from the perceived need to increase the population while addressing Italy's many economic problems, the regime ceased to promote the modern model of the working woman. Discouraging work outside the home by all available means, the regime aimed to relegate women to the home for most of their time. In the spirit of sacrifice for the Fatherland, and echoing the rhetoric of the First World War, women were now exhorted to concentrate on housework and to bear numerous children. Thus traditionalism came to be repackaged as a means by which women could take part in the building of the new Fascist state as mothers. In other respects women did not count for much. Their political and social involvement was restricted to participation in organisations strictly controlled by the Fascist Party and some Catholic lay associations. Within this framework basic physical education and some sports were considered to be affairs of state, offering a means to strengthen the bodies and spirits of young Italian women in accordance with the expansionist plans of the regime and current eugenic theories.

From the mid-1930s onwards, as Italy became involved in conflicts in Ethiopia and Spain, and then in the Second World War, some changes were made in the models of femininity that it promoted. Women were increasingly encouraged to participate more broadly in social and political life, so that they could become morally involved in supporting their husbands and sons as they responded to the call of the Fatherland. Strengthened by years of silent sacrifice and insistent patriotic propaganda, as well as by basic physical education, several combative women even participated in the world conflict. After the fall of Fascism in 1943 the subsequent civil war saw a number of women in northern Italy, part of which was still controlled by Mussolini, enrolling Fascist volunteers in the army of the shortlived '*Repubblica Sociale Italiana*', also known as the Republic of Salò. At the same time much larger numbers of women joined or supported the partisan groups that fought against both German Nazi and Italian Fascist troops for the liberation of the country. The involvement of women in these stirring and confusing events suggests that the role of women had indeed changed during the Fascist era, at least to the extent that some women had become more self-confident and more prepared to leave their homes and families for the sake of a political cause.

The revolutionary women of early Fascism, 1919–24

In Italy the end of the First World War ushered in a dangerous period that could easily have led to civil war: the country had been left with serious problems, notably a rise in violence, the impact of individualism and the fragmentation of society. Feminism was still admired by many Italian women, but in general it was regarded as being unsuited to the 'Latin temperament'. It was widely believed that Latin women had to pursue their own way to emancipation by adhering to a *femminismo latino* based on a strong sense of maternity, tradition and sacrifice, an ideology that, supposedly, could unify all women within a universal category[1]. On the other hand, the battle for suffrage and other civil rights was still raging (as discussed in Chapter 2). Against this background Fascism presented itself as one of the most constructive ideologies, capable of rapidly assuring the creation of a new, modern order in the tumultuous life of Italy.

The first Fascist programme, issued in June 1919, included demands not only for full freedom for citizens in general, but also for the right of 'integral' suffrage for women. Nevertheless, only a very small number of women joined the Fascist movement before it seized power. Just nine women had been present on 23 March 1919 when Mussolini and others, including

3.1 Revolutionary fascist women from Naples (1924)

assorted nationalists, socialists, Futurists, republicans and members of *Arditi* groups,[2] launched the *Fasci di Combattimento* at a meeting in the Piazza San Sepolcro in Milan. Among the nine were Giselda Brebbia, an active member of the Socialist Party, and the schoolteacher Regina Teruzzi, who was a capable organiser of lower-class women.[3] Between this event and the 'March on Rome' that brought Mussolini to power in 1922, only a few hundred women joined the movement: there were, for example, 200 female Fascists in Brescia, 28 in Verona and 100 in Florence.[4] Most of them were eccentric and bellicose women, interested in nationalism and/or socialism, who believed in the values of modernity and emancipation that Mussolini and his followers claimed to be spreading. Believing in the necessity for a 'new order', these women embodied the 'virile' and aggressive model of womanhood previously proposed by Futurism. Some of them even participated in violent actions against their opponents alongside male Fascists. At a gymnastics contest in Venice in 1919 a number of female athletes joined their Fascist friends in a scuffle with a group of 'cowards'.[5] In 1920, a certain Cesarina Bresciani participated in a bloody assault on the city hall in Verona along with her brother and other young Fascist men. In 1922, 30 armed Fascist women repelled a group of socialists from a Fascist centre near Udine.[6]

In its early years Fascism was also supported by aristocratic ladies, such as the marchionesses Cristina Malenchini and Corinna Ginori Lisci, and the countesses Luisa Capponi, Laura Scotti and Maria Grazia Vannicelli, as well as a number of middle-class women. Some of them had lost their sons, brothers or husbands in the First World War. Others had established reputations in politics or culture, including two Futurists, Eva Kuhn Amendola (known as 'Magamal') and Elda Norchi (or 'Futurluce'); the socialist Margherita Sarfatti; and the journalist Elisa Majer Rizzioli,[7] who founded a group called *Fasci Femminili* in Milan in 1921.

A separate *Fasci Femminili* group was also founded in Rome in the same year. It had about 20 members, who were very soon involved in skirmishes with anti-Fascists.[8] They supported the March on Rome by organising a number of first-aid stations in the capital, in expectation of a counter-attack by the Italian army. These women had to temporarily leave their families and work hard to prepare for the arrival of the marchers. One of the youngest of them, Piera Fondelli, wrote in her diary:

> I was away from home for four days and nights. We slept in arm-chairs for a few hours in the hotels where we were in charge of organising first-aid stations, and naturally the owners of the hotels joined the Fascist Party. I kept in touch with my mother by telephone. We could not believe that the country, the King, the army, the authorities, in short, Italy as a whole, would have delivered to us a handful of men, and a very small percentage of women, ready for action, aiming to restore order in every street, school and factory.[9]

On 1 June 1923 Mussolini attended a conference of the *Fasci Femminili* groups in Venice, where, for the first time, one of the most famous Fascist symbols, the black shirt, was worn by a number of women. They promised the *Duce* their fervour, faith and sacrifice for the Fascist cause.

Women who joined the Fascist movement thought of themselves as modern and emancipated, but in truth they still embodied the bourgeois model formulated by men long before, and their rights and needs were still underestimated by men in the new movement, who preferred to exalt the traditional 'feminine spirit of sacrifice'. Fascism was clearly a violent and misogynous ideology, and Fascists neither believed in nor supported the involvement of women in politics. An article in the Fascist daily *Il Popolo d'Italia* (27 December 1921) made this clear: 'The women's Fascist groups will devote themselves to propaganda, charity, welfare and other duties, but they are to be excluded from every political action led by the *Fasci di Combattimento*.'

Yet Mussolini's policy concerning women's rights remained ambiguous. At the start of his political career he had been a socialist, with a moderate sympathy for feminism, but later he had set out to conciliate the Church, restore the paternalistic traditions of the Italian people and emphasise the new myth of virility. In an interview published in the *Petit Parisien* (11 November 1922), Mussolini declared that he was in favour of universal suffrage for men, but not for women, because women would always vote in favour of male candidates.[10] However, during a Fascist women's conference in Padua in 1920 he had said that: 'Fascists do not belong to the crowd of the vain and sceptical who undervalue woman's social and political importance. Who cares about voting? You will vote!'[11] At a conference of the pro-suffrage International Alliance in Rome on 14 May 1923 he declared that:

> Given the Italian public spirit and the trend of our political develop-
> ment, the concession of women's votes finds no opposition in
> any party. As far as the government is concerned, I feel I am
> entitled to declare that, apart from unforeseen events, the Fascist
> Government stands firm for the right to vote for different categories
> of women, starting with local elections.[12]

Women's right to vote in local elections had indeed been granted, but this meant nothing after the end of 1925, when new 'emergency' laws that, among other changes, abolished local elections, were imposed by the regime. These laws remained in force until the fall of the regime.

Given these ambiguities, even some conservative Catholics deceived themselves into thinking that Fascism would help women's emancipation by promoting paid work for women. An article in the Catholic magazine *La donna italiana* (1924) declared that:

> The right to work is a holy human prerogative that has been
> sanctioned by religion, won through titanic battles, and fully
> accepted by common conscience nowadays. We should continue
> to claim that not only men but also women should have to earn
> their bread by the sweat of their brows, and that protection and
> respect should be given to those women who leave their quiet
> homes and enter the wild forest of the world.[13]

In fact, of course, Mussolini's policy concerning women's rights became anti-feminist as soon as power had been obtained.

At the beginning of 1920s, when the Fascists were fighting to assert them-selves, Italian women who were hostile to Fascism were too weak and divided to be capable of mounting strong opposition. On the other hand, the self-confident and aggressive women who fought alongside Fascist men were sometimes suspected of being lesbians. One such woman, Ines Donati, actively supported the Fascist cause, and in the early years the movement celebrated her as a heroine, but she was rapidly marginalised when she began to be suspected of being a lesbian, and therefore unsuitable as an example of the 'new woman'.

In the early years of the regime only a very few courageous women tried to support the anti-Fascist cause,[14] while many women joined Fascist groups. The rest of the female population looked on with little hope, or with quiet resignation.

'New women' as wives and mothers, 1925–35

The process of 'Fascistisation', which started in 1925–26, was aimed at the authoritarian integration, organisation and education of citizens within the new state. This state was no longer considered distant or extraneous, but was presented as a body within which all Italians would realise their goals. Alongside the 'virile' model of the 'new man', the model of the 'new woman' began to be propagated. This was a rather abstract image, however, as no woman had enough personal charisma or power to embody it convincingly. In any case, the official image of the Fascist woman was far from the modern model of womanhood developed from the beginning of the twentieth century and reinforced during the First World War, when emancipated working women had made their mark. The Fascist 'new woman' was simply a revival of the traditional model of femininity. Behind the modernist façade, women were still expected to be daughters, wives and mothers, and nothing else. Once the regime was firmly established, women were even considered incapable of controlling the organisations that they themselves had founded: the *Fasci Femminili* groups, for example, were placed under the leadership of a powerful male Fascist, Augusto Turati, in 1926.

At the beginning of the 1930s discrimination against female intellectuals culminated in the case of the writer Grazia Deledda. Although she had won the Nobel Prize for Literature in 1926, she was not allowed to become a member of the *Accademia d'Italia*, the most exclusive association of the cultural elite (which had originated in a proposal by Mussolini's inspirational muse and lover Margherita Sarfatti).[15] The poet Ada Negri was also prevented from joining the *Accademia*, which remained a bastion of male culture, but in 1930 she received a 'consolation prize' in the form of a Mussolini Prize. Women who still claimed their rights were ridiculed, depicted as 'emaciated and bespectacled old maids', and compared to the British Suffragettes.[16]

The Fascist 'new woman' may well have been inspired by Mussolini's view of his own mother, Rosa Maltoni, a primary school teacher whose high level of culture, religious faith, firmness of character, exemplary life and early death had left an indelible mark on the *Duce*. In his autobiography Mussolini wrote: 'My greatest love was for my mother. She was so quiet, so tender and yet so strong.'[17] Rosa Maltoni thus incarnated the stereotypical Italian mother of the nineteenth century, combining the image of the ancient Roman matron with the Catholic image of the *Madonna*. Her example was followed both by Mussolini's wife, Rachele, a silent, tolerant housewife, and, to some extent, by his favourite daughter, Edda, who had a vivacious and passionate nature that was said to resemble her grandmother's. However, Edda also usefully represented the younger generation of middle-class women who saw themselves as modern and emancipated but simultaneously respectful of traditional values. Edda herself enjoyed sport, travel and driving, and even wore trousers, but she was also hailed as an obedient daughter, a good wife and a busy mother. At the same time, women were exhorted to forget the American model of womanhood, incarnated by blonde movie stars, with their slender bodies, and their free and easy manners, in favour of the Mediterranean model of flourishing and modest womanhood, symbolised by broad hips and round breasts that, it was supposed, favoured maternity.[18] In addition, women had to make themselves fit and strong by practising physical education and sport, both at school and in the new state's organisations, in order to produce strong children for the Fatherland.

The propagation of the Fascist model of the 'new woman' was considerably eased by the suppression of all movements that offered alternatives. The Socialist and Communist parties, and their auxiliary organisations, were banned in 1925 and 1926, and only organisations linked to Catholicism were tolerated. In a speech to the Chamber of Deputies on 26 May 1927 the *Duce* openly revealed his true opinion of women:

> We have created a special Tribunal that is functioning perfectly without problems, and it will even improve its performance, especially if the female element, which brings the signs of frivolity into serious matters, is left outside its walls.

In the same speech Mussolini emphasised the regime's demographic policy as a means to increase the economic and moral power of the nation. This demographic policy and the campaign that it inspired were central to the regime's efforts to forge the 'new woman'.

In Rome, on 28 October 1927, the *Duce* officially received delegates from all the provincial groups of *Fasci Femminili*, for the first time. He told these important women, who were obviously convinced supporters of Fascism: 'I need births, many births. I wish that every year the country would add to its treasure new and healthy lives.'[19] This clear message was to be spread among all Italian women. Mussolini was convinced that 'size is power',[20] and intended to emulate more powerful nations by conquering new colonies, in which the nationalist dream of civilising new peoples under the Italian flag, and giving jobs to all citizens, would be fully realised. As a consequence, the 'new man' had to marry young and father numerous children for the Fatherland, while the 'new woman' had a duty to bring up her children and be a good housewife.

A new body protecting maternity and children's health, the *Opera Nazionale Maternità ed Infanzia* (ONMI), was founded in 1925, and special additional taxes on unmarried adults were imposed from 1926. In addition, a number of measures discouraging or limiting women's opportunities to obtain paid work were introduced. A royal decree of 9 December 1926 banned women teachers from teaching literature, Greek, Latin, history and philosophy. Another royal decree, dated 20 January 1927, reduced working women's wages to half the amount of men's wages. In 1928 the regime issued measures to discourage female students from continuing their studies

3.2 A big Italian family performing the 'Roman salute'

3.3 Mussolini congratulates a prolific mother and her children

at secondary school or university by doubling their taxes. Under another decree, dated 28 November 1933, restrictions were placed on women's employment in the civil service, explicitly on the grounds that they could not easily reconcile paid work with their maternal duties.[21] Under the Law of 14 June 1928 all families with six or more children were given financial support by the state and exempted from taxes. Nevertheless, the low incomes of most fathers compelled them to limit the number of children they produced and to let their wives go out to work: in 1931 about half of all Italian families lived on two incomes.[22] Finally, the new Penal Code, elaborated by Alfredo Rocco between 1926 and 1931, retained the old notion of 'crimes of honour': under Article 587 of the Code a man who murdered his adulterous daughter, sister or wife could be sentenced to three to seven years in prison, instead of the 30 years that was the standard punishment for other murders. The Code also outlawed abortion as a crime 'against the Italian race'.

Thus the family, theoretically a private institution, became more and more a target for public intervention. The demographic policy was celebrated with a special day dedicated to maternity and infancy in general, and to the most prolific Italian mothers in particular. In 1933 it was decided that this celebration would take place on 24 December, in order to emphasise that to be a mother was both a secular duty for the Fatherland and a religious vocation comparable to that of the Virgin Mary herself.[23]

The myth of maternity was spread all over the country by the media, especially the press and newsreels, which displayed images of mothers breastfeeding their babies, surrounded by their other young children. The periodical *Critica Fascista* claimed in 1933 that 'if one looks at Italy as a whole, from its poems to its pictures and churches, one finds that everything is a hymn to virginity and maternity',[24] and a wetnurse, Antonietta Girolamo, became popular when the press claimed that she could produce about 2.5 litres of breastmilk every day.[25] Many middle-class Fascist women were involved in the campaign for the protection of maternity, spending time visiting the poor, giving them food and clothing, and passing on advice about domestic economy. Poor families were also supported by ONMI and other organisations controlled by the Party or the Church. After all, the regime's demographic policy was in perfect step with Pope Pius XI's encyclical *Casti Connubii* (1930), in which he described paid work by women as 'a perversion for the family as a whole' and condemned all forms of birth control. The intermingling of politics and religion was symbolised in the heavily publicised annual ceremony known as the *Befana Fascista* (Fascist Epiphany), when Mussolini and other Fascist leaders gave toys and other presents to carefully selected children of the poor.

However, despite the combined efforts of the regime, the Church and the media, the demographic policy was a failure: indeed, the birth rate actually fell, from 29.9 per 1,000 of the population in 1921–25 to 27.1 in 1926–30 and then 24 in 1931–35.[26] The most prolific region was the South, where the traditional rural economy still needed children who could quickly become agricultural labourers, but infantile mortality was high there, due to low levels of nutrition and hygiene. For instance, in 1922, of every 1,000 children born in the South about 128 died during the first year of life and in 1940 about 103 died. In contrast, in the northern and central regions industrialisation had attracted many people from the countryside into the cities, which now housed increasing numbers of the unemployed, many of them too poor even to consider marriage, let alone raising children. Meanwhile, men and women who belonged to the aristocracy, the Fascist elite or the middle class, the only social groups to have living standards much above the poverty level, tended to have relatively few children, in the hope of being able to give those children they did have the best education and material goods without too much impact on their own lifestyles.[27]

Clearly, Mussolini's notion that producing more than four children was the best way in which a woman could defeat infant mortality and other 'negative factors'[28] failed to convince many women. The Fascist slogans – such as 'He who is not a father is not a man', or 'Through maternity a woman attains her greatest beauty' – were not effective either. Another slogan, 'War is for a man what maternity is for a woman', linked the demographic policy to Mussolini's hopes that a rise in the population would allow the regime to place about 8 million men under arms – another dream that was never to be realised.

The demographic campaign was obstructed not only by the economic problems arising from the worldwide crisis of 1929 but also by the under-developed state of the domestic economy, which was characterised by very low incomes and high unemployment. This tended to drive women to accept any job they could find, however low the wages, and to seek aid from any organisation that would give it, whether Fascist, Catholic or private. What the regime took to be public enthusiasm for the demographic policy may have been, at least in part, no more than the response of desperate families seeking financial and social support.

Mussolini tried to oppose the silent obstructionism of Italians by denying publicly that women were discriminated against or expected to be submissive to men. In his speeches the *Duce* often encouraged women to be fertile and demonstrated his personal admiration for 'Latin femininity'. In 1934, for example, he declared that:

> The Italian woman is a mother above all else: instinctively she is resistant to sterile masculinisation from overseas [meaning the United States], which estranges woman from her biological mission, which is also her higher spiritual mission: to continue the race and therefore history by giving birth.[29]

He added that the Italian women had the great privilege of not having to sacrifice their perfect femininity to any idol of the time. To speak of sub-mission to men, or of the persistence of old-fashioned ideas, was therefore absurd.[30] By emphasising this theme of women's 'biological mission', Fascism aimed to keep women burdened by family duties away from both paid work and culture. This policy, like the demographic policy to which it was linked, was wholeheartedly supported by the Church. In 1931 Pius XI issued a new encyclical, *Quadragesimo Anno*, in which he insisted that:

> Mothers should carry on their work chiefly at home, or near to it, occupying themselves in caring for the household. Intolerable and at all costs to be abolished is the abuse whereby mothers of families, because of the insufficiency of the father's salary, are forced to engage in painful occupations outside the domestic walls, to the neglect of their own proper cares and duties, particularly the upbringing of their children.[31]

From this point onwards priests handed copies of *Casti Connubi* to newly wed couples, along with wedding insurance papers and information on the state's natality prizes. This new custom underlined the convergence of Catholic religious faith and the Fascist notion of civic duty in the promotion of the demographic campaign.

The pseudoscientific belief that 'nature' compelled women to become mothers and housewives also received the support of some eminent scholars, such as Nicola Pende, the director of the Institute of Medical Pathology at the University of Rome, who was opposed to gender equality and the employment of women in most kinds of paid work. He recommended maternity as the overriding objective for all women, asserting, for example, that: 'A woman's body, and her moral and intellectual qualities, are suited to maternal functions, whereas a man's body and spirit are suited both to muscular work and to achievement in the arts and sciences'.[32] Pende's book, *Bonifica umana razionale e biologia politica* (1933), from which this passage is taken, is a highly original, if not really very scientific compendium of Fascist ideology, biology, psychology, anthropology, sociology, pedagogical theory and racism.

While the demographic campaign failed, the campaign to drive women out of the world of paid employment had some success. In the face of the legal changes outlined above, as well as informal pressures, the proportion of women workers within the total labour force of the country fell from 32.5 per cent in 1921, to 24 per cent in 1936. Those women who remained in factories and offices were portrayed in Fascist propaganda as ugly, man-like, if they were educated, while female secretaries were said to work only to get enough money to buy silk stockings.[33] Nevertheless, many middle-class and intellectual women continued to work and to fight for female emancipation, not only in private but also through national organisations, at least for as long as the regime permitted them to.

In 1935 the *Federazione Nazionale Laureate e Diplomate* (National Federation of University and Secondary School Graduates, or FILDIS), which had been founded in 1920, was denounced for being too involved in international feminist movements and was forced to cease its activities. However, organised activity on behalf of female emancipation did not entirely disappear from Italy. In 1930 Luigia Pirovano had founded the *Alleanza Muliebre Culturale Italiana* (Italian Women's Cultural Alliance), which declared itself anti-feminist, in line with the dominant ideology, but often fought against gender discrimination, especially in defence of working women from the lower middle class.[34] Another women's organisation supported by Fascism was the *Associazione Nazionale Fascista Artiste e Laureate* (National Fascist Association for Female Artists and Graduates, or ANFAL), which was headed by Maria Castellani Autentico, and was inspired by the example of the US-based International Professional Women's Organisation. ANFAL created a network of about 80 provincial sections in which intellectual women of good social standing organised work and art exhibitions at local, regional and even national levels. They tried to adhere to the Fascist model of the 'new woman' by spreading the notions that, when necessary, personal ambition should be sacrificed for family values, and that a subordinate social status was natural for 'Latin' women. Even so, ANFAL provided a milieu in which at least a small number of women who were willing to collaborate with the regime could take part in activities outside the home.

In addition, since the state censors paid much closer attention to the contents of newspapers than they did to the contents of periodicals, presumably on the assumption that relatively few people read them anyway, it was sometimes possible to express nonconformist opinions in specialist magazines aimed at women. For example, the *Almanacco della donna italiana*, which was published regularly between 1920 and 1943, presented different and contradictory points of view, some of which were incompatible with official Fascism. In the first half of the 1920s the *Almanacco* was clearly in favour of women's suffrage, education and employment. Later on it still occasionally carried articles that did not stress the official policy on women's role as housewives. Fascism regarded intellectual and professional women as just another negative aspect of bourgeois ambition and vanity,[35] but the *Almanacco* emphasised women's intellectual role in hundreds of biographical articles about self-confident and successful professional women. It also carried detailed reviews of books by Italian and foreign women writers.[36] It rarely gave explicit support to the official line on the role of housewives or the myth of the *Duce*, which were the main topics in other Italian women's magazines.[37]

Militarised women in the war years, 1936–45

Mussolini's low opinion of women did not change much, of course, but he was willing to adapt it a little to circumstances. As his foreign policy became more aggressive, in pursuit of his dream of refounding the Roman empire, increasing numbers of men were sent away to fight or to take part in the administration of the colonies, and women were encouraged to take jobs that had previously been reserved for men. The 'charming' Mussolini started to address his speeches to 'oceanic crowds' of women and his words were broadcast on the state's radio station, which could reach about 800,000 families by 1937.[38] In the years 1935–37 alone about ten of his speeches were specifically addressed to women, mainly to exhort them to further sacrifices.

By the end of 1935, while the Italian army was fighting in Ethiopia, women were being mobilised in a campaign for economic self-sufficiency intended to counteract the effects of the sanctions imposed on Italy by the League of Nations. In a speech to 850 women on 1 December 1935, the *Duce* expressed his indignation at the sanctions and asked his audience to help the

Fatherland. Many women responded to the regime's call for them to hand in their gold wedding rings: about 430,000 rings were collected in Rome and Milan alone.[39] At the 'Day of Faith', a theatrical ceremony held in Rome 17 days later, in an attempt to evoke the Roman empire, religious faith and Fascist civic duty converged once again, as the rings helped to symbolise a kind of wedding between Fascism and Italian women. Many housewives revealed a talent for transforming old pots, railings and other objects into supplies of metal for the Fatherland, and for replacing foreign foodstuffs and other imports with Italian products. According to the regime and its apologists, women thus demonstrated that, while their husbands and sons were far away in Africa, they too could actively participate in the foundation of a glorious Fascist empire.

On 7 May 1936 Mussolini, the conqueror of Ethiopia, spoke to the crowd from the balcony of the Venice Palace in Rome. It has been argued that it was at this point that the consensus between the Italian people and Fascism reached its apex. The *Duce*'s speech included words of congratulation to the 100,000 or more women in the square below the balcony:

> The victory of our troops in East Africa is also due to you, women of Rome and Italy. Fascist Italy … gave you a delicate and decisive task: to make a fortress of the Italian family in order to resist the sanctions. You women accomplished this task. The Fatherland pays tribute to you in its gratitude.[40]

The involvement of women as volunteers in programmes of social assistance increasingly became a state service and a political duty. From the second half of the 1930s uniformed *visitatrici* (district nurses), trained in special courses organised in collaboration with the Red Cross, visited poor families to provide charity, and also organised children's health resorts, domestic economy courses, handicraft laboratories and employment agencies for women. In addition, Decree no. 696, issued in January 1937, stated that the greatest care should be given to the mobilisation of women, and that their numbers and activities in Fascist bodies should be increased. Two new organisations were founded: the *Giovani Fasciste*, established in 1935 for young women aged between 18 and 21; and the *Sezioni Operaie e Lavoranti a Domicilio* (Sections of Women Working in Factories and at Home, or SOLD), launched in 1938. Ines Donati, who had earlier been marginalised (as mentioned above), was once again presented as an exemplary heroine, and her remains were transferred to the Chapel of Fascist Martyrs in the cemetery of Verano in Rome.

The regime was pleased with the results of the mobilisation campaign. In the African colonies uniformed women equipped with rifles stood guard in the army's camps, while in Italy the number of women enrolled in the organisations of *Donne Fasciste* (Fascist Women) and *Massaie Rurali* (Rural Women Workers) doubled between 1934 and 1937.[41] By the time the Second World War began in 1939 about one quarter of all eligible women were members of Fascist organisations. In 1940 about 750,000 women were enrolled in the *Donne Fasciste*, 1,480,000 in the *Massaie Rurali*, 500,000 in the SOLD and 450,000 in the *Giovani Fasciste*,[42] while about 3,600,000 schoolgirls were enrolled in the *Opera Nazionale Balilla* (ONB), then controlled by the central Fascist youth body, the *Gioventù Italiana del Littorio* (GIL). The regime had already arranged to celebrate the mobilisation campaign as early as June 1937, when ANFAL organised a colossal exhibition in Rome about health resorts and children's assistance schemes. About 60,000 women were present to hear Mussolini's speech at the opening of the exhibition, in which he expressed his admiration for an event that, he claimed, had no precedent in the history of the world.[43]

Step by step, the times were changing in favour of women. The cultural world, which had been dominated by men for centuries, now had to open up to a number of female intellectuals. Then came the 'revolutionary' but actually retrograde proposal by Ferdinando Loffredo that schools reserved for women be established, in which professional instruction would be avoided.[44] Even the Minister for National Education, Giuseppe Bottai, a relatively lucid and cultured Fascist who was also anti-feminist, criticised Loffredo's proposal. Loffredo, a brilliant Catholic social scientist, was an enemy of women's emancipation and therefore favoured traditionally patriarcal families. In 1938 he was still affirming, for instance, that:

> Feminine emancipation has not produced advantages in the fields of the sciences or the arts, but on the contrary has constituted the most serious danger, capable of destroying what white people's civilisation has already produced ... Women have to return to the absolute subjection of men, whether their fathers or their husbands; subjection because of their spiritual, economic and cultural inferiority.[45]

In spite of the views expressed by Loffredo and other influential men, not all women suffered from an inferiority complex. On the contrary, a number of intellectual women became more self-confident and found ways to improve the quality of their work. Consequently, they could not be left out of cultural events any more, and participated in some high-level national contests with brilliant results. The composer Barbara Giuranna gained first place in a national contest for musicians in 1937; the poet and journalist Fanny Dini won the annual competition for 'poets of the Mussolini era' in

1938; and in 1940 the poet Ada Negri at last became a member of the *Accademia d'Italia*. In the same year the *Accademia d'Italia* published the first volumes of a biographical encyclopedia on important Italian women throughout the ages. At a lower level, from 1938 onwards the *Littoriali* of Culture and Sport, a contest organised by the *Gruppi Universitari Fascisti* (GUF), was opened to female students, but separated from the male *Littoriali* until 1941, when male and female students began participating in *Littoriali* contests on equal terms.

There were even some initiatives in favour of enhancing women's involvement in politics, a clear sign that they were improving their lot. For instance, in 1938 the ruling party admitted women to the annual 'Fascist conscription' of new members, held on 23 March (the anniversary of the foundation of the *Fasci di Combattimento*); members of the *Fasci Femminili* were allowed to wear black uniforms; some women were employed as functionaries in Fascist centres and received salaries from the party; and from 1937 these women were placed under the supervision of female inspectors in the central committee of the *Fasci Femminili*.[46] In 1938 Mussolini proposed that one of these inspectors, Clara Franceschini, should be made a member of the Fascist Grand Council, but bowed to opposition from the more traditional-minded members of the Council and withdrew both this nomination and a proposal for the admission of women to the Chamber of *Fasci* and Corporations, the new 'legislature' created by the regime to replace the elected Chamber of Deputies.[47]

The professional and artistic women enrolled in ANFAL strongly supported the aggressive war propaganda of that time. They seem to have thought that they would have more opportunities in the working world if men were engaged on the battlefield.[48] On 28 May 1939 female auxiliaries of the party organised a political and folkloric event in Rome to display to the country the mobilisation of women. About 70,000 women gathered for this event, at which about 15,000 women in black uniforms, regional costume, working clothes or sportswear marched past the *Duce* and the other Fascist leaders. Groups of female cyclists, drivers and horse-riders paraded as well.[49]

Women were now expected to be truly Fascist, and therefore 'virile' and active in society, and at the same time to leave work and honour to men, and restrict themselves to being mothers of numerous children. The regime tolerated the presence of young women in workplaces, but still obstructed job opportunities for older women by upholding the ideal of maternity and the interests of working men. Yet the birth rate went on falling: having reached 24 per 1,000 of the population in the 1931–35 (as mentioned above), it fell to 23.4 in the years 1936–40.[50] In a speech delivered on 25 October 1938 Mussolini accused the Italian bourgeoisie of obstructing fecundity:

The bourgeois is an enemy of sport. He is the greatest enemy of anything that could disturb his perennial state of rest. He is a pacifist, easily swayed, always humanitarian and sterile. He is sterile because he thinks. In fact, fecundity is a state of instinct. Too much rationality is inimical to the primordial, irrepressible and profound forms of humanity.[51]

A decree dated 5 September 1938 provided that the number of women working in the civil service or in the offices of private firms had to be reduced to 10 per cent of the total workforce. This severe decree seems to have been the regime's main response both to the increasing presence of women in paid work, especially in the educational field, and to the failure of the demographic campaign.

By this time an ideal of women engaged in work and leisure had spontaneously developed alongside the imposed model of the modest housewife, in spite of – or, arguably, at least partly thanks to – the ambiguous Fascist policy on women. Yet in practice social and political activities mostly mobilised an elite of aristocratic and middle-class women, especially teachers and employers, or wives of employers, who could easily entrust their children to nurses and leave housework to servants. It is surely significant that the number of housemaids in Italy rose from about 380,000 in 1921 to about 585,000 in 1936.[52] In other words, emancipation for elite women largely depended on their ability to exploit women from the lower classes, which was hardly likely to promote female solidarity.

These lucky few who were free from heavy family duties and could engage in social and political life provided fascinating role models for a younger generation of women from backgrounds similar to theirs, if not for lower-class women. In 1939 Luigi Gozzini published an article in the *Almanacco della donna italiana* on the results of survey conducted in Rome.[53] A questionnaire distributed among female students by the city government showed that the inspirational model for most of these young women was completely different from the image of the 'new woman' propagated by Fascist ideology. Only about 10 per cent of them expressed any interest in housework, while about 27 per cent confessed that they really hated it. Any aspirations they had to start a family were vague, and they enjoyed talking about romance and dancing parties rather than about child welfare. Very few of them wished to become mothers, and those who did planned to have no more than one or two children.[54]

By the end of the 1930s and the beginning of the 1940s the regime was being compelled to come to grips with reality and to reconsider its policy towards women. On 30 September 1939, after the conquest of Albania, the forging of a military alliance with Hitler and the beginning of the Second World War, Mussolini exhorted women to further mobilisation:

> Fascist women have a very important task in the field of assistance among the families of the [common] people, especially those where the men are in the army. Many families live in misery and others suffer hunger.[55]

Then came the Italian participation in the Second World War. In 1940 all the restrictions on women's access to employment were suddenly abolished. Under a decree issued on 5 June that year women aged between 18 and 45 were ordered to seek employment in the place of men,[56] but they still had to manage their households and cope with the increasing shortages of food and other goods.

Despite this apparent shift in Fascist policy, the new Civil Code of 1942 did nothing to improve the position of women. The regime continued to stress the unity of the family under patriarchal authority and the subordination of families to the state.[57] Even in 1940 a young man could win a national prize by writing the following:

> due to its racial objectives, the regime has eliminated from work all categories of women whose activity has only the task of satisfying hedonistic requirements. Everyone knows that women's work … does not favour an increase in marriages and therefore in the population. As a consequence, the engagement of female workers has been limited in various ways, especially for those jobs that are peculiarly masculine.[58]

However, Italian women started to free themselves from the patronage of men and to learn how to make up their own minds. A number of women left their families and participated in the conflict as volunteers in the Red Cross. Others assisted the wounded in hospitals or supported soldiers with letters, or with homemade food and clothes. In 1941 Mussolini did not fail to declare his admiration for Italian women, especially those quiet and self-confident nuns who had previously been engaged as volunteers in Albania and were now active close to the front lines. On 18 December the *Duce* ended a speech addressed to all Italian women by demanding their 'total hatred' for the enemy.[59]

An increasing number of women were becoming critical of the aggressive policies of the government, which had sent their men into danger, consigned their families to misery and provoked the bombing of their homes. Like most

Italians, they did not believe in or support the racial laws, and many offered protection to persecuted Jews and deserters from the army. Support for Fascism was also weakening among men, in line with Italy's poor performance in battle. Mussolini had promised Italians a quick war and few casualties, but the conflict demanded excessive sacrifices from soldiers and civilians alike. Although Fascist propaganda emphasised occasional victories and ignored numerous defeats, more and more Italians were aware that Germany and Italy were losing the war. The first strong sign of popular discontent came with a strike organised by workers, of both sexes, at the FIAT works in Turin in March 1943. In spite of the Fascist decrees forbidding strikes, this one succeeded. Finally, on 25 July the same year the *Duce* was dismissed by the Fascist Grand Council and imprisoned by order of the King. Most Italians were hopeful the war would end soon, even if not victoriously. However, subsequent dramatic events, including Mussolini's escape and Nazi Germany's harsh reaction to Italy's 'treachery', led to the civil war, which lasted until 1945.

While the Allies were conquering the South of Italy, many daring women decided to participate in this fraternal conflict alongside their men. About 30,000 women were provided with arms and fought with Communist, Catholic and other groups of partisans against the Italian Fascists and their German allies. In addition, about 70,000 women were involved in the 'groups of female defence', which had been founded in Milan in 1943 in support of the resistance movement.[60] Six hundred and twenty-three women partisans were killed, 4,563 were imprisoned and 2,750 were deported to Germany.[61]

On the other side the *Repubblica Sociale Italiana* (RSI), the state founded by Mussolini in northern Italy on 18 September 1943, attempted to combat both the Allies and the Italian partisans. On 14 April 1944 Mussolini issued Decree 447, calling on women to join his army. About 6,000 answered the call.[62] Once they had reached the territory of the RSI these women were selected for special training courses and then were either given the uniform of the 'Feminine Auxiliary Service' (SAF), which was part of the RSI's army, or served in the *Decima Mas*, the *Brigate Nere* and other autonomous Fascist groups. Some were adults brought up in the true faith and long involved in Fascist organisations, but there were many idealistic but politically ignorant young women as well. These women were imbued with patriotic values and believed that they were defending the honour of Italy against 'traitors'. They were not armed, but had the delicate task of supporting the RSI's soldiers. Strengthened by two decades of physical exercises, speeches and sacrifices, and educated in the myth of the Fatherland, they thought that they could replace the 'cowardly' men who had delivered the country into the hands of foreigners. About 60 of these auxiliaries were killed before 25 April 1945, celebrated by their enemies as Liberation Day, and about 90 more were murdered after the civil war had ended;[63] if one also takes into account those involved in other Fascist groups, the number of women who died for Mussolini was about 300 in all.[64]

Both the female partisans fighting for the resistance and the auxiliaries engaged in the hopeless adventure of the RSI were looked upon distrustfully by most men, who still considered all women as weak and emotional, and therefore unfit for war. Yet these women revealed unexpected physical and moral strength, and became heroic combatants on both fronts. They served as exemplary nuns and dispatch riders in the zones behind the front, and at the same time supported the unfortunate families of fallen soldiers. This is made abundantly clear in recent publications on the civil war, including women's letters and diaries.[65]

Conclusion

The paternalistic ideology of the regime had built a cultural model of the 'true woman', the 'Latin' mother, which was propagated throughout the Fascist years, but, not surprisingly, this did not always coincide with reality. During the Fascist era the condition of Italian women was changing in line with the social dynamics of a country in which there was still a diffused yearning for emancipation. However, this process was hampered by the common beliefs that men were more intelligent, stronger and more capable than women, and that women could somehow be redeemed from their inferiority by fulfilling the supreme biological mission of maternity.

Although women worked not only in the home but also in agriculture, in factories and offices, in social assistance programmes and even in Fascist organisatons, none of this counted for much. Women were taught to love their country at school, in Fascist organisations and through nationalistic propaganda, but all political decisions regarding the destiny of the Fatherland remained firmly in the hands of men. Women trained their bodies within the regime's youth organisations, and even learned to march in perfect order and discipline like soldiers, but this was just a means for improving their health and making them better able to produce numerous children.

Nevertheless, during the long years of war Italian women learned at their own expense that international conflicts were their concern too. From 1935 to 1943 they suffered severe deprivation as a consequence of Mussolini's imperialistic plans. Women then had to undergo further suffering during a fraticidal war, due to the weakness, bewilderment, lack of preparation and lack of foresight of men. During the civil war a number of women rebelled against the 'spirit of resignation' ascribed to them down the ages and decided to transform themselves from victims of history into protagonists by partici-pating in the defence of the country. After years of sacrifice and restrictions, but also engagement, promises, hopes and nationalistic exaltation, their personalities had been notably strengthened. In spite of the prevailing climate of opinion these women emancipated themselves from traditional roles, and became sufficiently self-confident to join the partisans or support the RSI. Thus many Italian women not only learned how to stand up for their ideological choices and fight for their very lives, but contributed to the protection of a civil society that was being harshly tried by war, through a diffused spirit of feminine solidarity.

4

Sports medicine and female athleticism under the Fascist regime

This chapter and the next examine initiatives undertaken in Fascist Italy in relation to women's physical education and sport, in line with medical science, traditional habits and the drive to modernisation. In the first half of the 1920s the training of women's bodies was supported by the Fascist movement, which still retained some of the revolutionary spirit of its early years. In the second half of the decade, however, sportswomen came to be considered as both the ideal ambassadors of the new 'Fascist style', throughout the country and abroad, and as ideal mothers of strong children. Young women began to be trained within the ranks of the *Fasci Femminili*, which were under the control of the Fascist Party.

However, this new trend in favour of sport for women was bitterly criticised both by the Catholic Church and by old-fashioned elements of public opinion, which feared a 'masculinisation' of Italian women and girls, a loss of feminine modesty, and a decline in women's interest in family and maternity. As a consequence the scope for women's sport was considerably reduced. The prevailing opinion was that the competitiveness of sporting activities could be reproduced in everyday life, with the result that women could be distracted from their household duties, and might turn instead to work and politics. As many women in the industrialised areas of the country had already gained a certain degree of emancipation by working away from home, the danger that they could invade fields traditionally reserved for men seemed to many to present a real problem. In addition, it was rumoured that sport could make women infertile, which could only arouse the suspicions of Fascists committed to the regime's demographic campaign. Various measures limiting women's rights in relation to employment were imposed from 1926 onwards. Yet ever since its advent Fascism had encouraged the practice of women's sport as a sign of revolutionary modernity, so it was officially unable to oppose it. Being aware of the growing discontent with female athletes, who seemed to traditional-minded Italians to be too 'tomboyish' and too easy-going, the Fascist regime passed on to scientists the task of establishing activities that could be accepted as being more suitable for women.

This decision, which was taken at the beginning of the 1930s, effectively gave the *Comitato Olimpico Nazionale Italiano* (CONI) and the *Federazione Italiana Medici dello Sport* (Italian Federation of Sports Physicians, or

FIMS) a free hand to reshape women's sport, which was promptly put into a scientific and organisational 'ghetto'. Most physicians agreed upon the eugenic utility of basic physical education, which was highly recommended, while at the same time they advised women not to take up competitive sports. Non-competitive sports were also considered to be good for women's health, but they were limited to just a few activities, such as swimming, skiing, skating, tennis, basketball and athletics, and athletics itself was limited to just a few selected disciplines. Since most of these sports required specialised facilities and equipment, they remained no more than dreams for the majority of Italian women, who could enjoy them only vicariously, by reading newspaper reports about the activities of the elite of women's sport. Nevertheless, some of these activities were available to girls at school, and basic physical education was provided not only within the regime's youth organisations, but also, during the summer holidays, in the numerous health resorts all over the country.

Acting on the advice of physicians and other specialists, the regime then initiated programmes to select talented girls who could take part in competitive sports and help to confirm what the regime saw as Italy's pre-eminence among sporting nations. Although sporting activities for ordinary women were officially discouraged and unpopular, the regime did not hesitate to seek out new talent among girls taking part in physical activities at school and/or in the Fascist youth organisations.

Given the inadequate supply of qualified female staff who could train such talented girls, the regime also decided to create an elite of physical education teachers, who would be trained at a new university-level institution, the Accademia Nazionale Femminile di Educazione Fisica in Orvieto, from 1932 onwards (see Chapter 6). Other physical education teachers were recruited from among female primary school teachers and others who were involved in sport and imbued with the true Fascist faith. These teachers then set about selecting the girls who seemed most likely to become talented athletes. These girls could be trained without arousing much traditionalist opposition, since they were selected in accordance, not only with specific standards for each sport, but also with the official requirements of submissiveness and modesty. Their training was entrusted to specialised coaches, few of whom were women, and was designed to produce a sporting elite.

These carefully chosen young sportswomen were allowed a lot of freedom by the standards of the time. Because they took part in national and international contests alongside men, and displayed a certain lack of constraint in their manners and in the comradeship that they showed towards their team-mates, they inspired both perplexity and admiration. Their muscularity did not fit the dominant ideal of femininity, yet at the same time it made them symbols of the moral strength of Fascist women.

As in other countries, Italians had seen a variety of ideal feminine types come and go over the years. The long-established image of the 'Latin' woman with broad hips and round breasts that favoured maternity was still very powerful between the world wars, but meanwhile the slim, tomboyish woman of the 'roaring twenties' was supplanted by a new American ideal of slender and athletic womanhood, which in turn gave way in the 1940s to the increasingly accepted image of the muscular and patriotic sportswoman. The press and the fashion industry collaborated in stressing these different aesthetic canons, simultaneously and therefore incoherently, while works of Fascist 'militant-art' increasingly depicted strong Italian sportswomen.

Italian sports medicine and gender eugenics

The hygienic and moral implications of women's participation in sport were already being scientifically studied in Italy before the advent of Fascism. Among the important physicians who addressed these topics Dr Goffredo Sorrentino of Ancona, who taught at the University of Bologna, stands out as one of the earliest supporters of female athleticism in Italy. On 22 November 1921, Sorrentino published an article in the popular newspaper *La Gazzetta dello Sport* exalting Italian sportswomen as exemplary. Female athletes had clearly demonstrated that women could use their muscles to greater effect than in simply dancing the foxtrot or the quick step. In Sorrentino's opinion, sporting habits did not damage female modesty at all, but, on the contrary, helped to keep women healthy, and to steer them away both from wearing short skirts, transparent stockings or other provocative clothing, and from excessive flirting or use of make-up. On the basis of scientific studies by the French scholars Marey, Demeny and Hebert, Sorrentino proposed that sportswomen be tested throughout every stage of their activities. Italian physicians should test every improvement or deterioration in an athlete's physical condition, especially by investigating her heart, lungs and body weight. In addition, women should be trained gradually, using the basic scientific exercises suggested by Hebert and Heckel. Sorrentino believed that women should avoid the most dangerous sports, such as boxing, wrestling, football or rugby, but he recommended tennis, volleyball, basketball, track and field, and the use of medicine balls, as well as a few traditional ball games such as *sfratto* and *tamburello*.

Sorrentino shared the conventional view that athletics had to be adapted to suit the weaker bodies of women. For example, the weights of discuses, shots, javelins and hammers should be reduced by half, the sprint should be cut to 70 metres, the long-distance run should be cut to 1,000 metres, and the triple jump should be avoided altogether. In conclusion, Sorrentino supported female athleticism in Italy, since 'rational' training and sporting activity would not change beautiful Italian women into ugly circus performers.

On the contrary, once Italian women had adopted the habits of women in the most advanced nations and the proposals of eminent foreign scientists, they would be able to become more harmonious and robust through sporting activities in the open air. They would also be more likely to stay away from unhealthy drawing-room conversation and the morally dangerous dance-halls.

Leaving aside Sorrentino's questionable insertion of such moralistic asides into the scientific argument, which, as we shall see, was a habit he shared with many of his colleagues, he should clearly be considered a pioneer in the promotion of women's competitive sport. This was all the more remarkable at a time when few scientists or physicians, whether in Italy or elsewhere, approved of women's participation in sport.

In any case, even in the mid-1930s sports medicine was still a relatively new discipline, although it had begun to attract the attention of many Italian scholars and politicians. One of its pioneers was Dr Ugo Cassinis, who had been appointed in 1925 as director of a laboratory of sport-related physiology at the *Farnesina* Military School in Rome. This laboratory evaluated the physical condition of boys with sporting talent and assigned them to particular sporting activities; it also conducted periodic tests on athletes in order to evaluate their physical responses to training. Cassinis was also the official Italian observer at the First International Congress of Sports Medicine, held in Amsterdam during the Summer Olympics of 1928, which gave him opportunities to acquaint himself with developments in sports medicine across Europe, but especially in Germany. In October 1929, when another physician, Dr Giacinto Viola, founded the Medical Association of Physical Culture, Cassinis was elected to its national committee. In the following month the CONI, under the leadership of Augusto Turati, established the FIMS (already mentioned above), which was modelled on the International Federation of Sports Medicine[1] established during the Winter Olympics in St Moritz in the previous year. The FIMS rapidly became the main reference point for scientific research on sport in Italy. Cassinis was appointed a member of the technical committee of physicians that guided the initial activities of the new organisation. This committee comprised the most influential doctors interested in sports medicine, representing different areas of the country, such as Arrigoni and Poggi-Longostrevi from Milan, Viziano from Turin, Barbacci, Cartasegna and Pini from Bologna, Cassinis and Zauli from Rome, Polacco from Trieste, Podestà from Bari, and Sorrentino from Ancona. In 1929 and 1930 these doctors organised scientific and practical courses in sports medicine for general physicians, as well as courses for coaches and masseurs, in order to spread all over the country the idea that sports medicine was not limited to first aid, but was aimed at helping young people through active collaboration with physical education teachers, coaches, sporting societies and athletes themselves. In particular, a special course for female physicians, lasting two months, was held in Milan in 1929. It was conducted by Poggi-Longostrevi, who was particularly enthusiastic about women's sport.[2]

Among the many other initiatives undertaken around this time one of the most important was the establishment of Italy's first institute of sports medicine by the Fascist politician Leandro Arpinati in 1929. This very modern and efficient institute, which was housed close to the *Littoriale* Stadium in Bologna, aimed to evaluate the abilities of both students and professional athletes. In the years 1929–31 alone 1,383 boys and 1,022 girls were visited and evaluated by its sports doctors on at least two or three occasions, and 342 competitive athletes were evaluated to help them choose the activity most appropriate to their talents. In addition, in 1930 the CONI established a special hospital for traumatology in Rome, to provide treatment for injured sportsmen free of charge.

It was also in 1930 that the technical committee of physicians in charge of the FIMS discussed and approved its statutes and regulations, which aimed at nothing less than the co-ordination and control of all medical aspects of sport in Italy. Fourteen physicians from the FIMS were appointed as regional inspectors and 20 as provincial heads. Cassinis was elected Secretary of the FIMS; he became an 'extraordinary officer' in 1931, and then President from 1933 to 1941. The FIMS was abolished in the latter year and replaced by a new 'sanitary service', headed by the Secretary of CONI, which lasted up to the end of the Second World War.

At first the FIMS found it difficult to introduce qualified, specialised physicians into Italy's sporting societies. Most of these societies already had links with local doctors, who treated athletes' injuries and did not like the idea of calling in FIMS physicians who might try to take control not only of the athletes but of sporting activity as a whole. Many coaches and athletes also believed that FIMS specialists could obstruct their work and undermine their enthusiasm for sport. Despite this opposition, the FIMS became very active in the 1930s, not only in organising and diffusing sports medicine, but in improving scientific knowledge by holding periodical national conferences (in 1932, 1935 and 1938) at which physicians presented papers concerning their own experience and disseminated new ideas from abroad. The FIMS also published a periodical, the *Rivista di Medicina dello Sport*, edited by Dr Viziano.

The Italian school of sports medicine was to a large extent inspired by and dependent on international scientific activity, being relatively lacking in resources. However, it also did some original work, following in the footsteps of such nineteenth-century pioneers as Emilio Baumann, Achille De Giovanni, Luigi Pagliani, Paolo Mantegazza and, above all, Angelo Mosso (see Chapter 2). Naturally, these Italian scientists and physicians were well aware of the work of their German, French and American colleagues, such as Arnold, Anthony, Bach, Baker, Gordon, Latarjet, Magnus, Marchal, Rautmann, Süpfle and Thooris.[3] Among the Italian physicians of the Fascist era who specialised in sports medicine the most original were Giacinto Viola and Nicola Pende. Viola invented a new method for physically evaluating sportspeople, as well as new instruments such as the balance anthropometer and compasses of thickness. Pende, an expert in endocrinology, mainly focused on the interrelations between somatic structures and mental activity, from which he developed a complex methodology for classifying different constitutional types. In addition, by putting their methodologies together Viola and Pende developed the Viola–Pende evaluation schedule, which became well-known abroad. Italian sports physicians also conducted research in physiology and psychology, quoting in their papers the studies of influential foreign scholars such as Abramson, Asher, Atzler, Boigey, Bouardel, Casper, Christensen, Embden, Herxheimer, Jänsch, Knoll, Kohlrausch, Lagrange, Lorentz, Mülly, Orskov, Reich, Rosenbaum, Schmith, Simonson and Zuntz.[4] Some original contributions to research on the hygiene and nutrition of sportsmen were made by Calligaris, Cassinis, Baglioni, Chiurco, Davì, Del Guerra and Tavernari. In particular, they studied the effects of coffee and wine, the most popular drinks in Italy, on sporting activities, concluding that neither of them could damage athletic performance.[5]

In 1933 the FIMS started actively contributing to international sports medicine by hosting the second International Congress of Sports Medicine in Turin and Rome. After this congress, at which scholars debated the problem of how best to evaluate sportspeople,[6] the FIMS decided to pursue a number of important objectives:

(a) obtaining the full support of the academic world by ensuring adequate supplies of teachers, classrooms and especially laboratories;
(b) providing high-quality scientific and practical training for its own physicians;
(c) promoting general acceptance of FIMS physicians within all sporting societies; and
(d) evaluating all sportspeople from anthropological, morphological and functional points of view.

At the next International Congress, held in Chamonix in 1934, the FIMS was represented by Viola, who presented his methodology for evaluating the physical constitution of individuals in order to direct them to the sports most suitable for them. Viola's method not only met with international acceptance in Chamonix, but was widely applied in Italy through what became known as the biometrical schedule for physical evaluation.

By the middle of the 1930s the number of qualified sports physicians had increased, partly because the presence of FIMS doctors was perceived to be favoured by the Fascist regime. The regime was indeed interested in improving the efficiency of the country's sporting champions, as well as in building up medical support for the physical evaluation of young people as the starting point for its plans to strengthen the Italian 'race'. In 1935 about 2,000 members of the FIMS, under the direction of CONI, were placed in charge of medical matters within the existing Fascist organisations, the army and the sporting societies, and 17 regional and 74 provincial FIMS inspectors were appointed to control and co-ordinate sports medicine across the country. However, the FIMS still lacked sufficient resources to accomplish much scientific research.

Few Italian physicians opposed the regime. On the contrary, in their speeches and writings most of them did not fail to demonstrate gratitude to the regime for its placing of special emphasis on medicine, sport and health. Poggi-Longostrevi and Chiurco published popular books warmly praising Mussolini, and the numerous medical activities carried out within Fascist bodies concerned with sport, while Pende openly declared himself in favour of the racial laws of 1938.

The FIMS and female athleticism

At the beginning of the 1930s the Fascist regime regarded the FIMS as the body best qualified to resolve the very delicate problem of female athleticism. At a meeting on 16 October 1930 the Fascist Grand Council gave the FIMS a free hand in this area.

A number of papers on female athleticism were delivered at the first Italian national congress of sports medicine in 1932. These offer an interesting insight into the prevailing opinions concerning female sport, not only among physicians, but also among qualified teachers and coaches. For example, in a paper entitled 'May a Woman Practise Sport?'[7] Cassinis discredited the notion that physical activity could make women infertile by describing the sporting habits of the healthy and obviously fertile women of northern Europe. He then denounced the view that women should be confined to their homes in order to protect their morals. He pointed out that women were already living, fighting and working with the same rights and duties as men. Nevertheless, he considered that the main purpose of any woman's life was childbirth and he disapproved of hard work outside the home, especially if it was done in unhealthy conditions. He warmly supported physical activities in the open air, in the mountains, on rivers and by the sea, because he believed that it would help women to carry out their maternal functions even better. Such activities, besides strengthening the body and improving health, improved the willpower and made women's character more balanced by eliminating those states of irascibility and nervousness that could have a negative effect on children and husbands. Cassinis then looked closely at the issue of which physical activities best suited young women. He advised against athletic, acrobatic and competititve gymnastics, but recommended methodical, analytical and applied gymnastics, as well as callisthenics. In particular, he supported Ling's analytical gymnastics and, above all, respiratory exercises. The athletic disciplines he recommended most highly were the high jump and the long jump, the javelin and running, but he added that women should run only for fun, and should be banned from competing in 100-, 200-, 400- and 800-metre races. Hurdling, the discus, putting the shot and pole-vaulting were condemned as unsuitable for women. Cassinis thought that some sports, such as mountaineering, skiing, rowing, swimming and diving, were especially important because they encompassed physiological, anatomical and hygienic benefits. He recommended team games, such as basketball and volleyball, because they produced harmonious bodies, and stimulated discipline and emulation. Fencing or other indoor sports were not advised. Fencing was not as aesthetically suitable for women as callisthenics, rhythmic dance or ballet. Cassinis also discussed upper-class sports, such as golf, tennis and motor-racing, which he believed were no more beneficial than less expensive sports. Finally, he emphasised his view that the strongest nations should put physical education ahead of everything. Italian women who had neither strong bodies nor strong wills could never become perfect mothers for the 'new Italians' being moulded by the regime.

Another physician, Dr Viziano, presented the preliminary results of an ongoing investigation of the influence of exercise on menstruation.[8] Nineteen female athletes in the Gymnastic Society of Turin had responded to his questionnaire. He concluded from this staggeringly small sample that most female athletes did not feel any particular indisposition and did not give up their exercises during menstruation; indeed, some of them had found that sport seemed to be a remedy for menstrual pain. Two of the 19 women had declared that even while menstruating they had been able to participate in competition without any loss of form. Viziano concluded that the sports practised by these athletes appeared not to be unfavourably influenced by their menstrual cycles. Not all the participants in the congress agreed that sporting activities during menstruation were advisable. In a brief paper Dr Giaccone asserted, with no apparent supporting evidence, that menstruating women should avoid all sports, even the less strenuous ones, because 'during periods the female body, due to its increased requirements, is really in equilibrium ... [and] should not be unbalanced by exhaustion [from sport].'[9]

In the second part of his paper Viziano referred to important findings about female sport by Duentner and Helleland, Schlesinger, Runge, Casper, and McCloy. Viziano concluded by saying that, in general, sport need not be forbidden to women. The question of which sports were most suitable for women, in the sense of best enabling them to obtain an improvement in their physical conditions for the sake of future motherhood, was an open one for

Viziano: 'When considering female sport, we should emphasise quality as well as quantity, and the opportunity of starting at a convenient age after good preparation through the various levels of physical education.'[10]

A number of teachers and coaches also spoke at the congress. Female sport was defended against the accusation that it was dangerous to health by Marina Zanetti, who had become a famous athlete, sports manager and coach. In her opinion the greatest benefits for women could come 'from healthy, harmonious and non-excessive sports'.[11] In addition, due to the distinctive character of 'Latin' women, including Italian women, there was no danger of any sporting overload: 'Latin' women are endowed with so much harmony and grace that they 'instinctively avoid foreign, exotic overloads'.[12] Zanetti asserted that even uneducated people understood that athletics helped to strengthen women's reproductive organs. The lack of danger could be demonstrated by cases of women who had engaged in athletic activity for more than ten years without injury.

A physical education teacher, Mrs Lugnani, spoke at the congress in favour of female physical activity. She did not, however, support sporting activities: her emphasis was on gymnastics alone. She asked that special care be taken when choosing the type and intensity of exercise. She proposed a method developed by an American doctor, Bess Mensendieck,[13] based on static gymnastics without the use of apparatus. Lugnani wanted to integrate this method with the rhythmic and dynamic gymnastics of Delsartes, Stebbing and Kallmeyer, and the rigorous musical gymnastics of Dalcroze. Lugnani concluded her paper by suggesting that swimsuits be worn during gymnastics lessons, in order to give girls' bodies more freedom and more oxygen, and urged that athletes should shower following exercise. It is noteworthy that, while Dr Mensendieck had recommended exercising naked, her Italian disciple decided to adapt her method somewhat to prevailing Italian mores by suggesting swimsuits.

Professor Baglioni, who chaired the congress, summed up its proceedings by concluding that, in general, the speakers agreed that appropriate and moderate sport activity did not damage, but actually helped, the normal functions of the female sexual organs, such as menstruation. Physical activity helped young women to build healthy and harmonious bodies, and directed their energy away from the sexual excess stimulated by modern cinemas, dance halls and reading.[14]

At the International Congress of Sports Medicine held in Turin and Rome in 1933, Professor Rabino of Turin presented the results of a test concerning the relationship between menstruation and fatigue in sport. The answers given by 100 female athletes to his questionnaire showed that 48 of them did not stop training during menstruation; 20 very rarely stopped training; 15 switched to milder training than usual, cutting out running and jumping; and 17 did not train at all during menstruation. Among these 17 athletes,

12 admitted that they were influenced by the advice of their families and doctors, although only five of them suffered real pain. In addition, 76 of these 100 athletes said that their menstrual function had been improved by physical activity. Rabino concluded that well-trained female athletes could practise sport during menstruation, but only on the condition that they did not strain themselves too much.[15]

At the second national congress of sports medicine, in 1935, Dr Sirio Lentini presented a paper that was openly in favour of the political views of the regime in relation to female sport. Lentini emphasised that, following the regime's ideology, sports medicine should become a kind of social medicine. It should take care of the orthogenetic and physical education, and the sporting preparation, of all Italians from infancy to the end of puberty. Both forms of physical activity, Lentini said, contributed to the same end: 'the integral reclamation of humanity'.[16] On the specific question of female sport, Lentini considered that competition should be the exception rather than the rule, and that women should always practise sport with good taste and composure. He also suggested that physical education lessons should be given to female students within the *Gruppi Universitari Fascisti* (GUF), allowing them to practise many different activities, such as gymnastics, track and field, rhythmic dance, swimming, basketball, tennis, volleyball, skating, mountaineering and excursions. National sporting displays for women should also be organised, but certain disciplines, such as cycling and horse-riding, should be excluded from them, because they altered the statics of the spinal column and the internal reproductive organs. Indeed, according to Lentini they overdeveloped the muscular and skeletal apparatus to such an extent that the somatic femininity of Italian women, and their attitude to bearing and raising children, could be seriously compromised. Finally, Lentini drew quite a terrifying portrait of the 'virilised' female athlete, with 'a body abundant in muscles and lacking in breasts, a face turgid with blood vessels, a big neck and a hard expression, [and using] vehement language that is sometimes even violent'.[17]

Dr Tranquilli-Leali also spoke at the second national congress, presenting a series of data collected from young people who had suffered traumatic injuries while practising sport, and had been treated at the Arnaldo Mussolini Hospital in Bologna between 1930 and 1935.[18] Among the 704 cases, grouped according to sporting disciplines, only 23 involved girls. Of these 23 young female athletes, seven had been practising officially 'discouraged' sports, such as 'cheap' cycling, and 'expensive' horse-riding and motorcycling; nine had been practising the popular sports that were 'welcomed' by the regime, such as skiing, track and field, and skating; and the remaining seven had been taking part in motor-racing, a very elitist sport. The data, limited as they are, could perhaps be interpreted to suggest that in the 1930s male participation in sport was widespread but female participation in sport was limited, even in a relatively prosperous and modern city such as Bologna.

Only one paper presented at the third national congress of sports medicine, in 1938, dealt even in part with the topic of 'female athleticism'. A Dr Montanari-Reggiani[19] summarised the prevailing opinion of official medicine by asserting that women could undoubtedly practise a certain number of sports, with beneficial results for their levels of physical efficiency, and he also stressed the positive influence of sport on sexual intercourse, childbirth and breastfeeding. He argued that during menstruation women should avoid any competitive activity or stressful training. Female university students should practise only those sports recommended by GUF physicians as being suited to their physical and psychological constitutions. Montanari-Reggiani described how voluntary Red Cross nurses at the University of Modena had collaborated with him, when he himself was a GUF physician, from the first medical examination of new female students onwards. The nurses observed the students during their training, evaluating every physical and psychological change that occurred, and they also tested the students on three different occasions: first, at the beginning of the activity; second, in the days leading up to each of the university's *Littoriali* contests; and third, in the days following each contest. Montanari-Reggiani stated that the data collected by the nurses had been very useful for the GUF doctors in Modena and recommended that similar statistics on female athleticism in general be compiled under the auspices of the Central Sanitary Service of the GUF.

Controversies over female athleticism

The issue of female athleticism was also widely debated outside the FIMS by influential physicians of the time. In 1930, for example, Nicola Pende (already mentioned above) presented a paper to the first national conference of physicians involved in the *Opera Nazionale Balilla* (ONB), the Fascist organisation for schoolchildren. Pende used this occasion to emphasise the danger that some sports and physical exercises could 'deform' women's bodies and spirits. He was well aware of the decline in the birth rate and thought that it would be better to give women a basic, healthy physical education in order to prepare them for what he and the regime alike regarded as their fundamental function, producing children for the Fatherland. In his view, by practising sports Italian girls risked embodying the model of the infertile and masculine modern woman, by becoming *maschiette* (tomboyish).[20]

Initially at least, a very different view was put forward by Giuseppe Poggi-Longostrevi, one of the founders of the FIMS. In two articles published in *La Gazzetta dello Sport*, previewing and then commenting on a meeeting of the Fascist Grand Council on 16 October 1930, he declared himself in favour of female athleticism. In the first of the two articles Poggi-Longostrevi asserted that physical exercise outdoors was necessary if women were to become healthy, strong, robust mothers. He praised the recent displays at the women's athletic championship in Florence and the Women's World Games in Prague, where strength and *joie de vivre* had been celebrated in front of 30,000 spectators. In his opinion, 'Whoever criticises the wish to achieve records does not reflect that no progress would be possible in the world without competition.'[21] Women had as much right as men to obtain benefits from sport and to protect themselves from the damaging effects of sedentary work. They had the right to become more dynamic, as required by the tumultuous modern lifestyle. Physical exercise strengthened body and spirit, but sport and athletics formed character, and there was no reason why young women should sacrifice their grace and harmony even when striving to achieve sporting records.

In contrast, Poggi-Longostrevi's second article,[22] written after the meeting of the Fascist Grand Council, reflected the prudent position that had been expressed there by somewhat downplaying his enthusiasm for female athleticism. The Council had stated that anything that distracted women from their fundamental mission of maternity had to be avoided. Poggi-Longostrevi therefore informed his readers that the FIMS had a duty to decide what was the best age at which competitive female athletes should start training. True sportspeople would never impede the development of female athleticism, but, by moderating athletes' dangerously excessive enthusiasm, they could guide them along the desired path. Female athleticism would then be permitted only to a few women who had developed perfectly and thoroughly trained bodies over many years of basic exercises.

Poggi-Longostrevi went on to analyse the problem more deeply in a book, *Cultura fisica della donna ed estetica femminile* (1933), in which he concluded that women's sport had to be encouraged, but strictly under medical control. Athletes aged between 12 and 15 should be tested and directed to the sporting activities that were most suitable for them. Girls aged 18 and above should be allowed to compete in genuine sports. Every kind of sport was safe for a well-trained adult's body, but some were more suitable for young girls. Track and field was good, because women's races had shorter distances, while the high jump and the long jump were no longer dangerous because modern landing pits softened the fall. Even putting the shot, the javelin and the discus were safe now that lighter equipment, suitable for women, was available. Poggi-Longostrevi also recommended swimming, ball games, skiing, tennis and skating. Poggi-Longostrevi also wrote forcefully in favour of talented sportswomen. Strong female athletes, true champions, were exemplars of their disciplines and lived only for sport. They were the exception, the pride and glory of the nation, the improved model of the Italian 'race', to be admired everywhere. In contrast, ordinary women could harmoniously develop their bodies by practising motor activities as amateurs and by following precise hygienic norms in order to protect their sexual organs. Poggi-Longostrevi was quite convinced that physical culture and exercise offered the only possible therapy for the most critical periods of female life: the menopause and senility.[23]

In 1935 Professor Gian Carlo Chiurco of the University of Siena published an extensive study of Italian physical education and sports physiopathology, complete with an up-to-date bibliography of both Italian and foreign works of research on sports medicine. Having expressed his firm opposition to professional sportspeople in general, Chiurco made clear his support for the idea that motor activities should be practised joyously out of doors. He devoted several pages to meticulous descriptions of the activities that he felt were most suitable for women. His position was similar to Poggi-Longostrevi's. Both men believed that, even though women's anatomy and physiology were different from men's, sport and exercise could not be forbidden. On the contrary, they should be encouraged and adapted for women. On the basis of studies by Edith von Lölhöffel, Chiurco stated that tall women, short women and women of normal stature excelled at different sports. Long-distance races were acceptable because of their good influence, but hurdles, putting the shot, discus and pole-vaulting were all to be avoided unless prescribed by physicians. In any event, the most suitable activities for women were rhythmic gymnastics, skiing, swimming, rowing, racing and fencing.[24]

Chiurco also shared the opinion previously expressed by Cassinis that in the Fascist state women could not simply stay at home and take no part in healthy activities. Such activities contributed to shaping good mothers, with good, well-balanced characters, capable of producing strong and healthy children. Sport was particularly important for women who led sedentary lives, whether at home or in offices or laboratories. Chiurco agreed with Viziano and with many foreign scholars that sport had no adverse effects on women's sexual organs, and that it could be practised, in moderation, during pregnancy and after childbirth.

In 1936 the opposing view was expressed by Dr Ferdinando Loffredo in an essay on Italian families. He vehemently opposed every kind of sport for women, on the grounds that sportswomen had a number of sexual disturbances, such as painful menstruation, and reduced functioning of the womb and ovaries, and that their bodies showed obvious signs of masculinisation. Loffredo also claimed that in foreign countries sport had been the main cause of women's separation from their families and therefore of population decline and loss of womanly modesty. In addition, Loffredo was convinced that female sport could also encourage the 'ideal of nudity', already apparent in some foreign countries, with negative consequences for general morality.[25]

Finally, in 1940 Poggi-Longostrevi published *Medicina sportiva*, a book on sports medicine that contained a chapter on women's sport.[26] In the introduction he pointed out that the most advanced foreign studies, by Brandt, Droust, Duenter, Guggisberg, Merken, Schesinger and Roung, and the most advanced Italian studies, by Baglioni, Bolaffi, Nizza, Viziano and, especially,

Cova, all supported women's participation in sport. He also quoted a recent speech by Mussolini in which the *Duce* had praised the few Italian female athletes who, having married, had very quickly become healthy mothers of healthy children. Poggi-Longostrevi was clearly opposed to any limitation on female sport, as 'past experience has demonstrated that most physical activities were excluded because of excessive fear'.[27] Italian women were being prevented from taking part in sport by the traditional way in which they were educated, yet there was no moral or aesthetic justification for this, given that most sporting activities safeguarded femininity and modesty, and preserved women's gracefulness and their figures too. If Italian girls could follow the example of the balanced and fecund women of primitive societies, who practised a sort of 'natural' athletics, they too would be able to develop their abdominal muscles, favouring beauty and maternity at the same time. Poggi-Longostrevi also cited the positive attitude of a fellow-physician, Professor Cova, who warmly supported outdoor physical activities for women, arguing that they improved muscular energy, blood circulation and the genital apparatus, with great benefits from the point of view of increasing the population.

In the last part of his chapter on women's sport Poggi-Longostrevi pointed out that, although teams of Italian sportswomen had successfully participated in the Women's World Games in Prague in 1930 and in the Berlin Olympics in 1936, female athleticism was still not sufficiently popular in Italy. He reiterated his view that both sporting activity and training would improve the intrinsic qualities of women – their agility, their ability and their gracefulness – while keeping them in good health and developing their capacity for endurance. He too felt obliged to emphasise that women should avoid 'unsuitable' sports and should not try to emulate men's efforts. However, women should not abandon their physical activities, such as athletics, tennis, skiing, skating, golf, swimming or basketball, when they were menstruating, since in most cases continuing their activities had excellent effects on their capacity for sporting achievement and on their genital health. Poggi-Longostrevi concluded the chapter with a presentation of data on ten Italian women athletes who had taken part in the Prague Games, all of whom regularly practised their favourite sports during menstruation, nine of them with good results.

Conclusion

In line with the Fascist political programme for the moulding of the 'new Italian', the FIMS clearly supported the practice of sport by boys and men at every level. It applied its scarce resources largely to research on medical issues concerning males, sought to increase the health, strength and willpower of the 'race', and hoped to produce budding champions. FIMS physicians were aware of the damage that could be caused by excessive involvement in sport in the delicate periods of boyhood and adolescence, but they tended to assume that grown men needed no protection at all. Sports doctors advised boys aged between nine and 12 to confine themselves to swimming, wrestling, running over 25 and 50 metres, and ball games. They also advised boys aged between 13 and 16 to focus on gradually increasing the amounts of time they devoted to games and athletics, limiting running to distances of 100 or 200 metres. It was generally agreed that young men of 17 and above could safely engage in any sport, although they were advised to avoid long-distance running in order to avoid damaging their hearts and lungs. The most robust and talented among these young sportsmen could then become true champions.[28]

In contrast, the more limited and specialised discussion of female athleticism during the early 1930s demonstrates how much more protective the FIMS was towards women. FIMS physicians regarded women as delicate creatures in need of special attention and protection, and, following the consensus of the time, they took it for granted that their main goal was to help women to preserve modesty and femininity, and to prepare for motherhood.

However, the various combinations of genuine medical science and pseudoscientific moralising that the FIMS generated made little impact outside the specialist field of sports medicine. Most Italians were much more aware of, and much more deeply influenced by, the intransigent hostility of the Church to women's participation in sport. This hostility was exemplified by Pope Pius XI's objections to a women's gymnastics competition in Rome in 1928;[29] the Holy Office's severe criticisms of the regime's support for eugenic and sexual education;[30] and numerous articles in the Catholic press, such as the one published pseudonymously in *L'Osservatore Romano* in 1934 that claimed that spectators watched women's sport only in order 'to admire the competitors' physique, rather than their good form in the pure sporting sense'.[31]

Thus, even though most physicians came out openly in favour of a moderate version of female athleticism, their opinions made little difference to the conservative mood of the country. The Fascist regime completely supported the eugenic theory of 'race' and gave exaggerated emphasis to a reactionary conception of maternity.[32] Once the revolutionary vigour that had characterised Fascism in its early years had been exhausted, female athleticism was no longer encouraged, and the model of the dynamic and socially emancipated woman of the 1920s was replaced by the model of the flourishing and prolific mother, in spite of prevailing medical opinion.

Mussolini and the rest of the Fascist hierarchy were convinced of the intellectual and physical inferiority of women, and suspected that participation in sport did not favour maternity, even though most physicians had concluded that this was no more than prejudice. The regime gradually reduced the status of female athleticism, making it into no more than a marginal activity involving talented sportswomen, who were kept separate from ordinary sports amateurs. The regime's sports specialists were given the task of selecting only very talented young girls, who were then trained for competition by male coaches who, in many cases, had been recruited from other countries. For example, at the beginning of her career the athlete Ondina Valla was trained by a Mr Gaspar from Hungary, and then by a Mr Comstock from the United States, who was also in charge of training the Italian athletics team, of both sexes, for the Berlin Olympics of 1936.[33] These coaches trained elite sportswomen and sportsmen in roughly the same way, but even at a lower level coaches did not pay much attention to gender. However, the prevailing medical opinion in favour of a certain number of sports did not find practical application with regard to those girls who had not been chosen for competitive athletics. They had to go on practising a moderate, unexciting form of general gymnastics under the direction of female teachers of physical education, for whom the perfect and simultaneous execution of the exercises counted for more than technical content.

This in turn fitted the main objectives of the regime, which wanted to forge 'new men' through sport while leaving the forging of 'new women' to basic physical education, accompanied by the inculcation of eugenic, aesthetic and moral standards. Such women could then please the regime by producing strong and healthy children, please men with their beauty and grace, and please the Church with their modesty and composure. This is clearly indicated in Article 4 of the ONB's *Norme* (Standards) for members of the *Piccole Italiane* and the *Giovani Italiane*, its subsidiary organisations for girls aged between eight and 14, and those aged between 14 and 18, respectively:

> Female physical education has to focus on increasing the endurance of the body, and on increasing the aesthetic conformation of small and teenage girls, while every competitive or even athletic form is excluded, as well as any professional tendency that is not suitable to the female disposition of the female body.[35]

Only at the end of the 1930s did the issue of female athleticism move out from conferences of sports physicians to become a topic of wider debate, as the Fascist regime started to consider female athleticism as an important way of displaying to the world that Italian women were not old-fashioned, or weaker than foreign athletes, and that their 'athleticisation' could improve the quality and numbers of their children. The regime also hoped that this would increase women's support for Fascist ideology. Consequently, female athleticism became a subject for further scientific investigation and popularisation.

After years of research, disseminated through speeches, papers and books, Italian sports physicians had demonstrated abundantly that sport was not necessarily antithetical to the regime's eugenic and demographic goals,[36] yet even in the early 1940s female athleticism still aroused some suspicion, among many Italian families, of possible dangers to women's health, their chances of successful maternity and their very femininity. The question remains whether this was really a problem peculiar to Italian Fascism. Would Italian physicians have produced much the same kind of partly medical, partly moralistic texts if they had been living in a non-Fascist country? After all, the same superficially rational arguments against women's 'excessive' participation in sport were being propagated in many other countries at the time, including not only, and predictably, Nazi Germany, but also Britain and the United States.

The education system and the Fascist youth organisations

The physical and sporting education of Italian girls and young women had to be adapted to the pedagogic goals pursued by the Fascist regime, and therefore to the models of femininity that promoted. Like the regime's institutions for sports medicine, hygiene and therapeutics, schools also promoted eugenics for the sake of the Italian 'race', slowing down the development of women's sport in a nation that had long defined itself as 'athletic'.

Schools and physical education before the Fascist era

Educational gymnastics had become a subject for all pupils in Italian schools in the late nineteenth century. Following the passage of Daneo's Law in 1909, a serious attempt was begun to modernise physical education courses by opening them up to a wider range of activities. However, the implementation of the Law was hampered by the hostility of the more conservative physical education teachers, and then the loss of lives and the damage to buildings inflicted on Italy during the First World War served only to accentuate the chronic lack of teachers and facilities.

The economic and social crisis that immediately followed consumed all the energies of the authorities, and the problems of physical education in schools remained unaddressed. Meanwhile, experts in the field carried on offering different proposals for the revitalising of physical education, reflecting the ideological and pedagogical divisions in their ranks. Giuseppe Monti, the influential head of the institute for the training of female physical education teachers in Turin, and a follower of the nineteenth-century educationist Emilio Baumann (see Chapter 2), took the view that discipline had to remain at the heart of the school system as an integral part of the educational process. Others, such as General Luigi Gasparotto, wanted to reform physical education in particular so that it could serve the needs of the army. A third school of thought, typified by Romano Guerra, the director of the teacher-training institute in Rome, sought to separate physical education from the conservative traditions of the school system. Guerra wanted a new form of physical education, inspired by Swedish scientific methods and British sporting practices, and provided by a modern and autonomous organisation outside the schools.

One notable trend within the world of physical education during these years was the increasing 'feminisation' of the student body in the three main teacher-training institutes: Guerra's institute in Rome, which trained male physical education teachers, and the institutes in Turin and in Naples, which trained female teachers of the subject. The second decade of the twentieth century saw a notable increase in the proportion of women among those preparing to become physical education teachers, from a mere 6 per cent in 1911 to 42 per cent in 1921.[1]

Nevertheless, in general schools, universities and other institutions involved in educating girls and young women continued to be deeply influenced by old and new prejudices about their mental and physical abilities, and more or less openly hindered their emancipation. This can be inferred even from a cursory examination of the laws on education, the curriculum in force at the time, and the types of gymnastic and sporting activities chosen for girls and young women.

The school system under the Fascist regime

Following the advent of Fascism, the project of transforming schools into political institutions serving the new ideology could not be entrusted to the men now in power, who were more prone to action than to theoretical considerations. The project was therefore passed to the philosopher Giovanni Gentile, who had been appointed Minister of Public Instruction by Mussolini. Gentile promulgated his School Reform Law (Law no. 684) on 15 March 1923. His aim was to find a compromise between the liberal and Catholic ideologies that had dominated pre-Fascist Italy and the new Fascist culture, which needed to create its own ruling elite and at the same time to 'Fascistise' the Italian masses through the school system. However, even though Mussolini himself called Gentile's Law 'the greatest revolutionary act attempted by the Fascist government',[2] it failed to meet the Fascists' expectations. Gentile wanted the school system to train the future ruling class through narrow historical and philosophical studies in secondary schools, which were attended only by members of the upper classes. His Law made little provision for the professional and technical training of the lower classes: instead it stressed the selective and class-oriented character of the school system. In addition, by granting autonomy to private schools, which in Italy were traditionally mostly religious, Gentile's Law managed to disappoint both the Fascists, who wanted more control over the programmes and activities of such schools, and the liberal secularists, who were ideologically hostile to confessional schools.[3] In other words, Gentile's Law broadly continued the educational policies first laid down in Casati's Law of 1859, while making concessions to religion, and did not adequately provide for the 'fascistising' of the masses.

Gentile's Law underwent numerous amendments during the following 15 years, notably following the signing of the Concordat between the Fascist regime and the Catholic Church in 1929, which made it easier for Fascist ideology, myths and rituals to penetrate the school system. The Ministry of Public Instruction became the Ministry of National Education, a more appropriate name for an institution that had taken on the duty of educating the population in the new ideology. Authoritarianism and hierarchy were strongly emphasised. New textbooks were introduced and any teacher who expressed anti-Facist ideas, even in private, could be subjected to deportation. In 1929 all teachers in primary and secondary schools were compelled to take an oath of allegiance to Fascism. The following year university professors were also forced to swear allegiance: of 1,225 professors, only a dozen refused to do so.

These changes had a particularly marked effect on women teachers, whose activities became more closely controlled and whose numbers were reduced. Ironically, this would have pleased Gentile, who was a fervent anti-feminist and had opposed the entry of women into the teaching profession. According to Gentile, women did not possess, and would never possess, the 'originality of thought, nor that iron spiritual vigour, that constitute the superior intellectual and moral forces of humanity, and that must be the pillars of any school that aims to train the superior spirit of the country.'[4]

Despite the fact that such views were widely shared, the percentage of girls attending school rose under Fascism. The female illiteracy rate fell from about 50 per cent in 1911 to 24 per cent in 1931. Nevertheless, the number of boys in primary schools was consistently about twice the number of girls. In 1926 there were 3,634,556 boys and 1,736,420 girls on the primary schools' registers; in 1931 there were 4,761,690 boys and 2,266,333 girls; and in 1940 there were 5,213,004 boys and 2,504,232 girls.[5] While about 28 per cent of boys and 23 per cent of girls aged between 10 and 14 had attended junior high schools in 1901, by 1931 these proportions had risen to 65 per cent and 53 per cent respectively. As for senior high schools, in 1931 girls were definitely at a disadvantage because they made up only 25–30 per cent of the total enrolment of 379,000 students.[6] In addition, during the Fascist era the drop-out rate in all three types of school was higher among girls, presumably because the schools, the girls' families and society in general expected less of girls, and/or because there seemed little purpose in preparing girls for jobs that they would not be able to obtain.[7] A small minority of girls, mostly from the upper class, attended single-sex schools, inspired by Gentile's philosophy, in which they studied a little of everything, from the arts and humanities to traditional 'feminine' household activities. However, these schools aroused opposition from 'emancipated' women and lasted for only four years (1924–28).[8]

On 18 March 1931 Mussolini told the Council of Ministries that Gentile's Law had been 'a mistake due to the times and to the frame of mind of the former Minister'.[9] On 19 January 1939 the Minister of National Education, Giuseppe Bottai, proposed a 'renovation' of the school system at a meeting of the Fascist Grand Council. This led to the promulgation of Bottai's *Carta della Scuola* (School Charter), which was intended to launch the regime's most determined effort to 'fascistise' the school system, but, because of Italy's participation in the Second World War, was never implemented. Nevertheless, its 29 clauses usefully summarise the Fascist approach to education. The goals of education were to include political and military training as well as moral and cultural development; all Italians were to be educated up to the age of 21, either in the mainstream educational institutions or through the Fascist youth organisations; and there were to be separate schools for Jews.[10] The Charter also, not surprisingly, emphasised the secondary status of women. Bottai proposed a clear-cut distinction between female and male education, the former being aimed at preparing girls to perform the roles of wife and mother. Clause 21 of the Charter asserted that:

> The destiny and social mission of women, distinct in Fascist life, are based on different and special institutions of education. The transformation of mixed schools is to be carried out according to the definition of the new 'work of women' in the co-operative order. The feminine order consists of a feminine institution, [with courses lasting] for three years, which receives girls from junior high schools, and a teacher-training course for all the girls who graduate from the feminine institution. These institutions spiritually prepare females for managing households and teaching in pre-school institutions.[11]

The way in which girls were educated under Fascism is perhaps more clearly indicated in a composition written by one girl at an elementary school, dated 9 December 1939 and headed '*Quando indosso la mia divisa di Piccola Italiana penso ai miei doveri di donna Italiana*' (When I wear my Piccole Italiane uniform I think of my duties as an Italian woman) – a reference to the Fascist organisation that she belonged to:

> I am a Piccola Italiana. … I wear my uniform when I have to go on parade. When I wear it, I feel in my heart a great love for Italy, and deep honour for my country. … Even when I am a woman I shall wear my uniform. Italian women must imitate ancient Roman women. They stayed at home to raise their children and educate them. They wove cloth and they cleaned the house. We should follow their example, stay at home, and clean, wash and cook. These are the duties of a real Italian woman.[12]

From the ENEF to the ONB, 1923–27

Somewhat paradoxically, the specific provisions of Gentile's Law affecting physical education had gone against the spirit of his own educational philosophy, according to which physical education should be part of 'spiritual education' and should therefore be fully integrated into the school system. Instead his Law had provided for the implementation of Romano Guerra's approach to the issue. The teacher-training institutes in Rome, Turin and Naples were closed down, and physical education was removed from junior and senior high schools and placed in the hands of a new body, the *Ente Nazionale per l'Educazione Fisica* (ENEF), which would have the duty of assigning school pupils to courses in designated gymnastic and sport clubs.[13] Gentile's Law thus relieved local authorities of the burden of providing gymnasiums and sports grounds, which became the responsibility of the ENEF.

The ENEF was clearly intended to be a vehicle for significant improvements in the country's provision for physical education and sport. In practice, however, lack of economic and organisational support, and confusion over the methods to be adopted, led to the failure of the ENEF. Teachers were now to be paid from taxes imposed on the pupils themselves, which proved difficult to collect; and, now that the teacher-training institutes had been abolished, there was no provision for the training of new teachers of the subject. ENEF proved incapable of controlling the activities of the numerous different sports clubs scattered throughout the country, many of which were unwilling or unable to collaborate in organising activities for schoolchildren.

On 3 April 1926, while the ENEF was still struggling to cope with its responsibilities, the regime promulgated Law no. 2247, establishing the *Opera Nazionale Balilla* (ONB), which was to take charge of assisting, and providing physical and moral education, for all Italians under the age of 18, with a particular emphasis on preparation for military service.[14] Then, on 12 October 1927, the Council of Ministers decreed that the responsibilities of the ENEF would be passed to the ONB. Under a royal decree (no. 2341) dated 20 November that year ENEF was closed down and ONB was given the additional task of dealing with the physical education of pupils in public elementary schools, which Gentile's Law had neglected. However, the ONB lacked sufficient funds to take direct control of these children's physical education and under another royal decree (no. 1594) dated 9 August 1929 it was given the role of 'guidance and supervision' of their physical education, which remained subject to the goodwill of the schools and the availability of teachers.

The conception of the ONB as a totalitarian institution involving children and young people of all social classes had come directly from Mussolini, who had entrusted its implementation to Renato Ricci. Ricci then finalised the structure and activities of the ONB by taking ideas from such bodies as the *Balilla* Inspectorate, an arm of the *Partito Nazionale Fascista* (PNF) con-cerned with young people; the youth wing of the *Milizia Volontaria per la Sicurezza Nazionale*; and the two main Catholic bodies involved in physical activities, the scouting movement[15] and the *Federazione delle Associazioni Sportive Cattoliche Italiane* (FASCI).[16]

The vexed issue of how the sports clubs were to be controlled had already been resolved before the disappearance of the ENEF. Starting on 2 March 1927, those clubs that had not closed down were required to join one of the 32 national sports federations. These federations, which had a combined membership of 423,763 individuals in 1926, were in turn required to affiliate to the *Comitato Olimpico Nazionale Italiano* (CONI).[17] This completely 'Fascistised' body was given additional powers and funds to carry out its twin functions of representing Italy in dealings with the Olympic movement and supervising sport within the country.

The Concordat between the Holy See and Italy ensured that FASCI and other Catholic sports associations would survive for a few more years, although by 1927 they had only 27,000 members left. In 1927, however, the Catholic scouting movement was 'Fascistised', and its members were required to display the *fascio* symbol and the initials 'ONB'; the movement was then dissolved the following year. The organisation *Forza e Grazia* (Strength and Grace), which had been founded in 1923 to organise gymnastic and sporting activities as an affiliate of the *Gioventù Femminile di Azione Cattolica* (Young Women of Catholic Action), with subdivisions in Milan, Cuneo and Acireale, was also abolished in 1928.[18] Finally, in September 1931, all gym-nastic and sporting activities other than those organised under the ONB were strictly prohibited.[19] From then on the ONB became the sole patron of sporting activities for children and young people.

Through the ONB the Fascist regime not only tried to remedy the effects of the ENEF's failure in physical and sports education, and in the military training of schoolboys, but also aimed to achieve an important goal that Gentile's Law had failed to address: the moulding of young Italians, from primary school onwards, according to the principles of Fascist aesthetics and the 'Fascist style'. The ONB also devoted itself to spreading these principles among young people who had left school, and to supplementing the social assistance provided by the *Opera Nazionale Maternità ed Infanzia* (ONMI) to younger mothers and children. In addition, the ONB set about replacing the teacher-training institutes that had been abolished in 1923. From 1928 onwards male teachers were trained at the *Accademia Nazionale di Educazione Fisica* in Rome; a separate academy for the training of female teachers of the subject was established in 1932.

The activities of the ONB, 1926–37

During its brief existence the ENEF promoted a physical education programme for schoolgirls that was completely different from the one for schoolboys, basing it on the notion that girls should develop grace, elasticity and aesthetic sense. The ENEF also tried to prevent girls from practising sports that might induce them to want to imitate boys.[20]

With the ENEF out of the picture the ONB initially busied itself with re-organising physical activities for boys, leaving provision for girls entirely in the hands of the *Fasci Femminili*, the women's auxiliary of the ruling party, which was now placed under the supervision of the ONB but retained some control over the physical education and assistance programmes that it had been organising since its foundation in 1921.

In 1925 the *Fasci Femminili* had launched a newspaper, the *Rassegna Femminile Italiana*, to promote its activities. An article in its very first issue declared that:

> Men make laws, women make customs. We do not write poems … we are talking only of mothers and not of Spartan mothers, who are too conventional and academic. We are talking about the saintly Italian mothers who blessed their children departing for war and waited till later to cry. … Re-establishing women in their own realm, the home, will give them back their mission.[21]

The young recruits of the *Fasci Femminili*, which was led by Elisa Majer Rizzioli, followed a programme of activities that was better suited to the tastes of upper-middle-class ladies than to the expectations of young women from lower classes. It was centred on recital competitions, domestic science, gymnastics, 'fun get-togethers and instructive field-trips, sports and singing'.[22] Simultaneously, the organisation expected each of its members to:

(1) Fulfil the duties of daughter, sister, scholar, and friend with kindness and happiness, even if work is sometimes tiring.
(2) Serve the country as the greatest mother of all Italians.
(3) Love the *Duce* who has made the country stronger and greater.
(4) Gladly obey superiors.
(5) Have the courage to oppose anyone who suggests evil and ridicules honesty.
(6) Educate the body to overcome physical strain and the soul to fear no pain.
(7) Avoid futile vanity and love beautiful things.
(8) Love work: it is life and harmony.[23]

Through the *Fasci Femminili* the Ruling Party supervised three more organisations aimed at sections of the female population: the *Piccole Italiane*, for girls aged between eight and 14 (such as the elementary school pupil quoted above); the *Giovani Italiane*, for girls aged between 14 and 18; and the *Giovani Fasciste*, for young people of both sexes aged between 18 and 21. In 1926 there were 35,000 *Piccole Italiane* and 2,000 *Giovani Italiane*;[24] In 1927 their memberships rose to 128,000 and 19,321 respectively[25] (there appear to be no figures available for the *Giovani Fasciste*). This rate of growth was deemed inadequate, and Ricci launched an overhaul of the organisations. In 1929 the *Fasci Femminili* withdrew from any connection with the activities of girls under 18, to focus instead on the *Giovani Fasciste* and the *Opera Nazionale Dopolavoro* (OND), which provided spare-time activities for working people (see Chapter 1). By this point there were 364,300 *Piccole Italiane* and 100,153 *Giovani Italiane*, but following another promotional campaign by the ONB, which now had direct responsibility for both organisations, their combined membership rose to 741,302 in 1931–32.[26] In other words, they now had nearly three times as many members as the *Unione Femminile Cattolica Italiana*, which had been founded in 1908 and had 250,000 members in 1931.[27] By this time the ONB was working more closely with the school authorities. In 1929 Ricci, who was to remain at the head of the ONB until 1937, had been given an additional post as Undersecretary for Physical and Youth Education in the Ministry of National Education. He took care to use this position to safeguard the autonomy of the ONB, in the face of the intrusiveness of both the CONI and the PNF.[28] Ricci's balancing act probably helped to accelerate the spread of physical education, now a monopoly of the ONB, both within schools and outside them. Indeed, given that all children and young people were required to take part in some form of physical education, and that outward conformity to the regime's wishes was highly advisable, if only to stay out of trouble, membership of the ONB, although it was never formally made compulsory for all Italians below the age of 18, certainly became effectively compulsory for the vast majority of them. Not surprisingly, the ONB was jealous of its prerogatives. In 1930, for example, a publication of the ONB's provincial committee in Vicenza spelled it out:

> In accordance with the Sports Charter of 1928 athletic training of young people up to the age of 17 is the exclusive concern of the ONB. The CONI may supervise the training of minors below the age of 18 only for specific sports and only if they are enrolled in the ONB. The CONI may not in any way take charge of children under the age of 14, even if they are enrolled in the ONB. Only the ONB may organise or authorise gymnastic or sporting festivals in Italian schools.[29]

Under Ricci's leadership the ONB paid special attention to the harmonious psychological and physical development of children and young people of both sexes, as well as to the preparation of collective military displays. Motor activities aimed at strengthening health were carried out in gymnasiums in swimming pools, and on sports grounds, most of which were, apparently, brand new. In 1928 there were only 502 such facilities in the whole of Italy, but by 1933 there were 4,199.[30] However, it is not now possible to ascertain how many of these facilities were genuinely new and of good quality, and how many were created by hasty overhauls of existing facilities.

Under constant pressure from the ONB the numbers of pupils taking physical education classes in state schools also increased, from about 220,000 in 1928 to 324,000 in 1933. In the latter year there were also 110,000 pupils taking classes in private schools.[31] The ONB's affiliates were expanding too: in 1933 there were 1,952,597 boys aged between eight and 14 in the *Balilla* organisation and 535,974 youths aged between 14 and 18 in the *Avanguardisti*, alongside 1,637,689 *Piccole Italiane* and 200,971 *Giovani Italiane*.

Having established a new facility for training male teachers of physical education (as mentioned above), the ONB saw to an increase in the number of qualified teachers from just 166 in 1928 to 638 in 1933.[32] Their non-qualified colleagues included elementary school teachers and other professionals who had both expertise in physical education and a commitment to inculcating Fascist principles. In 1930, in an effort to ensure their loyalty to the regime, the Fascist Grand Council ruled that all new teachers had to be able to prove membership of the PNF for at least five years. One side-effect of this ruling was that teachers who had been in post before 1930 also had to display orthodox beliefs and attitudes, or risk losing their jobs to younger and more enthusiastic rivals.

The children and young people who joined the ONB's affiliated organisations received special benefits and assistance, sufficient to attract those who, whatever their interest in politics, were keen to engage in sport. However, they were also given copies of an instruction booklet that recounted the history and achievements of Fascism in simple language and with captivating images, and included a list of their numerous duties to the Fatherland, religion and the family. Commitment to the ONB did not imply any exemption from scholastic duties. High marks in physical education courses were taken into account in assessing their work at school, but they made little impact on the process of advancement through the school system, which remained as selective and narrowly focused as ever.

The ONB tended to downplay competitive sport and to favour educational gymnastics, following the recommendations of Eugenio Ferrauto, a follower of Romano Guerra (mentioned above), and of Emilio Baumann and Angelo Mosso (see Chapter 2), who supported Ricci's work in his capacity as head of the ONB's Central Service for Gymnastics and Sport. Ferrauto and his colleagues were concerned to match physical activities to the different needs of children of different ages and genders, and to provide ample time within the curriculum for traditional gymnastics, marching practice and group choreography. They did not entirely neglect competitive sport, but they did tend to regard them as primarily suitable for boys and young men only. The problem was that, while some of Ferrauto's ideas were excellent, many were never realised because of the continuing shortages of money and qualified personnel. The financial restraint on Ferrauto's plans partly reflected the fact that Ricci devoted a large proportion of the ONB's budget to the creation of the Mussolini Forum in Rome (see also Chapter 1), a monumental sports complex with stadiums, swimming pools, sports grounds, gardens and fountains that was intended to symbolise the regime's commitment to the promotion of sport among the young.[33]

Midway through the 1930s the ONB began enrolling children under the age of eight in yet another organisation, the *Figli della Lupa* (Children of the She-Wolf), around the same time that one particularly fanatical physician published a book promoting gymnastics for infants.[34] Following Italy's

5.1 Male and female Children of the She-wolf

Italian Fascism and the Female Body

5.2 Parade of ONB children

5.3 Checkpoint for gymnastics female teams

acquisition of more colonies in Africa the ONB also expanded its operations there, enrolling the daughters of colonists in the *Gruppi Giovanili Fascisti* within which the age limit for membership of the *Piccole Italiane* was raised to 16. By this time the ONB was beginning to attract attention from other European countries. The Hitler *Jugend* (Hitler Youth) was to some extent modelled on the ONB,[35] and in 1933, the same year that Hitler seized power in Germany, Robert Baden-Powell, the founder of the international scouting movement, publicly praised the ONB's work, although, like many other British visitors who were impressed by Mussolini's regime, he recanted later on.[36]

Girls and young women in the ONB

All the children and young people who enrolled in the ONB's affiliate organisations had to swear the following oath:

> In the name of God and Italy, I swear to carry out the orders of the *Duce* and to serve the cause of the Fascist revolution with all my strength, and, if necessary, with my blood.[37]

The first set of regulations for the *Piccole Italiane* and the *Giovani Italiane* was outlined in 39 articles in a pamphlet, but they were later expanded and reissued.[38] The new rulebook, distributed to the district managers of the ONB, contained 128 articles, which declared, among other things, that it was the 'duty of the ONB … to train the new generation of females in the principles of the Fascist doctrine' (Article 1), 'by instilling moral education and culture, as well as [the idea of] social assistance, in all girls and young women, not necessarily belonging to the school population, through methodical and pre-arranged activities in physical education' (Article 2). These activities were to 'aim at elevating the power of the organism to resist, and at improving the aesthetic conformation of girls and young women, refraining from any form of competitiveness or athleticism, as well as any tendency not suitable to female natures and bodies' (Article 4). This latter provision was in keeping with the prevailing opinion among sports physicians, most of whom shared the regime's anxiety about helping women to avoid dangerous physical activities and to retain their traditional 'Latin' femininity. Yet for the most part physical education for girls and young women hardly differed from its male equivalent, being centred on the same army-style exercises – discipline, formation and marching – aimed at stimulating the 'warrior spirit' of Italians.

The rulebook also specified (in Article 5) that:

In moral, political, civil and religious education special attention must be paid to infusing a deep sense of duty and responsibility, in order to nurture the perfect Fascist woman, conscious of the tasks allotted to her and in spiritual unison with the regime. Girls and young women must therefore be educated to love religion, their country and their family, to respect sound traditions, and to be faithful to Fascism.

and (in Article 7) that:

Girls and young women must be prepared to worthily perform their duties as wives and mothers: it is essential for young women to be prepared to organise and manage the household, raise children, and assist their relatives if the need should ever arise.

Other articles established how offices for the training of girls and young women were to be organised within the ONB's district committees (Articles 14–17), and how activities in its centres, known as Houses of the Young Italian, were to be managed. Each was to develop 'cultural, physical, professional and domestic programmes', and was to be equipped with an infirmary, a conference room, a laboratory, a library, study halls, a kitchen for lessons in domestic science, a gymnasium, a swimming pool and sports grounds (Articles 18–19). However, more realistically, the rules also provided (in Article 20) that it would be acceptable to provide activities for girls and young women in any suitable establishment, so long as they were kept apart from boys and young men, and had access to a conference room and a kitchen.

The *Piccole Italiane* and the *Giovani Italiane* were to be divided into groups, and each group was to be composed of three, four or five centuries, each century of three maniples, each maniple of three squads and each squad of nine members (Article 24 of the rulebook). Each of these formations was to be managed by a leader chosen from among the members (Article 25). This quasimilitary hierarchy, which closely resembled that of the *Balilla* and *Avanguardisti*, was meant to evoke the army of ancient Rome, in keeping with the regime's propaganda to the effect that Fascism was making Italians into worthy heirs of the greatness and glory of the Roman empire. The members of these organisations were required to perform the 'Roman salute' devised by the regime and to wear regulation uniforms, complete with badges and insignia of rank, both during meetings, ceremonies and parades, and when taking part in gymnastic and sporting activities (Articles 27–34). The uniforms, designed by a painter named Mario Pompei, had to be purchased by the members' families, who also had to pay their annual ONB membership fees on their behalf. Disciplinary shortcomings could be punished with oral or written reprimands, suspension, or, in more serious cases, expulsion from the ONB, although it was recommended that any punishment should take into account the 'distinctive sensitivity of girls and young women', and be aimed at 'correcting and educating [them]' (Article 38).

The 'leaders' within the ONB's female affiliates (provided for in Articles 42–44) had to be members of the PNF, and were usually primary or secondary school teachers, or physical education teachers, although anyone who had a senior high school diploma and demonstrated goodwill could be appointed a leader – another indication of how the regime's reach so often exceeded its grasp. These leaders, who enjoyed a certain amount of power within schools and some prestige in society, were mostly aged between 18 and 45, fitting the youthful image that the regime wished to project. They too were organised in a hierarchical pyramid. As Central President of the ONB, Ricci supervised the district presidents, who were all men. They supervised the female district officers and their deputies. Below them came municipal, rural, section and neighbourhood officers, all of them female. The heads of groups, centuries and maniples formed the base of the pyramid. All these women, numbering about 50,000 as of 1936 (including commanders of the *Figli della Lupa*),[39] had precisely detailed duties (Articles 42–75). In addition, annual training courses were organised for young women who aspired to the leadership of groups or centuries, ending with examinations that determined which of them would obtain a licence to lead (Articles 76–88).

Article 92 of the rulebook stated that:

> Every initiative regarding female physical education will be clearly and absolutely separated from initiatives for males. Tennis, basketball, volleyball, the traditional Italian games of *palla rilanciata*, *volantino*, *palla ribattuta* and *tamburello*, ice-skating and roller-skating, rhythmic gymnastics, swimming, walking, hiking, pre-athleticism as a means of physical culture suitable for *Giovani Italiane*, etc., will be the preferred exercises, in accordance with the distinctive programmes, integrated with the necessary precautions, that are contained in the publication of the Central Presidency …

Many of these activities were available only in the larger and more prosperous Italian cities, where the right equipment was available. In small country towns much was left to the goodwill of teachers and trainers, and to young women's initiative and their ability to improvise.

The ONB's physical education programmes, approved by the Ministry of National Education,[40] were different for the two sexes, except for children aged between eight and 11, who all performed 'general corrective and recreational exercises of moderate intensity'. Boys aged between 11 and 14 were required to perform 'moderate [and] general formative, corrective, developmental and disciplinary exercises'[41], while girls in the same age-group had 'moderate recreational, corrective, developmental and grace exercises'.[42] Young men aged between 14 and 16 were to be kept busy with 'elementary pre-athletic and practical training exercises',[43] while their female counterparts had to make do with 'grace, developmental and disciplinary exercises of moderate intensity'.[44] Finally, young men aged 16 to 18 had a completely different pro-gramme from the one for young women in that age-group, centred on sports and pre-military training, and including 'pre-athletic, athletic and practical training exercises'[45] in track and field, gymnastics, fencing, canoeing, cycling, swimming, boxing, horse-racing, hiking, target-shooting, Graeco-Roman wrestling, skiing, tennis and skating. Walks over distances of 15–20 kilometres and topographical expeditions into the countryside were also required. In contrast, young women aged between 16 and 18 followed a programme of 'easy rhythmic exercises, elementary developmental exercises in pre-athletic style, [and] precise disciplinary and sports exercises'.[46] Athletic activities, where it was possible to hold them, were limited to the javelin, the shot, archery and running distances of up to 70 metres, while the prescribed sports were volleyball, basketball and skating.

The remaining articles in the rulebook fleshed out the main provisions with a striking amount of extra detail. Special courses were to be provided for those needing physical education for medical and correctional reasons; small-scale, non-competitive athletic displays were to be held to strengthen members' willpower, and to instil in them a healthy spirit of emulation; and health resorts were to be organised to accommodate the needs of the youngest girls (Art. 93–95). The rulebook also recommended that leaders should encourage 'women's sense of dignity, illustrating their mission in society and the duties they faced in the name of the Fascist nation' (Article 98), and 'illustrate the ethical goals of the ONB, arousing in young women the desire to belong to it' (Article 99). The penultimate section (Articles 101–27) concerned the provision of courses in religious education, Fascist doctrine, general culture, artistic culture (such as music, drama, figurative art, plastic arts and applied arts), and working activities (such as cutting and sewing, foreign languages, shorthand-typing and bookbinding. Courses in domestic science, child welfare, hygiene and assistance to the sick were highly recommended, and special courses in gardening, beekeeping, horticulture and livestock husbandry were to be held for young women in rural areas. The final sentence (Article 128) reiterated the requirement that all female activities within the ONB were to be kept completely separate from those of male members, in order to avoid any mixing between the sexes.

This highly ambitious and optimistic outline of the ways in which Fascism hoped to mould the bodies and minds of girls and young women, so that they could fulfil their prescribed destinies as models of the 'new woman', never came close to being fully implemented. Teachers and equipment were in short supply, and most of whatever money became available from time to time tended to be spent on activities for boys and young men. The implementation of the ONB's elaborate plans was also hampered by the reluctance of more traditional-minded parents to allow their daughters to take part in extrascholastic activities of any kind, particularly if they were adolescent, regardless of the traditionalism that pervaded the ONB itself. It seems likely, too, that, while younger girls might have enjoyed ONB activities, its ostensibly classless vision of harmonious and healthy activity would have held little genuine appeal either for upper-class young ladies or for young women from poorer homes, who hardly needed the ONB to train them in housework, and had little time to spare, whether they were burdened with domestic chores or earning money, or both.

Nevertheless, it is arguable that, to the extent that the ONB did attract willing participants to its courses and facilities, it helped to initiate Italy's first experience of the social integration of the female population. Previously, girls and young women had left their homes only to attend school, or to work in the fields and factories, the rest of their time being devoted to helping their mothers. Prestigious professions, diversions and cultural interests, as well as politics and sports were all reserved for men only, apart from a small number of privileged women favoured by birth and/or education. In contrast, under the Fascist regime all girls and young women were encouraged to step over the threshold of the family home and join in new collective experiences. Yet it is difficult to gauge the extent to which the Fascist form of social integration through the ONB really influenced the thinking of its members, as opposed to simply providing facilities that they could enjoy without necessarily making any real commitment to the regime. By the time the ONB was in a position to enrol the majority of children and young people, all rival organisations had been suppressed, so it is not possible to make any worthwhile comparisons or contrasts between them and the ONB.

The ONB certainly made itself ubiquitous – indeed, in the mid-1930s it started mailing congratulatory letters to the parents of newborn children in envelopes that also contained ONB enrolment forms and details of how to pay the fees. Most schoolchildren enrolled in the ONB's affiliates, at least partly because their teachers prompted them to do so, but, arguably, also because they enjoyed wearing uniforms and/or participating in the activities of which the ONB was the monopoly provider, or simply out of a desire to conform. Fascist ideology spoke to the imaginations of at least some of these young people. Although they naturally tended to become more critical and less impressionable as they grew older, many young adults continued to participate in Fascist organisations, whether out of sheer habit, for the sake of the benefits membership conferred on them, or because they felt a real ideological affinity. Active involvement in the ONB and then in the PNF also provided significant advantages, and contacts, when the time came to choose a career. Conversely, membership of either body was not compulsory, except for certain categories of state employees, and those who did not join were usually not persecuted as opponents of the regime, but were treated dismissively as 'lazy bourgeois', neutralists or, at worst, defeatists.

The activities of the GIL, 1937–43

Halfway through the 1930s the Fascist regime became increasingly enamoured of the idea that sporting victories, creating national and international records and celebrities, would be the most effective means to show the world the greatness of Fascist Italy. The CONI was also lobbying the regime over what it saw as an urgent need to start raising future sporting champions from a tender age.[47] Renato Ricci and the ONB, committed to promoting sport and physical education while opposing competitiveness as unsuitable for the young, seemed to stand in the way of these ideas. The ensuing dispute within the PNF led to Mussolini's withdrawal of his support from Ricci, who had always operated with a worrying degree of autonomy.[48] Under a royal decree dated 27 October 1937 the ONB was suppressed, and all its responsibilities for physical, sports, political and military education of the young were taken over by a new organisation, the *Gioventù Italiana del Littorio* (GIL). The transfer was confirmed when the decree was reissued as Law no. 2566 on 23 December.

Enrolment in the GIL was compulsory, at least formally. Article 1 of the Law stated that:

> GIL, a unitary and totalitarian organisation of the young forces of the Fascist regime, is established within the PNF under direct supervision of its Secretary ... Young people of both sexes between the ages of six and 21 belong to it, and are assigned to the subdivisions of male Giovani Fascisti, Avanguardisti, Balilla and Figli della Lupa, and female Piccole Italiane, Giovani Italiane, Giovani Fasciste and Figlie della Lupa.

Article 5 stated some of the fundamental duties of the GIL, such as:

> Spiritual, sport and pre-military training; the teaching of physical education in elementary and junior high schools in accordance

with the programmes issued by the GIL in agreement with the Minister of National Education; the creation and functioning of courses, schools, colleges and academies pertaining to the goals of the GIL; assistance realised through sports grounds, health resorts and scholastic patronage, or through other means provided by the Secretary of the PNF, a minister, a secretary of state or a general; [and] the organisation of trips and cruises.

The Secretary of the PNF at this time was Achille Starace, who was also President of the CONI. The Law now made him *ex-officio* Director of the GIL. In 1935 Starace had instituted the *Sabato Fascista* (Fascist Saturday) to spread the 'Fascist style' through political, military, cultural and sporting activities.[49] Through the GIL Starace could finally carry out the project of centralising all youth activities in the hands of his PNF Secretariat, in the hope of turning Italians into a nation of determined sportspeople, and this time with the priceless support of the CONI. In 1938 he issued regulations ensuring that all the sports programmes of the GIL would be established and managed in agreement with the CONI.[50] Starace also enjoyed the support of the Minister of National Education, at least in principle. As we have seen above, Bottai's *Carta della Scuola* was never implemented, but its endorsement of the GIL's activities, aimed at 'obtaining harmony of development, validity of training, moral elevation, self-confidence, and a high sense of discipline and duty', shows what was intended.[51]

However, despite the continuous proselytising campaign conducted by the GIL, the number of enlisted members was higher in the North than in the South, and enrolment decreased with age.[52] This latter tendency became even more pronounced as the years went by because even the young people born and raised under Fascism found it increasingly difficult to believe in its ideals, and saw the GIL's choreographic rituals and celebratory parades as pompous and meaningless.[53] At its foundation the GIL inherited 2,478,768 *Balilla* members, 960,118 *Avanguardisti*, 2,130,350 *Piccole Italiane* and 483,145 *Giovani Italiane* from the ONB, but by the end of 1941 there were only 1,865,290 *Balilla* members, 988,733 *Avanguardisti*, 1,759,625 *Piccole Italiane* and 454,204 *Giovani Italiane*. Enrolment in the new *Giovani Fasciste*, an organisation for young people aged between 18 and 21, was also below expectations: in 1941 it had only 1,313,900 male members.[54] It is noteworthy, too, that about 85 per cent of the partisans who fought in the civil war against the Fascists and their Nazi allies were under the age of 22, which suggests that the ONB and GIL activities that had been carried on throughout most of their lifetimes were not very effective as means of indoctrination.[55]

The creation of GIL came at a time when the regime was seeking public support for its turn to a more aggressive foreign policy, which would require more and more Italians to become soldiers and colonists. The alliance with Nazi Germany and the desire to imitate its organisations served to reinforce the regime's wish to arouse the admiration of the whole world through sporting achievements. This in turn led it to place even greater emphasis on the moulding of champions and the transformation of sports into showbusiness. As part of this overall mobilisation of Italians the GIL tried to make junior and senior high school students more competitive through its *Ludi Juveniles* (Youth Games), which included tests of sports of a paramilitary nature. More broadly, all GIL members were expected to take part in spectacular displays, organised jointly by the GIL and the CONI in the hope of discovering new sporting talent. According to the PNF's official pronouncements, the GIL's goals were to ensure 'control of sporting disciplines for the training of future champions'; to assist in 'the perfecting of sport for young people, which is essential from the point of view of the Olympics, and in military preparation'; and to direct 'the selected forces of Fascist sports, not only in national competitions, but also in international ones, in order to claim once again the growing spiritual boldness, physical value and aggressive geniality of Mussolini's Italians.'[56]

Physical education and sport in universities

In 1920–21, before Mussolini came to power, Fascists active in the universities created the *Gruppi Universitari Fascisti* (GUF) as a rival to the Catholic student organisation, the *Federazione Universitaria Cattolica Italiana* (FUCI), and the various socialist and YMCA-linked groups on the campuses. The GUF also created the *Comitato Olimpico Studentesco Italiano* (COSI), which in April 1922 organised artistic, literary and sporting competitions under the banner of the the the *Olimpiadi Nazionali Universitarie*.[57]

However, during the first years of the Fascist era nothing was done to promote sport in universities, because it was considered an 'Anglo-Saxon' custom alien to Italian traditions.[58] The GUF survived, but with some difficulty, because it lacked moral and financial support from the PNF. Then, in December 1927, the GUF was invited to draw up its first agreements with the CONI on participation in the regime's massive sports campaign. Lando Ferretti, then President of the CONI's board, carried out a thorough campaign in favour of university sports among members of the PNF, urging them to 'break down the bronze doors of the universities in the name of Fascism and sport', and to 'create a *Casa dello Studente* [Student House] in every institution of higher education'.[59] Playing on the nationalistic and imperialistic spirit of the regime, Ferretti convinced the PNF's leadership by claiming, for example, that 'just as the British colleges have prepared the basis for British imperialism for centuries, our Student Houses will prepare the basis for

Italian imperialism.'[60] The GUF duly became a more powerful and better-resourced organisation, providing cultural and sporting activities that were in principle open to any university student. In practice, while admission to the universities was not 'Fascistised', except at a late stage when the racial laws were applied and Jews were excluded, admission to the GUF's facilities was conditional on joining the GUF.

The first positive outcomes were achieved towards the end of the 1920s at the national sports championships and, later, at the World University Championships, where, according to Ferretti, students belonging to the GUF had made an impact as 'athletes with a statuesque build ... who lacked nothing compared to their peers from Oxford, Cambridge, Harvard and Yale'.[61] The agreements between the GUF and the CONI were officially reconfirmed in December 1928 through the *Carta dello Sport* (Sports Charter – see Chapter 1). Article 5 stated that 'university groups must sustain all their activities

5.4 Singing the fascist anthem

through federations or sports clubs, in full enforcement of the proceedings stipulated in the CONI–GUF pacts'.[62] The GUF thus became officially dependent on the CONI under its successive directors, Augusto Turati (1928–30), Iti Bacci (1930–31), Leandro Arpinati (1932–33) and then Starace (1933–39).

In 1930, when the organisation *Fasci Giovanili di Combattimento* was created by the PNF for young men aged between 18 and 21, Ricci sought to draw the GUF into the ranks of the ONB, but that proposal was firmly rejected.[63] Every sporting and cultural activity on university campuses remained in the hands of the CONI, the PNF and the GUF, operating jointly. In the first months of 1931 an attempt was made to enrol high school students in the GUF,[64] but this was done without Ricci's knowledge and was not supported by Mussolini, who publicly denounced it at a meeting of the Fascist Grand Council on 6 June 1931.[65] On 29 May the same year Mussolini, in a telegram to the provincial prefects, ordered the suppression of the FUCI. The GUF organised two sets of cultural and sporting competitions: the national *Littoriali della Cultura e dello Sport*, first held in Bologna in 1932; and the local Agonali, in which representatives from faculties on each campus competed from 1934. The complex ceremonial of the *Littoriali* was centred on the swearing of the following oath:

> I will fight to overcome every trial, to conquer every record. With strength in contests and with knowledge in intellectual gatherings, I will fight to win in the name of Italy. I will fight as the *Duce* orders: I swear![66]

Participants in the *Littoriali* had to be either students or graduates below the age of 28, and also had to perform satisfactorily in a preliminary target-shooting contest (another example of the militarisation favoured by the regime). The *Littoriali* held in Turin in 1933 involved both male and female students for the first time. About 100 female athletes competed in a limited number of athletic disciplines (swimming, basketball, track and field, tennis and fencing) gathered under the generic denomination of 'female games',[67] but their presence, alongside the male athletes caused both astonishment and bewilderment, and attracted the attention of the Church. Towards the end of the 1920s the Vatican had expressed support for the ONB's programmes for girls and young women, stating that:

> barring all excesses, eliminating every gymnastic form pertaining to male physical exercises, prohibiting coeducation, we gladly see Christian foundations being carried out in this very delicate

section of public education: in other words, we see perfect harmony between the just concern for women's health and physical development, and the strict guarantees necessary to ensure their modesty and gentleness. The *Opera Nazionale Balilla*, thus solving a widely debated issue by [relying on] tradition, custom and the good sense of our people, deserves the most sincere gratitude of Christian families.[68]

Yet the Vatican had always been hostile to the presence of women on sports grounds, especially if they were in mixed groups. This firm opposition had already prevented the CONI from sending women athletes to the Olympics in Los Angeles, and the *Littoriali* in Turin once again raised the same troublesome issue. To prevent further disagreement it was decided to confine participation in the *Littoriali* to men only.

On the international level GUF members were trained for the World University Championships, in which they achieved good results. The best male athletes were also selected for the Olympic Games, and won significant victories in Los Angeles (1932) and Berlin (1936).[69]

In 1937 the GUF was absorbed into the GIL, along with every other Fascist youth organisation. Under the GIL mass involvement in sport resulted in the creation of separate female *Littoriali dello Sport*, also in 1937 (separate *Agonali* games for female students had been instituted in 1935.)[70] Finally, in 1941, conformism and traditionalism having been abandoned in the name of the Fascist cause, university students of both sexes once again took part together in the *Littoriali*.

Throughout its existence the GUF had few female members, chiefly because there were relatively few female university students. In the academic year 1920–21 about 18 per cent of graduates and about 17.4 per cent of enrolled students were women, most of them training to be schoolteachers.[71] Female students were often mocked by their male colleagues and subjected to tasteless chauvinist pranks,[72] and they were not usually encouraged by their parents to apply themselves to their studies. Consequently, in 1936–37 only 16 per cent of university students were women.[73] However, the general mobilisation brought about during the Second World War had some positive side effects and in 1941–42 about 22 per cent of university students were women.[74] Presumably this figure is somewhat inflated, reflecting the absence of many men who would have been studying in peacetime but were now in the armed forces, yet there was a real increase in the numbers of women graduating from universities, from 1,929 in 1936–37 to 3,012 in 1941–42, a rise of about 34 per cent.[75] By this time increasing numbers of women were studying not only in the universities, but also at the *Accademia Nazionale Femminile di Educazione Fisica* in Orvieto, as well as at four other university-level institutions directly managed by the PNF – the *Scuola Superiore Fascista per Istruttrici d'Infanzia*, the *Scuola Superiore Fascista delle Maestre Rurali*, the *Scuola Superiore Fascista di Economia Domestica* and the *Scuola Superiore Fascista di Assistenza Sociale* – which trained women for posts as, respectively, pre-school teachers, teachers in the countryside, experts in domestic science and social workers.[76] Arguably, this rising presence of women in work and politics, aided by the removal of many men into the forces, led to a certain degree of acceptance of women in the public realm, with favourable effects in culture and in sport.

6

Girls and young women at health resorts

Health resorts were not, of course, an invention of the Fascist regime. However, they grew in numbers and their prestige was enhanced as a result of initiatives undertaken by the regime in the name of the people's health.

In Italy health resorts had originated from seaside hospices, institutions affiliated to major hospitals that were opened in summer for the treatment of children and young people with scrofula, rickets and lymphatic disorders. The first such hospice appears to have been started in 1822, on the initiative and at the expense of the main hospital in Lucca, which sent some of its young patients from poor families to the sunny beaches of Viareggio. Similar initiatives followed, largely thanks to the work of Giuseppe Barellai, who, from 1853 onwards, took great pains to help a number of sick children, especially tuberculosis patients, to enjoy 'heliotherapy' and 'thalassotherapy', or, in plain language, the benefits of sun and sea. Numerous seaside hospices were built, above all in Liguria, Tuscany, Emilia–Romagna and Marche, and similar hospices were established in various mountainous regions.

The efficacy of the treatment given at these institutions can be deduced from a reading of their annual reports, which claim, for instance, that in the 15 years between 1871 and 1885 25 per cent of about 5,000 patients admitted to the hospices were 'restored to health', 50 per cent showed 'considerable improvement' and about 17 per cent 'showed some progress'. Since the children sent to these hospices were from very poor backgrounds, part of the improvement in their health must have been due to improved nourishment and hygiene alone. Although the hospices received patients of both sexes, they were kept separate by being treated at different periods. In July 1892, however, a mixed group of 11 boys and ten girls stayed at Camandona, near Biella, for two months.[1]

The results of treatment at these hospices seem to have been more encouraging for boys than for girls; doctors speculated that this may have been because boys had 'greater organic resistance to cosmic influences, greater constancy of sea-bathing and a longer resistance on the beach'.[2] The hospice doctors also reported that, unlike girls, boys remained naked for one hour or more after being bathed in burning hot sand, which, they claimed, contributed 'very much to strengthening the constitution of these [boys] more than that of those [girls]'.[3]

At the end of the nineteenth century additional seaside and mountain health resorts were founded for poor children who were considered to have delicate constitutions, due to lack of food and hygiene, but were not affected by specific illnesses. These new institutions worked closely with the existing therapeutic hospices. The huge expenditure on managing and organising the hospices and health resorts was usually covered by wealthy benefactors, by charitable institutions such as the *Opere Pie*, by private firms or by co-operatives.[4] During the First World War a new era began, characterised by a certain form of state intervention, as the Health and Education Ministries endeavoured to provide direct financial support for summer health resorts that gave places to children of soldiers. The state also introduced a system of inspections in regions where hospices and children's health resorts were more numerous, with the aim of controlling, cataloguing and organising the different kinds of intervention, ranging from the therapeutic and prophylactic to the merely recreational.

Official statistics show that in the six years between 1916 and 1921 the health resorts run by the *Opere Pie* for poor children of delicate constitutions tripled in number, from 13 to 35.[5] In 1902, 25,000 children had been treated in summer hospices and health resorts, but by 1922 there were 100,000 children in these institutions, which had become deeply rooted in social custom.[6]

Expansion under Fascism

After the establishment of the Fascist regime the organisation of children's health resorts was undertaken by the state and there was a considerable increase in the numbers of children using them, from 350,000 in 1932 to about 700,000 in 1936.[7] There were several reasons for the state's enhanced interest in health resorts. First, there was a general sensitivity, shared by Fascists and non-Fascists alike, to the damage caused by industrialisation and urbanisation. Second, there was an increasing interest in, and respect for, the achievements of medicine. Third, the regime considered it a matter of urgency to improve the health of the population, and thus strengthen the 'race', by way of:

> the formation of physically and morally strong and healthy generations, through the protection and assistance of maternity and infancy, physical education, and the moral preservation of young people.[8]

Finally, of course, the resorts and hospices offered yet another avenue for the ideological manipulation of young people.

Just as in families, schools, workplaces and sporting activities, everything that happened at the health resorts was, at least in principle, to be controlled by the regime. Accordingly, the Fascists subjected the private charities that managed most of these institutions to strict political control, or even absorbed them into the regime's own organisations, in order to manipulate the young people who were in their care. Thus Fascism took possession of one of the last remaining areas of freedom: young people's holiday time.

It was in 1927 that the *Opera Nazionale Maternità ed Infanzia* (ONMI) first spent its own funds on sending about 180,000 children to health resorts. Then, under the direction of the *Partito Nazionale Fascista* (PNF), and with the assistance of the *Fasci Femminili*,[9] the Italian Red Cross and the *Opera Nazionale Balilla* (ONB), the OMNI extended its involvement from 1930 onwards, with the result that the number of children that it sent to resorts rose from 100,000 to 250,000.

Between 1931 and 1937 the organisation of health resorts was also co-ordinated by another Fascist entity, the *Ente Opere Assistenziali* (EOA), which was concerned with various programmes of social assistance. Finally (as we have seen in other chapters), from 1937 until the collapse of the regime in 1943 every kind of educational, recreational and charitable activity was firmly under the control of the *Gioventù Italiana del Littorio* (GIL).

The regime paid special attention to children of the numerous Italians who had emigrated. From 1927 onwards they were regularly invited by the

6.1 Flowers given to Mussolini visiting a seaside health resort

PNF to spend holidays at seaside or mountain resorts in Italy. The main objectives of this programme were to maintain close ties between emigrants and their native country, and to bring up children in Mussolini's ideology so that eventually they could help to teach the rest of the world 'to believe, to obey, to fight'.

The following statement, made in 1934 by Piero Parini, the director of the network of *Italian Fasci* in foreign countries, exemplifies the connection between these holidays and the regime's ideological motives.

> By ordering that the beautiful seashores and the picturesque Alpine landscape be opened to young Italians from abroad, the *Duce* has achieved the most tenacious conquest: that of the soul. Our young people are worthy of that. They redeem the ancient miseries of emigration, and in the future, however events may turn out, they will show that their faith will come forth as strong as granite.[10]

During the Fascist era the network of health resorts was greatly expanded and spread throughout Italy. In 1927, 410 health resorts provided treatment for 80,000 patients; in 1938, 4,357 health resorts treated 772,000 patients. No fewer than 4,262,000 children stayed in the health resorts covered by the regime's statistics for varying lengths of time during the years 1931–38. If the additional health resorts affiliated to farmers' and religious organisations are taken into account,[11] it appears that Mussolini's ambitious aim of providing treatment for 1 million young people by 1938 was not far from being realised. (National statistics on the total numbers of children sent to health resorts ceased to be compiled in 1938; however, official documents and other publications indicate that the resorts were still functioning up to 1944.)[12]

The regime's efforts to provide holidays in the sun for Italian children appear to have satisfied most citizens' expectations for the health of the rising generation. At the same time they constituted both part of a more general plan, aimed at increasing the population and improving their health, and a precious tool of propaganda available for use in the manipulation of young people's minds. The colossal buildings erected at the leading resorts during the 1930s – monuments of Fascist rhetoric capable of accommodating up to 1,500 people at a time – encouraged depersonalisation and uniformity among young people by offering them a way of life that increasingly resembled that of a barracks rather than that of a traditional holiday resort. The activities imposed on the young people who, needing fresh air, sunshine and adequate food, were sent to these health resorts offer clear evidence of these attitudes. Whether boys and girls resided at entirely separate facilities, or used the same facilities but at different times, their movements were rigorously organised.

6.2 Daily exercise at the mountain health resort of Mottarone

Given traditional attitudes to the rearing of girls, it cannot have been easy at first for the regime to convince families that even girls could live in such institutions, far removed from their parents and their homes. In the summer of 1927, for example, while about 50,000 members of the two Fascist organisations for boys and young men, the *Balilla* and the *Avanguardisti*, were sent to health resorts, only 4,000 members of the girls' organisation, the *Piccole Italiane*, were sent to them.[13] In the following years, however, the proportion of girls increased in response to the eugenic propaganda of the regime, which took it upon itself to reassure their parents by promising the constant presence at the resorts of trained assistants with high moral standards. Parents' reactions seem to have been broadly positive regarding both girls and young women. In 1929, for example, 1,433 young working women spent some time in 12 health resorts reserved for them,[14] while others, given the lack of suitable accommodation for such young women at children's resorts, were sent to ordinary boarding houses at the seaside, again at the PNF's expense. Then, during the summer of 1930, 1,421 children spent one of three residence periods at the health resort of Marina in Igea, near Rimini, of whom 683, or just under half, were girls.[15] In the same year some beds at a children's seaside health resort called *Duce*, in Romagna, were reserved for working women, so that in three 15-day shifts 45 of them could enjoy the benefits of the resort.[16]

Recruitment of female patients and training of female staff

Further information on the female presence at health resorts can be gleaned from the *Bollettino del Comando Generale* (Bulletin of the General Headquarters) issued by the PNF. According to this publication, the *Fasci Femminili* in each province was expected to provide information about girls needing treatment at health resorts to the province's sanitary committee, which supervised the work of every health resort within the province, even those managed by private entities; the committee gave each candidate a check-up and chose the health resort most suitable for her.[17] Any girl for whom treatment was sought had to provide a medical certificate, a certificate of membership of the *Piccole Italiane* and, to prove that she was older than seven and younger than 14, her birth certificate. Depending on her specific needs, she could then be admitted to one of the resorts, which were classified into six types: seaside, mountain, sunlight, riverside, iodine-treatment or lakeside.[18] The Secretary of the PNF was responsible for issuing an annual report based on the numerous inspections carried out to ensure that the health resorts were being properly managed.[19]

The task of training the female assistants and directors of children's health resorts was also entrusted to the *Fasci Femminili*, which from 1929 onwards organised regular courses aimed 'at the sanitary and moral assistance of guests' in each provincial capital. In order to be admitted to one of these courses for training as a health resort assistant, women had to be younger than 35; had to demonstrate their past loyalty to Fascism, through membership of one of the PNF's affiliated organisations; and had to have certificates of secondary education, usually of the type that qualified them to teach in primary schools. The working programme over the 40 days that the course lasted was intense: at least in principle, the students would have to be trained in physiology, nutrition, medicine, prophylaxis, general hygiene, dietetics, first aid, climatic therapy, 'heliotherapy', 'thalassotherapy', physical education, history, 'Fascist culture', and the statutes and regulations on health resorts.[20] Those students who successfully completed the course were awarded diplomas and given part-time postings to health resorts for the four summer months. Candidates for directorships of health resorts had to be enrolled in one of the PNF's organisations, have an assistant's diploma, show evidence of having given good service in health resorts for at least three years and pass another examination.[21] The stated aim of the training for both assistants and directors was to ensure that they could help the children who stayed at health resorts 'not only … to flourish in health, but also to elevate their little souls towards the supreme ideals of Fascism, to love their country, and to have a deep religious feeling and a precise moral education'.[22]

The realisation of all these aims seems unlikely if we consider that children stayed at health resorts for 30 days on average, the minimum perod being

6.3 The 'Roman salute' of female children in a summer health resort

6.4 Leaving by bus

20 days and the maximum 40.[23] It should be remembered, however, that all children and young people were subjected to the same kind of indoctrination all year long, at school, within their families and during their spare time. Members of the *Piccole Italiane*, for example, were expected to learn:

> the value of the race, its mission in the world from ancient times up to the present, ... pride in their descent and a yearning to perpetuate and hand on that glory to future generations; ... [and] to have a profound veneration for the home [and] for the family, ... seen as deep-rooted and wise training in what their mission as mothers and brides will be.[24]

Dr Grasca Diaz, a director of a health resort, set out the requirements of the job in 1921 (before the Fascists took power):

> a sum of energies is required that can be appreciated only by someone who knows how much sense of responsibility, what a lot of tact, how much goodness of health and readiness of mind, and what a lot of physical endurance are necessary for this very important task. Do not believe that being the director of a children's health resort is a holiday. The place may be enchanting and very healthy, and the resort may be operating wonderfully, but who-ever assists children never has any peace or rest.[25]

Treatment at the health resorts

The young people who, year after year and in increasing numbers, attended the health resorts received a homogeneous and standardised treatment that, in the name of efficiency and 'massification', glossed over individual differences. 'Heliotherapy', climatic cures, well-balanced if simple nourishment, and attention to personal and environmental hygiene were offered – all of them being largely unknown to most children from large, poverty-stricken families – together with a full programme of compulsory activities, which followed one after the other throughout the day. The nature and order of development of these activities, which were laid down by the authorities in some detail, did not leave any room for personal initiative. All the children in the health resorts were considered as passive subjects, simple mechanisms of a system that had to function perfectly and uniformly throughout Italy, aiming to make them perfect young Fascists able 'to believe, to obey, to fight'. The daily pro-gramme, which made no significant distinctions between the sexes, was clearly stated. In the mornings it included rising at half past six; personal hygiene; gymnastics in the open air; prayers; breakfast; hoisting the flag and singing patriotic songs; 'heliotherapeutic' cures and, at the seaside resorts, sea-bathing; and then lunch. In the afternoons it included 'educational' activities, notably readings praising Fascism and its achievements; more gymnastics and games; a snack; lowering of the flag, accompanied by more singing of songs; dinner; and then bed.[26]

A strict hierarchy assigned a well-specified role to every person in every health resort. At the head of each institution were the director, who was always female, a medical officer and a number of assistants. Then came a small number of qualified nurses, and finally the ancillary staff employed in the kitchens, the laundry and other service areas.[27] The children were divided into squads of about 30 members each;[28] all children assumed the name of the squad to which they belonged. For instance, in 1932 the boys' squads at the health resort in Riccione, near Bologna, which, unusually, accommodated both sexes at the same time, were called 'young eagles', 'young cocks', 'chicks' and 'crickets', while the girls' squads were called 'swallows', 'dragonflies', 'butterflies' and 'fireflies', apparently in imitation of the customs of the Boy Scouts and Girl Guides.[29]

Later, when the political purpose of the regime became more aggressive, girls at the health resorts had to submit to the harsh rules that had already been imposed on other organisations for children and young people, and that now transformed the health resorts from healthy holiday homes into barracks. Following the military model derived from ancient Rome, the *Piccole Italiane* were organised into maniples (squads of 24), centuries and cohorts,[30] each carefully controlled by the assistants and by the heads of the squads, chosen from among the fittest, who had to direct their groups as if they were corporals in skirts.

Throughout their periods of residence at health resorts girls had to wear the prescribed bathing suits, dresses, evening-wear and night-shirts that were given to them. Sometimes they also received hats and woolly vests of uniform shape and colour, depending on the climate.[31] These uniforms also had the effect of cancelling out visible differences between the poorer children and those who were not so poor.

The daily rituals of raising, saluting and lowering the flag were practised in all children's health resorts from the start of the Fascist era, although as time passed they were expected to be performed with ever greater military precision. The children were compelled to march like little soldiers every time they moved, either inside the health resorts or in the streets outside; in the latter case they were expected to put on the uniforms of whichever Fascist organisation they belonged to.[32]

The ideological indoctrination and militarisation of the children at the resorts was also carried out through the exaltation of the care of the body, the strengthening of which was said to contribute to the health of the Italian 'race'. Particular emphasis was put on the eugenic education of girls as future mothers: health and strength were required of them, as well as a spirit of sacrifice and devotion to the *Duce*'s ideals, so that they could raise numerous progeny in the service of the Fatherland.

As the timetable sketched out above suggests, a great deal of time was dedicated to physical education, and in particular to corrective gymnastics, which was to be practised for one hour in the mornings and one hour in the afternoons. At the larger health resorts – those that had more than 150 children in residence at a time – the gymnastics programme was co-ordinated by a female 'manager of gymnastics' specially trained and qualified in teaching the subject in health resorts;[33] at the smaller resorts the assistants had to follow detailed instructions provided in an official handbook.[34] Thus all the girls were compelled to complete a series of regimented and elementary exercises, such as jumping and vaulting, as well as corrective exercises, special exercises after sea-bathing and team games. The handbook directed the assistants to:

> Keep in mind that gymnastics wisely taught and applied in the right amounts can make a delicate child become a strong one. Physical education is the medicine of the race ... Children at health resorts are generally frail: for them gymnastics constitutes a very good prophylactic measure. Make sure that respiratory gymnastics and exercises performed while lying on the ground are done in the right way.[35]

Particular attention was paid to any imperfections of the spine discovered during the girls' initial medical examinations. With their backs exposed, the better to display their movements, the *Piccole Italiane* were subjected to a series of specific exercises, the efficacy of which was verified during a final visit by the resort's physician. The goal was to send the girls home prettier and more vigorous than when they arrived.

The available evidence from the medical examinations conducted at the beginning and at the end of each period of residence suggests that, in general, the children who spent time at health resorts registered considerable improvements in chest circumference, weight and muscular strength. The sunlight and fresh air provided free of charge to growing number of children, among whom, as we have seen, the seriously ill were in fact a minority, clearly contributed, to a significant improvement in the health of large numbers of young Italians.

Nevertheless, as might be expected, there is also evidence that the children, of both sexes, missed their parents a great deal, and vice versa. The improvement in their physical health may have gone some way to compensate children and parents alike for these separation pangs. In addition, given that the boys in particular would have been continuously subjected to militaristic propaganda from a very early age, some of them at least may well have enjoyed the pre-military training, and may have acquired pride and self-confidence as a result. Girls, of course, were encouraged to place domestic duties above military values, even in the last years of Fascism, and may well have found it harder to leave their mothers behind. Predictably, the Fascist press did not report on any of these questions, but there is oral evidence that some problems did exist.

Indeed, far from asking how the children felt about their experiences at the health resorts, the press and the regime's other propaganda outlets presented as much good news as possible, in as much detail as possible, about the progress achieved at the resorts, as part of the regime's general drive to secure broad consent, or at least acquiescence. In 1937, for example, the regime organised in Rome a large-scale exhibition about health resorts and other forms of social assistance for children, to illustrate how much Fascism had done for them. Meanwhile, in 1937 as in every other year under Fascism, the press was filled throughout the summer with articles on children's health resorts, covering openings of new resorts, visits by Fascist leaders, government inspections, the departures and arrivals of batches of children, and public displays by the inmates, often copiously illustrated with photographs. The various items of news were used to compose colourful pieces of sentimental, patriotic and ideological prose. In general, these articles seem to have been welcomed, not only by the authorities – whose censors saw to it that nothing critical ever appeared – but also by the children's parents, who naturally wanted to be told that sending their children to health resorts was a good idea.

From the late 1930s onwards, as has already been mentioned, the rising militarism of the regime also affected life inside the children's health resorts. The Fascist censors ensured that no reliable evidence survives as to the success or failure of this policy. However, we do know that the time given to some of the activities that had been practised at health resorts such as educational courses, corrective gymnastics and team games, was considerably reduced. On the other hand, parades and displays, requiring hours and hours of training in uniform and perfect synchronisation, took up more and more hours in each day at the resorts.

While boys were given physical and moral training aimed at transforming them into strong and obedient soldiers, girls were given similar training, but with the emphasis being on improving their general health, making them sturdier and therefore more likely to give birth successfully, and moulding their spirits so that in due course they would become submissive, modest and well-behaved housewives. Even so, it might still be argued that the experiences that these girls underwent at the health resorts may unintentionally have made some contribution to their emancipation, if only to the extent that they were encouraged, often for the first and only time in their childhoods, to take part in communal activities away from both their families and the Fascist organisations that dominated their everyday lives.

7

The *Accademia Nazionale Femminile di Educazione Fisica*

By the end of the 1920s the idea that physical education and sport should be diffused not only at school but throughout society was fully accepted by the Fascist authorities, which took on the task of convincing the people to join in these activities and encourage their children to do so too. For example, the provincial head of the *Opera Nazionale Balilla* (ONB) in Udine stated in a speech delivered in 1929 that:

> Sport should be universalised, so that all children of any and every social class can usefully engage in exercise. A healthy and diverting sports training should be given both to children of the workers, who should be sometimes removed from workshops or unhealthy houses, and to the students from wealthy families, who should be removed from their studies. This is also a problem of social morality.[1]

One of the obstacles in the way of the regime's policy for expanding physical education was (as mentioned in previous chapters) the severe shortage of teachers who were both qualified in the subject and committed to the regime's values. Between 1923 and 1927 the shortlived precursor of the ONB, the *Ente Nazionale per l'Educazione Fisica* (ENEF), had organised a special university course to train physical education teachers, in Bologna in 1926, and similar initiatives had been undertaken at other universities, but none of these experiments lasted long.[2] The ONB was then given the responsibility of solving the problem under the terms of Law no. 2341, dated 20 November 1927, Article 8 of which directed it to establish one or more Fascist teacher-training schools for physical education, with functions equivalent to those of universities, including the capacity to award degrees.[3]

In 1928 Renato Ricci, the head of the ONB, saw to the establishment of the *Accademia Nazionale di Educazione Fisica* in Rome. This institution, which was exclusively for male students, did much to help increase the number of qualified male teachers of physical education in Italy, from a total of just 1,000 in 1926 to about 14,000 ten years later. These teachers were employed not only in schools but also in the Fascist youth organisations (see Chapter 5). In addition, local summer courses were held from 1929 onwards

7.1 Archery in the Academy of Orvieto

to train primary school teachers.[4] Ricci tried to involve primary school teachers more deeply by organising provincial and regional courses for them, and there was even a national course for them provided within the *Accademia Nazionale*. Those who attended this course were fully reimbursed and received diplomas that opened the way for them to teach physical education in junior and senior high schools as well.[5]

Ricci then turned his attention to mounting a campaign in favour of a separate academy to train female teachers of physical education. After experimental ventures with various courses for women[6] the *Accademia Nazionale Femminile di Educazione Fisica* was finally opened in Orvieto in 1932, under the control of the ONB and the Ministry for National Education.[7]

In 1937 the ONB was abolished, and total control of physical education was assumed by the new *Gioventù Italiana del Littorio* (GIL) and the *Partito*

Nazionale Fascista (PNF). Under the GIL a third year of studies was added at both the male and the female academies. The academies continued to be closely supervised until 2 August 1943, when the PNF was abolished as a consequence of Mussolini's dismissal. They then passed into the hands of the Ministry for National Education, while the *Repubblica Sociale Italiana* (RSI), the Fascist state founded by Mussolini in a part of northern Italy, started new physical education academies for men and women in Gallarate and Castiglione Olona respectively.[8] Both these academies found it difficult to operate in conditions of civil war and, following the hanging of Mussolini and his mistress, and the collapse of the RSI, they were finally closed in June 1945.

Forging the 'new woman' in Orvieto under the ONB, 1932–37

The *Accademia Nazionale Femminile di Educazione Fisica* occupied an imposing complex of restored old buildings and specially constructed new buildings that was complete by the mid-1930s. In these buildings, which were surrounded by extensive gardens, there were dormitories, dining-rooms, kitchens, a swimming pool, a library, a theatre, an infirmary, and several gymnasiums, laboratories and classrooms. A church and a stadium were also provided. The academy was located on a forested hill near the small, quiet town of Orvieto, but far enough away to allow the staff to keep control of the students. All the members of staff were, of course, committed Fascists, and displayed the 'elevated morality' that the regime deemed appropriate in people who were to take young women away from their parents and direct every aspect of their waking lives for months at a time.

The students of the academy were selected from all over the country. They were required to be unmarried and aged between 17 and 23; they had to have senior high school diplomas, and healthy and robust physical constitutions; and they also had to be members of the ONB or, after 1937, the GIL. These young women, whom the regime hoped would become exemplars for others, left their families and moved to Orvieto hoping to have the kind of exciting experiences that female students in the United States were depicted as having in the popular films of the period. Obviously, much of the surviving evidence about the academy and its personnel must be treated with considerable caution, since its records were compiled by convinced Fascists; anything that outsiders wrote about it was censored if it was not entirely positive; and the memories of former students, recorded by interviewers decades later, are not necessarily accurate or complete. It is striking nonetheless that all the former students of the academy who were interviewed in the 1990s declared that their years there were unforgettable: they had met very important people, enriched their knowledge in very different fields and developed a certain *esprit de corps*.[9]

It was relatively expensive to study at the academy. Only food and accommodation were free. The annual fees of 5,000 lire, insurance (at 150 lire), books, travelling expenses and uniforms all had to be paid for by the students' families, who often had to make considerable financial sacrifices. Nevertheless, the former students interviewed many years later all mentioned that their mothers in particular had been very supportive, partly because the academy's diplomas would give their daughters career opportunities that most of the mothers had never had, either in teaching or, after another training course, on the staff of the ONB or the GIL. Until 1937, when the ONB was abolished and Ricci was dismissed, he helped the best students from poorer backgrounds, not only providing special annual grants of 3,000 lire through the provincial committees of the ONB, but also reducing the fees by one half for students who already had older sisters studying at the academy or whose parents were on the ONB's staff.[10] As a result students from different social classes and regions lived together, and were trained in the niceties of etiquette as if they all came from the wealthiest families in Italy. They were served by a number of housemaids and supported by personal tutors, and in return they had to act in accordance with their privileged status whenever they went outside the academy, for example by wearing white leather gloves, travelling only in first-class train carriages and never carrying their own luggage.

The students' lives were totally organised, and they were strictly controlled both in class and during their spare time. Their teachers and inspectors enforced a rigorous discipline, and all rules had to be strictly obeyed. The students were forbidden either to go around Orvieto on their own, or to leave the campus without getting prior permission and providing detailed information about their journeys, which was then passed on to their families. In short, the academy combined the features of an upper-class college, a military barracks and a convent. Within its walls women were encouraged to develop their strength and camaraderie, freed from romanticism, and inspired, at least in theory, to embrace Futurist values, such as 'revolution', 'dynamism' and 'modernity'. However, the academy was not in any real sense a place in which women could emancipate themselves from either Fascism or the traditionalism with which it had such ambivalent relations. This was, after all, a totalitarian institution in a dictatorial state: all the students had to study Fascist law, courses in moral and religious education were also compulsory, and nothing was done that could possibly offend His Holiness the Pope. Even Elisa Lombardi, who was to be the last head of the academy (see below), said later that when she first saw its high walls, as a student, she thought that it was not a school for physical education but a convent.[11] This puts into proper perspective the more enthusiastic accounts of the academy written at the time, such as the claim by one female educationist that the academy's students 'constitute a revolutionary power against any hidden seclusion at home, [and against] physical and mental laziness'.[12]

The courses taught at the academy were the same as those taught to male students of physical education in Rome, except that military training was replaced by instruction in 'feminine work'. All the courses were divided into scientific, 'literary' and technical groups. As of 1932 the scientific group comprised classes on human anatomy, general and applied physiology, and anthropometry and traumatology. The 'literary' group comprised general and applied pedagogy, the history of physical and youth education, Fascist laws and regulations, and one foreign language. The technical group comprised general theory, technology, training and command; formative and corrective exercises; pre-sporting and sporting exercises and games; dance, music and singing; 'feminine work'; and organisational techniques. In line with the consensus among Italian sports physicians of the time (see Chapter 4) not all sporting activities were practised at the academy, which provided instruction and facilities only for swimming and diving, gymnastics, fencing, roller-skating, skiing, athletics, archery, tennis and basketball.[13] Teachers of scientific and 'literary' courses were recruited from the universities, while experts in physical education and sport were brought in from secondary schools. In 1932 there were eight female teachers and one male teacher, whose speciality was pedagogy.

7.2 Ski training of female students
from the Academy of Orvieto

In their spare time students put together material for their yearbook, such as drawings, poems, stories and interviews, wrote sketches to be performed on special occasions, and created new dances and costumes for their performances. They had only a few contacts with their families during the academic year. Their parents could sometimes reach Orvieto for weekend visits, but in general their communication was by letter or telephone. The students were largely secluded from the local population as well. It has been claimed that they were received with respect and admiration when they walked to the cathedral for Mass every Sunday,[14] and they also interacted with local people at the academy's annual exhibitions, and when they went into the town to visit the poor or do teaching practice at its primary schools. Given the prevailing mores of Fascist Italy the unusual sight of their bare legs emerging from their shorts or skirts doubtless also aroused comment from local people, not all of it respectful. On the other hand, these students had some opportunities to interact with outsiders at the national level and even abroad. They were invited to visit other countries or were visited in turn by foreign delegations, for whom they put on displays of dance and sports, and they were frequently taken to Rome to attend political ceremonies and sporting displays. On these occasions they marched in formation or put on displays with their male counterparts from the academy in the capital. Sometimes they were taken to Rome to see exhibitions, or on skiing trips to Italian resorts, as part of the academy's attempt to transform them into simulacra of upper-class ladies.

7.3 Rhythmics gymnastics in the Academy of Orvieto

This process was managed by the academy's female teachers, who were all unmarried. The first Rector of the academy was Ismene Robecchi of Turin, herself a former physical education teacher, but she was required to leave her post when she got married. The second Rector, Maria Costa, controlled the academy from 1933 to 1937. She has been described by some of her former students as a very talented, humane and beautiful person.[15] The image of the academy that these dedicated Fascist women sought to promote received characteristically hagiographic expression in an article by Angelo Cammarata, entitled 'Fucine della Rivoluzione: Le accademie dell'ONB' (Forges of the Revolution: The Academies of the ONB) and published in 1936:

In the promotional booklet ... for the Fascist female academy in Orvieto the Leader [Mussolini] wrote: 'Feminine Fascism is destined to record a splendid history, leave memorable signs, [and] give a deeper and deeper passion and working contribution to Italian Fascism'. ... The revolution had to found these academies rapidly. They are an inspiration of its spirit, intended to arouse the enthusiasm, discipline, strength, harmony and values that the new education should constantly diffuse among Italians ... The academy in Orvieto, with its vast rooms, facilities and programmes, set in a peaceful landscape, has faced a very important problem: that of the totalitarian preparation of Fascist female educators, i. e. grace and strength, kindness and vigour, smiles and severity, the splendour of spirituality in a firm physical harmony, maternity, and the future. Whoever has seen how much has been done in just a few years, across the whole of Italy, for the physical and moral improvement of the Figli della Lupa, the Piccole Italiane and the Giovani Italiane can judge the value of the academy in Orvieto, where young people have been pushed to new achievements that directly or indirectly (by decisively affecting female educators and mothers) concern the delicate flower of our race. ... In the feminine Fascist academy life is varied and preparation is fruitful. The female students acquire habits and virtues that will benefit young women, the sex for which the new education has eliminated the adjective 'weak'.[16]

It is interesting that this article mentions subjects that were not taught at the academy in 1932, notably, in the scientific group, eugenics, hygiene, demography, child welfare and first aid; and, in the 'literary' group, Fascist pedagogy, Fascist culture and two foreign languages, English and French, the study of which was intended to assist in 'the propagandistic task of spreading the universal Fascist ideology all over the world'.[17]

By the time this article appeared the atmosphere in Italy had changed considerably. The new empire needed new soldiers for further expansion, and women were asked to produce numerous children, provide stronger social support and accept broader Fascist indoctrination. These goals were to be diffused among the female members of the ONB and its affiliates by every woman who graduated from the academy in Orvieto.[18]

Forging militarised women in Orvieto under the GIL, 1937–43

Even before the two physical education academies became affiliated to the GIL (under Law no. 866, issued on 22 May 1939) their courses had begun to be changed to make them fit into the GIL's plans. In 1937 the regime, increasingly influenced by Hitler's racist ideology, replaced courses in English and French with courses in German, which became the one and only foreign language to be taught in the academies. In 1938 the new racial laws were imposed, excluding students belonging to 'non-Aryan races'. As a result one student was expelled from the academy in Orvieto in 1940.[19]

In 1939 a special school was established near the academy. About 150 younger women, selected from schools in the various regions of Italy, were trained in physical activities in this school and given the right to move on to studies in the academy, without any further selection process, once they had left the school. In addition, during the summer holidays about 1,500 members of the *Giovani Italiane* organisation attended special GIL courses in physical education and sport at the academy of Orvieto. This proved to be an effective source of new recruits for the academy.

By then Fascist indoctrination permeated all the activities in the academy, and a new group of 'political' courses had replaced the previous 'literary' group. The students now had to spend even more of their time studying the history of the Fascist 'revolution', the history of Fascist policy and doctrine, Fascist policy itself, the institutions of Fascist public law, the structures of the PNF and other organisations, and the principles of Fascist pedagogy. New courses were added to the scientific group to ensure indoctrination in what was called 'biology of the human races', as well as to instruct the students in biotype studies and 'social hygiene', while a course in umpiring was added to the technical group. All these additional courses were given formal recognition in the academy's new statutes, which were approved by Mussolini on 1 February 1940. The statutes also imposed a third year of studies, intended to prepare the students to become managers and instructors in the Fascist youth organisations, or teachers in any kind of school. Finally, all the academy's students were now to be employed by the GIL during the summers to organise sporting contests.

7.4 Forward dive from five-metre springboard

7.5 Perfect synchronisation and symmetry in gymnastics

From February 1937, when Maria Costa left the post of Rector, the academy was headed by Elisa Lombardi (already mentioned above), a Piedmontese who was appointed, not Rector, but Commander of the academy, in order to stress the new military spirit of the institution. She also taught courses in religious instruction. She was only 25 years old when she was appointed. She had been educated in traditional disciplinarian style in a large middle-class family, and is said to have had an independent and lively personality. She had joined the Catholic *Forza e Grazia* society in Cuneo in her teens, but after studying at the academy in Orvieto from 1932 to 1934 she had gone on to organise all the female affiliates of the ONB in Bolzano, a city on Italy's border with Austria, where the different cultures and languages of the Italian-speaking majority and the German-speaking minority had to be handled with tact and diplomacy.[20] She was transferred from Bolzano back to Orvieto by Renato Ricci himself, who had become a friend of hers and whose ideas were to influence Lombardi's work even after the academy had been taken over by the GIL.[21]

There is some evidence (which must be treated with due caution, as mentioned above) that Elisa Lombardi's style and energetic personality, and even her sense of duty, made her successful with the students, at least some of whom may have considered their Commander as setting an example to be imitated.[22] Even though the students' discipline and diet were strictly controlled, and they were forbidden to use make-up, smoke, or read uncensored letters, it has been claimed that she was unanimously loved by her students – which, if true, would surely be almost unique in the history of educational institutions anywhere – and that she displayed a 'sweet severity'. Under the GIL's regulations all the members of the academy's staff had to wear 'Sahara' uniforms modelled on those of the Italian officers fighting in Africa, but the students were allowed to keep both their elegant, feminine uniforms, which had been made by the Botti Sisters' fashion house since 1932, and their brightly coloured working aprons. The students' lives became even busier than before, because Lombardi added classes in piano and other musical instruments to the curriculum, but they were also permitted twice a week to see films that they themselves selected from among those being shown in the local cinemas.[23]

Under Lombardi's command the students also continued to function as part of the Fascist regime's propaganda machine. In 1937 they were sent on a special 'Train of Youth' to Berlin, where Hitler watched them parade. In 1938 they marched in front of him once again when he visited Rome. In 1939 they put on a display of gymnastics in Rome in honour of the British Prime Minister Neville Chamberlain, who was visiting Italy in his futile quest to avert war. Mussolini visited the academy in Orvieto twice: in 1939, when he expressed his admiration for the students' strength and grace, and in 1940, when they organised a special dance performance for him.[24] Other visitors included representatives of Spain, Hungary, Romania, China, Japan, the United States and Germany.[25] The students also continued to put on displays on the occasion of the most important Fascist holidays, such as 24 May, commemorating Italy's victory in the First World War, and 28 October, the anniversary of the 'March on Rome' in 1922. In addition, they participated in the GIL's national sporting contests, such as the *Littoriali dello Sport*, and in other more martial activities, such as a display of archery and javelin-throwing in Rome in 1940.

In 1940, just after Italy had officially entered the Second World War, some of the academy's students were selected to appear in a propaganda film, *L'Accademia dei venti anni* (Twenty Years of the Academy), produced by the GIL section in Orvieto and directed by Giorgio Ferroni.[26] This film portrayed the daily life of the academy through footage of the students' sporting, scholastic and spare-time activities. The film was shown at the Venice Film Festival in 1941.

7.6 Hitler reviews the female squad of the Academy (1937)

Conclusion

According to the propagandistic booklets issued by the academy every year, about 800 students graduated between 1934 and 1943.[27] One of these booklets claimed that 'female youth struck from the coin of Orvieto was a perfect alloy of femininity and "virility", which did not result in "masculinisation", but made their femininity more splendid and stronger'.[28] These 800 young women, Vestal Virgins forged in the temple of Fascist women's physical culture, formed a distinctive elite. Taken away from the love and discipline of their families, and placed under the total control of the academy's staff, they were indoctrinated in Fascist principles, which included an insistence on traditional femininity, and yet at the same time they were prepared for independent lives as career women working side by side with men. Their years in the academy isolated them from the problems that affected other Italians, even during the war years, when the only effects that the world conflict had on the academy was that the uniforms became more military in style and the quality of the food deteriorated. Even though the students were subjected to constant indoctrination in the principles of Fascism, those former students who were interviewed by researchers many years later claimed that life in the academy was not much affected by politics, and that they were more concerned about their future careers than about current events, which they were only disjointedly aware of. They appear to have enjoyed the privileged time they spent training, chatting and cultivating friendships that helped them to develop a strong sense of identity and independence, and deeply influenced the rest of their lives.

The collapse of the Fascist regime in 1943 put an end to their isolation, shocking the students out of what seems to have been a dreamlike state, and opening their eyes to reality.[29] Having been treated as celebrities fit to be invited to major events, admired and photographed, they now felt not only that they counted for nothing, but that they were being looked upon with suspicion, as living symbols of the widely detested Fascist ideology. Some of them rejected Fascism, and others made their way to the RSI to work for their hero Mussolini, but apparently most of them went into hiding to avoid persecution.

Did the education provided at the academy in Orvieto contribute to the emancipation of its students in particular and/or of Italian women in general? If one assumes that there are two different types of education towards emancipation, the 'inner' stressing emancipation in the domestic framework and the 'outer' concerned with struggling for equal conditions outside the home, it could be argued that the students received both types of education at the academy.[30] The Fascist regime said a great deal in favour of the modernisation of society, but to the extent that this process went beyond rhetoric it involved men much more than it involved women. However, the academy in Orvieto was a privileged place where students could receive a well-organised education towards both 'inner' and 'outer' emancipation. The first was available through the subjects that stressed traditional 'womanly' values, such as grace, elegance, modesty, religiosity, child care and 'feminine work'. The second was based on modern sports science and Fascist policy, similar to the instruction given in the academy for male students in Rome. 'Outer' emancipation was also promoted through the students' social life and their frequent participation in public events, although all these activities were, of course, firmly under the control of the staff. This kind of modern and collective education, albeit framed within the totalitarian structure of Fascism, had no precedent in the experience of most Italian women. Former students of Orvieto told their interviewers that their main objective in life had been to become fully independent and get good jobs, even if that meant moving far away from their families and hometowns. Deeply influenced by the examples set by Commander Lombardi and her colleagues, these former students said that they had learned not to be afraid to work confidently alongside men in a spirit of comradeship.

In supporting the academy in Orvieto as the best way to train capable teachers who could accomplish the goal of forging a healthy people, the regime may well have underestimated the impact of this new kind of modern woman on the more traditional-minded Italians they came into contact with. Of course there were very few women trained in Orvieto in comparison to the 20 million more or less old-fashioned women living in Italy at the time, but they were at least able to start to modernise the habits of Italian girls through sporting activities. By stressing healthy bodily habits, organising gymnastics displays and directing students in competitive disciplines, and sometimes even in mixed groups, these teachers helped to free a number of girls from the overprotective control of their parents. However, it is difficult to assess to what extent these teachers influenced the general trend towards the emancipation of women. The sudden collapse of Fascism prevented the academy from producing still more physical education teachers, who might have been able to popularise the new model of womanhood.

Spare-time activities in the
Opera Nazionale Dopolavoro

While the *Opera Nazionale Balilla* (ONB) and, later, the *Gioventù Italiana del Littorio* (GIL) organised and ideologically manipulated physical education and sport for children and young people, and the *Gruppi Universitari Fascisti* (GUF) did the same for university students, the spare-time activities of workers were placed under the control of the *Opera Nazionale Dopolavoro* (OND – *dopolavoro* means 'spare time')'.[1] The OND took autonomy away from Italian workers, offering them in its place a range of rationalised and assisted leisure activities practically free of charge. Many working people were attracted to the OND's clubs, through which they could not only train their bodies, but also buy goods, visit beautiful places and try out many other activities, even those previously reserved for the upper class. The OND seems to have become genuinely popular among Italian workers, of both sexes, many of whom enjoyed the pleasant sensation of being at the centre of the regime's attention.

Organisation and objectives of the OND

The OND was founded under a royal decree dated 1 May 1925. The choice of this particular date, which had previously been celebrated as International Labour Day, was, of course, not an accident. The decree was reissued as Law no. 562, dated 18 March 1926, and was amended by three later royal decrees (no. 1936, dated 11 November 1926; no. 516, dated 7 April 1927; and no. 817, dated 24 May 1937). Through the OND the Fascist state aimed at the nationalisation of workers' spare time, which had previously been mainly a private affair, although there had also been a collective dimension to it, organised by Catholic or leftwing unions, or, more importantly, by manufacturing companies in northern and central Italy. The regime saw to it that the Catholic and leftwing rivals to the OND were swiftly marginalised and then dissolved, while the companies' various in-house leisure organisations were absorbed into the OND's network. These included the *Unione Sportiva Operaia* at FIAT in Turin; the *Scuola di Educazione Fisica* run by Cantoni, a cotton fabric producer in Castellanza; the *Gruppo Sportivo* at Cucirini, a coat-maker in Milan; the *Società Sportiva* at Magneti Marelli in Sesto San Giovanni; the *Gruppo Sportivo Dopolavoro Ferroviario*, a spare-time sports club for railway workers in Milan; and the *Società Sportiva* at Venchi Unica in Turin.

Initially at least, political activity was forbidden within the OND, which was ostensibly a provider of services rather than an ideological organisation. Nevertheless, from the outset the leading posts within the OND were all held by members of the *Partito Nazionale Fascista* (PNF), who made its true objective quite plain: within the OND 'the worker rises again from Bolshevik abjection, and quietly evaluates his rights and duties regarding the Fascist state'.[2] Less than ten years later Mussolini's turn towards a more aggressive foreign policy inevitably affected the OND as well as the other Fascist organisations. Fascist symbols, along with portraits of the *Duce* and slogans based on his sayings, became increasingly prominent at the OND's local clubs.[3] In 1940 an official publication setting out rules and standards for OND managers stated just as plainly that: 'OND is disciplined, co-ordinated and strengthened by the PNF, on which it depends. As a consequence, OND has a double function: educational and political.'[4]

The OND presented an outline of its objectives and programmes in the first issue of its official bulletin. Every local *Dopolavoro* club under its control was to acquire suitable sporting facilities. The declared target of the OND was not to present workers simply with opportunities for amusement, or to emphasise different ideologies and classes as in the past, but to improve individuals for their own benefit and that of the Fatherland. The bulletin also declared that:

> While young people of the highest social classes practise gymnastics at school, and later sport in pre-military and military courses for officers, the working class and farmers practise gymnastics and sporting activities only during military service. For the rest of their lives they do manual work that does not improve their bodies but, on the contrary, damages them. Every kind of sport is therefore encouraged by the OND, which regards sporting activities as a uniquely powerful instrument for physical and moral improvement, cohesion, loyal competitiveness and reciprocal respect among workers.[5]

By the mid-1930s the *Dopolavoro* clubs had become locales for interaction among people from the working class and the lower-middle class, who could meet and relax away from concrete problems of money and jobs. Anyone who enjoyed cultural events or recreational activities such as card games, chess, music, drama, choral singing, dancing or sport, or was keen on tourism, could find companions and interesting activities at the clubs. Workers could also attend the OND's classes on cultural subjects, or join its technical courses in order to improve their knowledge in the fields of agriculture, industry, commerce and insurance. The OND was a colossal organisation. Its registered membership rose from about 1,744,000 in 1932 to about 2,376,000 in 1935, and had reached 3,832,248 by 1939. There were *Dopolavoro* clubs for different categories of employees in the civil service, the armed forces and the merchant navy, and for artists, teachers and other professionals. Manual workers were enrolled in OND sections attached to factories, small businesses and farms. By 1935 OND owned numerous cinemas, theatres, libraries and choir schools, and supervised 2,066 companies of amateur actors, 2,130 orchestras, 3,787 bands, and 10,302 professional and cultural associations.[6]

Membership of the OND was cheap, costing five lire a year in 1940,[7] and it was easy to join. Any working woman who was aged 12 or above, and any male worker aged 18 or above, could become a member if an OND official was satisfied that their moral and political behaviour was good; in addition, from the mid-1930s young men below the age of 18 were admitted if they were already members of the GIL. University students could join too, but Jews were excluded from 1938 onwards under the new racial laws.[8] All OND members could buy books, travel by train, or go to cinemas, theatres, museums or sporting events at reduced prices,[9] or buy relatively expensive goods, such as furniture, radio sets or sewing machines, on the instalment plan.[10]

Physical activities for all

The OND's programmes of physical activity and sport encompassed both tradition and modernity. A number of traditional games that were not recognised by the national sporting federations under the *Comitato Olimpico Nazionale Italiano* (CONI) could be played in OND facilities, depending on the facilities available and the prevailing customs in each region. These activities included rowing in boats with fixed seats; *bocce*, a popular kind of bowling; the traditional ball games *tamburello*, *elastico* and *sfratto*; and tug of war. There were also more modern activities such as marching, target-shooting and volleyball.[11]

Initially, OND members could play football as well. However, in 1929 Augusto Turati, an influential member of the Fascist hierarchy, decided that football was not suitable for Italian workers, and it was replaced by *volata*. This game was intended to evoke Italian tradition, but it was in fact merely one of Turati's bizarre inventions, and it did not go down well at all. Within three years it had disappeared from the OND's sports programmes.[12]

The OND also had to contend with pressures from rival organisations in the field of sport. In 1927, for example, the PNF's press agency published the results of two meetings involving representatives of the PNF's central sporting office, the leadership of the CONI and its federations, and the head of the OND, held on 14 July and 17 August.[13] They had decided that the CONI was to look after the most talented sportspeople while the OND met the needs of the masses. Those enrolled in the CONI's federations could not take part in OND contests, which were to be organised independently of the CONI. Those OND members who obtained significant technical results had to leave the OND immediately and enrol in one of the sporting federations. This agreement, which averted a serious dispute, was ratified in the *Carta dello Sport* (Sports Charter) of December 1928 (see Chapter 1). However, the fact that the most talented members of the OND had to train within the CONI's system did not mean that they had to give up their OND member-ship, simply that they had to train for their favourite sport under the CONI's control. As a result many Italians owned more than one membership card. The official statistics deliberately obscured this fact in order to inflate the membership figures for both the OND and the CONI's federations, making it appear that almost all Italians were engaged in sporting activities.

From 1932 onwards the OND was engaged in rivalry with another Fascist organisation, the GUF, this time in the search for potential champions for the annual contests known as the *Littoriali dello Sport* (see Chapter 5).[14] The OND, with its much larger membership and broader social range, became the most important vehicle for the development of amateur sport as well as for the selection of professionals. The number of OND competitions reached its peak in 1933, when it organised 191,773 sporting events.[15] In 1935 it had 11,159 non-competitive sports sections and 4,704 competitive sport sections.[16] It was said to have organised about 130,000 contests in 1937, although this figure included such events as chess competitions, which would not generally be regarded as physical activities.[17]

On paper the OND catered for a wide range of sports, but in practice only a few were really popular. For example, in 1937 it was reckoned that of about 8,000 OND sections for competitive sports, 6,434 were for *bocce* only.[18] This traditional game, which does not need expensive facilities, just some wooden balls and some solid ground, was played or watched by many Italians of different classes, including General (later Marshal) Pietro Badoglio, the musician Mascagni and Pope Pius XI.[19] Although in its early years in power the regime had not encouraged *bocce*, which was not considered sufficiently dynamic and 'virile' for the forging of the 'new man', it came to accept that the game could not be suppressed.[20] In 1936 the OND organised the first national *bocce* championship in Rome to celebrate the foundation of the Italian Empire with the playing of a 'truly national sport'.[21]

In the 1930s skiing became a popular activity in many OND sections. The middle classes enthusiastically participated in cheap OND excursions at the weekends and went to exclusive winter sport resorts, imitating the habits of the wealthier classes.[22] Following Italy's single victory in the 1936 Winter Olympics,[23] the OND organised local and national championships in 'Alpine skiing and target shooting', which involved both male and female teams.

By the end of the 1930s the OND had become a powerful body in the sports world under the effective control of the GIL. New regulations, issued by the PNF on 29 February 1940, required that an OND representative had to be included on each of the local and national boards within all the sporting federations affiliated to the CONI. The OND organised championships in the following disciplines: gymnastics, fencing, target-shooting, roller-skating and, partially, athletics. Other sports disciplines were still controlled exclusively by the CONI, but at a basic level they could be practised in the OND's sports sections.[24]

Female members of the *Dopolavoro* clubs

Most female workers had little time for recreational activities, especially those who had children. In any case, the idea that a working woman would spend spare time out of doors on her own, away from her family, was too innovative to be easily accepted in Italian society.[25] However, even before the advent of Fascism a small number of pioneer female workers had practised some physical education, gymnastics and athletics in their spare time, especially in the industrialised and modernised regions of the country. Such women had trained within the workers' societies founded by important companies (such as those mentioned above)[26] and they continued to do so after the OND was established.

Women formed a very small minority within the OND. In 1929 there were 10,901 *Dopolavoro* clubs for men but only 183 for women,[27] and from 1930 onwards the OND did not even take the trouble to compile national statistics on the numbers of female members or women-only sections. However, there are some locally compiled reports that give some idea of the trend. For example, in Potenza, in the deep south, 549 women were members of OND sections in 1935, as compared to 6,736 men.[28]

In the first few years, however, the OND's organisers, far from discriminating against women, had sought to encourage them to participate. A woman lawyer, Adele Pertici Pontecorvo, had helped to draw up the OND's rules.[29] In 1928 the OND–FIAT sports section in Turin included mixed-gender groups both for the 'masculine' sport of rowing, with 400 men and 50 women taking part, and for the 'feminine' sport of tennis, played by 40 men and 60 women.[30] However, in 1929, when the traditionalist leaders of the *Fasci Femminili* had to give up control of the *Piccole Italiane* and the *Giovani Italiane* (see Chapter 5), they turned their attention instead to the women taking part in OND activities and helped to push them back towards more 'womanly' activities, such as domestic economy, hygiene or social assistance. According to the results of an enquiry conducted in 1930 the majority of the 100,000 working women enrolled in the OND claimed to enjoy cinema, theatre, travelling and sport, the very pastimes enjoyed by their male counterparts, much more than 'womanly' activities.[31] The Catholic Church did not fail to infer that the OND was promoting feminism, the 'masculinisation' of women, their eroticisation and, ultimately, infertility.[32] Thus it appears to have been against most women's wishes that the OND, like the ONB and the GIL, marginalised women's sport, restricting its female members to gymnastics and other graceful, quiet 'feminine' physical activities. Even the gentle game of *bocce*, which was traditionally played only by men, could not be played by women, but simply watched. Even those 'feminine' physical activities that were approved of were not practised much, since the available gymnasiums and other venues were normally reserved for the training of amateur sportsmen.[33]

Controversy over dancing

A different kind of motor activity became and remained very popular in the *Dopolavoro* clubs: dancing.[34] By involving mixed couples, and therefore the moral and sexual behaviour of Italians, this activity predictably aroused controversy. Dancing was supported by ordinary Italians, whatever their social background, who were used to dancing in private and in public, and saw no reason why the OND should frown upon it. It was opposed, however, both by the Church and, in principle, by the Fascist regime. In 1936, for example, an article in the newspaper *Diario Cattolico* claimed that when boys and girls left dancing parties, those places of depravity, they were not the same people anymore, having come to detest any expression of pure affection and love for the family. These people, undermined by sin and indifference, would provoke a fatal weakness and decadence in their own children and the Fatherland.[35] The fascists were not so consistent as the Church and put out contradictory messages. On the one hand, dancing was defended as a physical exercise that could improve people's health. Mussolini himself enjoyed dancing and was said to be especially good at the waltz. As one biographical article put it, referring to the *Duce*'s younger days:

> Once he finished his studies, Benito [Mussolini] dived once again into Sunday dancing parties and feasts. He danced on threshing-floors, in taverns and in front of churches, with the energy of a colt, [being] capable at all physical exercises, [and] naturally breathing rhythm, melody and music.[36]

On the other hand, dancing was widely practised among the bourgeoisie, whose degenerate habits were, in theory, despised by Fascists. For the sake of the Fascist conceptions of sobriety and civil ethics, the PNF's press tried to convince people to abandon this 'pleasure-loving custom',[37] and 'to give up dancing and [holding] cocaine parties [!] at night'.[38] Yet even though official Fascist publications carried on giving space to moralists to inveigh against dancing,[39] Italians never gave it up and the regime had to compromise. After all, dancing could provide a further opportunity for attracting popular support and encouraging people to spend time in supervised activities under the Fascist banner. From 1931 onwards dancing parties were organised by the OND in its local sections and even the PNF permitted dancing at its local centres, the *Case del Fascio*. Mussolini, his children and other relatives, prominent members of the Fascist hierarchy, and local dignitaries all participated in these parties for the sake of both enjoyment and propaganda. However, the tolerance of dancing did not extend to African-American dances, or the music associated with them, which the regime denounced as likely to contaminate the 'purity' of the Italian musical tradition and the 'Latin' race. The regime kept up a propaganda barrage against black music and in favour of Italian music for many years.[40]

Finally, the problem of how to safeguard public morality, health and traditional values even when people were taking part in a pastime disliked by the Church and by many Fascists was solved, to the regime's satisfaction if not necessarily the people's, by organising folklore displays by dancers in regional costumes. These shows were performed by mixed groups of amateur dancers, musicians and singers, all members of the OND, at the dancing parties held by the local sections. Members and their families had to stop dancing and watch. Clapping their hands and singing along with the performers may have provided some compensation for being interrupted.[41]

9

Sportswomen's contests and displays

In the early years of Fascism little information was published about women in sport in comparison to the coverage given by the media to men's sporting endeavours. Even though Italian society was living through a time of dynamic change and a number of modern women were enjoying taking part in 'manly' sports, their achievements did not interest many people. The specialist newspapers and magazines of the time contain a few articles on female motor activities,[1] and the non-specialist press commented on this kind of news from time to time, usually ironically. Sportswomen were still widely considered to be eccentrics, to be looked upon with astonishment and/or suspicion, even as the numbers of sportswomen were growing, and their performance was improving, in many other European countries and in the United States.

Nevertheless, the phenomenon of female athleticism had started to make its mark at the very beginning of the 1920s, before Mussolini took power, and partly in response to the growing popularity of international athletics. In subsequent years the Fascists appropriated, organised and at the same time channelled this phenomenon from on high, stressing the diffusion of those sports that did not seem likely to interfere with its maintenance of male hegemony. The history of women's sport under Fascism can be roughly divided into three periods. The first, lasting from 1923 to 1929, was a time of discovery of women's sport. The second, from 1930 to 1936, saw the definition of a framework within which sportswomen could function. The third, from 1937 to 1943, was a period of popularisation and mass achievement in women's sport.

Since the regime wished to uphold and even enhance the image of Italy as the sporting nation *par excellence*, while exploiting that image for its own benefit, it had to give sport a high level of 'visibility', chiefly by ensuring that both male and female physical activities were often shown to the public. This drive for greater visibility involved gigantic performances, combining both sporting and Fascist ritual, in Rome and other important cities. Those events were received positively by the media – hardly surprisingly, given that negative coverage would have been censored or punished – and were disseminated across the whole country. As a sporting nation, however, Fascist Italy needed a wider international visibility, so that it could exploit the results of its efforts to forge the 'new Italian'.

Modern women and sport in the 1920s

When the Fascist regime was established gymnastics and other 'cheap' sports were already being practised by a number of female students and working women from the north, while 'expensive' sports were regarded as the preserve of women from the upper classes, some of whom gave their energy, time and passion to training regularly and competing in exclusive sports championships. Their models were the sportswomen of the nobility and, above all, the royal family. King Victor Emmanuel III had an inferiority complex about his small stature and his main pastime was hunting, but many other members of the House of Savoy were keen on sport. The King's mother, Queen Margherita, was a pioneer in mountaineering, hiking and cycling. Among her grandchildren, Princess Jolanda and her three younger sisters were trained in gymnastics, horse-riding and fencing, and Jolanda in particular grew into a 'militant' sportswoman, enjoying outdoor sports such as hunting, downhill skiing and horse-riding. She continued riding after her marriage to Count Calvi of Bergolo and the birth of her children, and won some prizes for it.[2] Jolanda's sister-in-law, Princess Maria José of Belgium, who married Crown Prince Umberto, was good at mountaineering, tennis,

9.1 Choice of ends and service

skiing, skating, swimming, horse-riding and fishing, and was often seen in press photographs wearing elegant sportswear.[3]

Exclusive sports such as golf, fencing, motor-racing and tennis were generally indulged in by the children of the upper class and the wealthier families among the middle class. The specialist sports magazines of the time publicised the deeds of such female golfers as Paola Medici of Vascello, Maria Bernasconi of Cernobbio, Carla Visconti of Modrone and Isaline Crivelli-Massazza, who took part in international mixed championships in the sport. Crivelli-Massazza was also adept at hunting, swimming, skiing and tennis.[4] Tennis was also played by aristocratic ladies, such as Baroness Levi and Countess Aline Macchi of Cellere, as well as bourgeois women, notably Lucia Valerio, who became national champion in 1929; Sandra Perelli, who was especially good at doubles; and Rosetta Gagliardi (later Prouse), an all-round sportswoman whose husband was a competent tennis player too.[5] They were all members of the Tennis Society of Milan and all took part in international contests. (In 1920 Rosetta Gagliardi had become the first Italian woman to participate in the Olympic Games, going to Antwerp as the only woman in the Italian team. She did not qualify to play

9.2 A fencing room

in the Games, but she did attract press attention as one of the bearers of the Italian flag.)

In the 1920s some sports excluded or discriminated against women more than others. For example, specialist physicians joined with technical experts to criticise women who were involved in fencing. On the occasion of the first women's fencing championship, held in 1928 in Treviso,[6] Nedo Nadi, who had won five medals at the Olympics in Antwerp, declared that he did not like to see women fencing at all and confessed that during a mixed contest in Cremona he had left the gymnasium in disgust when the women's team started fencing. A year later, however, Nadi expressed some doubts as to whether fencing might not after all suit some modern women, at least in the lighter discipline of the foil. He had been positively impressed by the female foiler Germana Schwaiger, from Treviso, who won the Italian championship in 1929.[7] Nadi's perception turned out to be accurate, for Schwaiger also came first at the European meeting in Florence in 1931.

9.3 A smart figure-skater

Elite motor-racing attracted wealthy male drivers and some eccentric women, in many cases under the influence of the Futurist myth of engines and engineering. The first woman driver was Maria Antonietta Avanzo, who from 1920 onwards participated with some success in important contests such as the *Targa Florio* and the *Mille Miglia* Cup,[8] driving Packards and Alfa Romeos. Once, on the 423.5-kilometre circuit at Brescia, she came third and achieved a notable average speed of 107 kilometres per hour.[9] Her astonishing enterprise, and the fact that she was a happy mother as well, gave her a special place in the Fascist media and probably some genuine popularity too. In 1928 she wrote in favour of more women driving:

> When I drove my car along Italian streets for the first time I saw people trying to save themselves by jumping onto the pavements. Today, [however,] a woman can easily drive with the same safety and ability as a man. In this tumultuous life a car is increasingly necessary. … Does a woman driver lose her aesthetic femininity? I do not think so. On the contrary, I suggest that her elegant figure perfectly suits the line of a car and that they complement each other.[10]

9.4 *Giovani Italiane* marching with clubs and hoops

Yet in 1927, when the first women's motor-race was organised in Tuscany, just one competitor entered. Evidently, although the small minority of Italians who owned cars included some women – for example, of about 30,000 driving licences issued in Turin in 1934 1,700 were issued to women – there was still a long way to go before women could easily move on from driving on ordinary streets to entering motor-racing contests.

9.5 The *Milanese* team of 4 x 100 m relay race,
       holding the Italian record in 1941

9.6 National championship of athletics in Florence,
       1941: the 80 m hurdles final

In the 1920s sports such as athletics, basketball and gymnastics involved a number of middle-class and working-class women in the industrialised regions of north and central Italy. Their involvement sent a clear signal that through their schools and/or their jobs they had freed themselves from traditional patterns of femininity, and were ready to become as competitive as women in other European countries. The most important initiative in this regard came from Patricia Milliat,[11] who organised the first Monte Carlo Games in 1921. These games were publicised in Italy as the *Olimpiadi della Grazia* (Olympics of Grace), in an attempt to avoid offending traditionalists. They attracted one Italian team, from Busto Arsizio in Lombardy, to cross the border into Monaco and compete, unsuccessfully, in the high jump, the

9.7 Training for relay race

9.8 The female downhill skiing team from Turin

60 metres and the 4 x 75 metres relay. However, their experience was given approving coverage in *La Gazzetta dello Sport*[12] and probably helped to encourage the subsequent development of women's sports in Italy. It was also in 1921 that the *Pro Patria et Libertate* society in Busto Arsizio organised a women's gymnastics, athletics and basketball contest, involving about 100 women, while Milliat founded both the *Federation Sportive Feminine International*, which Italy joined, and the Women's World Games, which continued until 1936.

A number of Italian women participated in athletics and basketball at the next Monte Carlo Games, in 1922, but better results were achieved at the Games in 1923, when Maria Piantanida and Lina Banzi competed honourably and were congratulated by Patricia Milliat herself.[13] (The Monte Carlo Games were then discontinued, although similar Games were held in London in 1924 and 1925.)

The Italian Federation for Women's Athletics (FIAF) was founded in 1923 and the first women's national championship was organised soon afterwards. This championship was the target of negative comments from spectators and press alike. According to the daily *Il Giornale d'Italia*, for example, 'the first women's championship was not followed by many

9.9 Sportwomen in parade

9.10 Basketball game held in Bologna in 1940

9.11 International basketball match in 1928: Italy–Canada

spectators, and was not approved by right-thinking people, who believe that it is necessary for a woman to keep strong and healthy, but not through deforming athletic exercises'. Luigi Roffarè, a prominent sports fan, declared that any woman who engaged in such disciplines as the discus, the javelin and the shot could easily become the kind of woman who is fired from a cannon at the circus.[14]

In 1924 a FIAF team went to London for the Women's International Games, which involved six countries, and was placed last. In later years women's activities were restricted to domestic championships, apart from one unsuccessful competition with a French team. However, a number of athletics disciplines, such as long-distance and cross-country races, were added, and some women demonstrated real ability, notably two all-round athletes and basketball players from Turin, Andreina Sacco and Marina Zanetti. After brilliant careers at the national level, these sportswomen continued to work in favour of women's sport both in Italy and abroad. Sacco became a competent technical specialist and the founder of modern rhythmic gymnastics;[15] Zanetti was appointed national technical commissioner for the women's athletics team.[16]

This happened just after the FIAF was abolished, 1928. Members of the FIAF were automatically transferred to the *Federazione Italiana di Atletica Leggera* (Italian Track and Field Federation, or FIDAL), one of the sporting federations affiliated to the *Comitato Olimpico Nazionale Italiano* (CONI). By the end of the 1920s there were still no more than 100 professional sportswomen in Italy, but local sporting societies had female memberships ranging from 3,950 in Lombardy and 3,116 in Piedmont, to 717 in Latium and 154 in Sicily.[17]

In Milan in 1928 a Canadian women's basketball team beat an Italian team by 68 to two. In the same year Italian women's gymnastics and athletics teams were sent to Amsterdam for the Olympic Games. The six women in the athletics team qualified only for the final 4 x 100 metres relay, in which it was placed last, while the young gymnastics team, from Pavia, won a silver medal.[18] As far as can be ascertained it was at Amsterdam that for the first time an Italian woman, a Mrs Bonaretti, served as a judge at the Olympics.[19]

Gymnastics remained one of the physical activities most widely practised among Italian women. In 1920 a new national women's committee was founded within the *Federazione Ginnastica Nazionale Italiana* (FGNI), and new rules and programmes were introduced, stressing not only traditional gymnastics, but also modern 'female sports and games'.[20] After a gap of nine years the third national women's gymnastics contest was held in Trento in 1921. The fourth such contest, renamed the first, was held in Rome in 1922, with about 1,800 girls taking part, including, for the first time, girls from southern Italy. The activities included target-shooting, javelin-throwing and putting the shot.[21] The FGNI's women's committee worked hard in favour

9.12 Female target-shooting

of gymnastics and its teams were placed with honour at international meetings, such as the Antwerp Olympics and the gymnastics contest held in Dinard in 1929.[22] However, the programme of 'female sports and games' was progressively abandoned by the FGNI, which left it to the FIAF to organise them while it lasted.

Annual gymnastics and athletics displays were also organised by the Fascist organisation for young women aged between 14 and 18, the *Giovani Italiane*, on 24 May, which was celebrated as a holiday commemorating Italy's victory in the First World War. In 1928, after careful selection, the most talented members were sent to Rome for the first *Concorso Ginnico–Atletico Nazionale*, in which 151 teams from 71 provinces competed. The *Concorso*, or contest, was aimed at stressing the physical strength and combative spirit of modern Fascist women,[23] but it provoked trouble even before the performance was held. Its programme, which included 'virile' athletics disciplines and even target-shooting with muskets, aroused not only enthusiasm among the Fascist organisers, but also the indignation of the Church and the usual right-thinking people.[24] By displaying their young bodies in public, the girls would lose their womanly modesty, and in the holy city of Rome, of all places.

As has been shown throughout this book, there was ambivalence and confusion about women and sport in the minds of the leading Fascists. Some were totally in favour of women's participation in sport, for the sake of their own modernity and the health of the 'race'; others, including Mussolini, were more doubtful; still others were opposed, claiming that the 'athleticisation' of women could be responsible for the decline in the population and excessive emancipation. By the end of the 1920s women's sport appeared to be a problem to be looked at very carefully and solved as soon as possible.

'Suitable' sports and spectacular displays, 1930–36

In the 1930s track and field became the most popular sport among girls and young women, while gymnastics gradually lost support, mainly because it was a highly technical and selective discipline requiring qualified teachers, gymnasiums and apparatus. Outdoor athletics seemed more 'natural', healthier, cheaper and easier.

The problem (as the Fascist regime saw it) of female athleticism was much discussed among sports physicians, who quickly reached a consensus on the view that, while women could engage in basic physical education, gymnastics, roller-skating, basketball and athletics, and the wealthier among them in skiing, fencing and tennis, competitive activities were to be discouraged (see also Chapter 4.) Football remained strictly a men's game, although one women's football team from Milan was permitted to train in 1932–33 by Leandro Arpinati, then heading the CONI, on condition that it did not play in public.[25] The only other occasion on which women donned football gear during the Fascist era, so far as is known, was in 1928, when ballet dancers in Turin put on 'Futurist' tops and shorts to perform a ballet entitled *Foot-Ball*.[26]

The Church kept up its opposition too. In 1926 for example, the Catholic magazine *Azione Muliebre* had backed a campaign to separate the sexes on beaches;[27] five years later, in 1931, it launched an enquiry among religious families asking for their opinions on female sport. Predictably enough, mothers who responded agreed that, while moderate sporting activity was a good thing, mixed groups presented a real danger.[28] In 1934 a public swimming pool in Florence reserved for women was closed because it had attracted men who concealed themselves and spied on the swimmers.[29] Indeed, it was largely because of pressure from the Church that amateur swimming was restricted and policed, just as cycling was. At the start of the 1940s the Bishop of Trento forbade women from swimming in front of male spectators, and banned the mixing of the sexes in swimming pools and on beaches, while female cyclists were told not to wear shorts.[30]

More generally, the Fascist regime, trying to keep up a reasonably good relationship with the Vatican, ruled that all training and contests had to be separated by gender. In 1932 the FIDAL issued strict regulations obliging sportswomen to wear long trousers over their shorts whenever they were not actually competing in an event.[31] The Bishop of Aosta denounced the well-known athlete Vittorina Vivenza to the authorities simply because she used to arrive at the stadium wearing comfortable and modest shorts.[32] Nevertheless, within the context of the Fascists' plans for the massive physical regeneration of Italians all the state bodies in charge of people's physical activities continued to push women towards motor activities, while the CONI sought new female champions to enrol in its federations.

By the end of 1936 there were fewer than 5,000 sportswomen in Italy,[33] among whom 3,000 competed in track and field, 800 in basketball, 500 in gymnastics, 80 in swimming and 70 in foil fencing. In addition, 225 university students were recorded as taking part in undefined 'sporting activity', and about 300 women competed in mountaineering and skiing. Among nearly 5,525 women whose activities were monitored by the official statisticians 3,273 were members of the *Giovani Italiane*, among whom about 2,500 were involved in track and field, while others were members of *Dopolavoro* clubs (see Chapter 7), mainly playing basketball.[34] The most important national meetings were the annual athletics championships organised by the FIDAL[35] and the national displays organised by the *Opera Nazionale Balilla* (ONB). The latter involved many girls in athletics and choreographed gymnastic exercises, some of which included the use of small-scale apparatus. In preparation for these displays detailed programmes were sent out to the ONB's provincial centres, distributed to its local sections and taught to young female members step by step. The best girls performed in the celebrations in Rome every 24 May. From 1934 onwards they also participated in a new event, the *Concorso Nazionale di Ginnastica* for members of the *Giovani Italiane*, also held in May, with a programme that included not only gymnastics but also other sports championships, starting with tennis and roller-skating but increasing in number and range year by year.

In 1936 the ONB founded a series of provincial contests, known as the *Agonali* of the ONB to distinguish them from university *Agonali*,[36] for children and young people aged between eight and 18. They were mixed contests involving culture, art and sport; in addition, there were military contests for the boys and contests in typical 'feminine work' for the girls. At first only girls aged between 14 and 18 were allowed to compete in the sporting events in these *Agonali*.[37]

During the 1930s international events engaged Italian athletes with varying degrees of success. In 1930 an Italian women's team was sent for the first time to take part in the Women's World Games, the third set of which were held in Prague that year. The best result any of them obtained there was third place in the discus for Vittorina Vivenza; overall the team was placed only sixth. Marina Zanetti, the technical commissioner of the FIDAL, organised the first women's international sports meeting ever to be held in Italy itself. It was not easy to overcome the usual prejudices and Zanetti had to seek support from Mussolini himself. The meeting went ahead in Florence in 1931, with about 150 athletes from 11 nations participating. It was dubbed an *Olimpiade della Grazia*, as the Monte Carlo Games had been, because, as Zanetti explained:

the poetry of this name was a necessity, because it was difficult for Italian girls to do sport and compete against strong adversaries without causing a great fuss and getting involved in the usual polemics.[38]

The event did not produce any victories for the Italian women taking part and it was not repeated. In 1932 the Italian women's athletic team did not participate in the Los Angeles Olympics, but did compete in the fourth Women's World Games, in London, again with no success. In 1933 Ondina Valla became a star of track and field, helping the Italian team to beat France. The Italian team won against France again in 1935, and at the Berlin Olympics in 1936 Valla won the 80 metre hurdles, while Claudia Testoni and the 4 x 100 metre relay team came fourth.

From the mid-1930s onwards the Fascist organisations involved in providing facilities for physical activities stressed sporting activity as the main way to create consensus among Italians, show the world that Italy was a modern nation and emulate Nazi Germany. The CONI and its federations were involved as well. In 1936, 30,000 sporting events were held and about 40 million spectators were said to have watched them. However (as will be further discussed below), like most official statistics from the Fascist era this figure needs to be treated with caution. It is probably an aggregate of the numbers of spectators at all events, with no account being taken of the fact that many spectators must have attended several.[39]

Other statistics compiled in 1936, for all that they too need to be treated with caution and, in particular, do not indicate gender at all, may nonetheless help to give a general picture of the importance of sport in Italy at this point. At the national level sports championships (including those for traditional games), which had apparently involved just 2,506 people in 1929, are said to have involved 31,181 people in 1935. At the provincial and local levels they reportedly involved about 3,000 people and 3,719,507 people respectively in 1935. While there had been 1,034 provincial and local managers, physical education teachers and sports judges in 1929, there were 14,038 in 1935. Finally, while the second *Concorso Ginnico–Atletico Nazionale* for members of the *Giovani Italiane* had involved 452,501 girls in 1929, the one held in 1935 involved 1,991,871 girls.[40]

Mass displays and championships, 1937–42

In 1937 all the Fascist bodies involved in sport and physical activity for the young were brought together under a new organisation, the *Gioventù Italiana del Littorio* (GIL), which took charge of a programme for mass 'athleticisation' from then until the regime collapsed in 1943 (see Chapter 5). One of its first initiatives was to enhance the activities of the *Giovani Fasciste*, the organisation for young people of both sexes aged between 18 and 21 (not to be confused with the *Giovani Italiane*, which catered for girls aged between 14 and 18). While 9,819 members of the *Giovani Fasciste* took part in national sporting displays in 1936, 23,977 did so in 1937.[41]

Under the GIL's leadership mass displays by young people of both sexes were organised at both the national and local levels, sometimes for mixed groups, in an attempt to promote the regime's aggressive foreign policy, which needed popular support, cohesion and visibility. The organisation of local displays involved GIL managers and teachers in each province, who had to work hard to try to understand the physical exercises prescribed in the booklets sent down to them from Rome. Boys and girls were trained according to this programme, and the best, or at any rate the most compliant, were selected to go forward to provincial and national meetings.

There is evidence that there was a serious mismatch between the grandiose plans made in Rome and the execution of those plans at lower levels. Local units of the GIL's affiliated organisations lacked financial support and suitable facilities, especially for anything involving girls or young women. However, the organisers, most of whom were genuinely enthusiastic about sport, whatever they may have felt about Fascism, used a number of stratagems for managing and overcoming obstacles, or hiding deceptive practices when they seemed necessary.

The GIL's national sporting events were virtually Pharaonic performances, imitating those of the German Hitler Jugend, costing large amounts of money and drawing in thousands of competitors. The technical content of the physical exercises mattered much less than their uniform execution. Royal and Fascist flags were flown alongside those of sporting societies and provinces, and patriotic and Fascist songs were sung by both participants and spectators at these theatrical shows. The state-controlled media gave these performances extreme prominence, and photographs, radio broadcasts and newsreels reached people all over the country.

The GIL's programme of activities was ambitious and wide-ranging. In 1941, for example, there were national winter sports championships for both sexes and also for military officers in February; training courses for teachers at health resorts in April; a national gymnastics festival, and a national physical education contest for *Avanguardisti* and *Giovani Italiane*, in May; the opening of the GIL's summer camps and health resorts in June; national courses for Fascist culture and physical education, involving GIL managers and teachers, in July and August; national courses for future officers and GIL assistants, also in August; the start of pre-military courses, and the celebration of the GIL's foundation, in October; and finally, the celebration of *Balilla* Day on 8 December.[42]

The most important women's displays organised by the GIL were still those of the *Concorso Nazionale di Ginnastica*, which, as mentioned above, had been held for *Giovani Italiane* since 1934 but, from 1938 onwards, included female members of the *Giovani Fasciste* as well. The *Concorso* included not only gymnastics but also an increasing number of sports; for example the *Concorso* in Milan in 1937, featured swimming, fencing, and track and field.[43]

In 1936 Mussolini decided to enhance women's sporting activities within the *Opera Nazionale Dopolavoro* as well (see Chapter 8). The first gymnastic and athletic contest for female members of the OND was organised in 1937, alongside the one for male members that had started in 1928. Ninety-four provinces were invited to select and train a total of 350 teams, from which 180 teams were chosen to compete in Rome. Half of the teams were composed of industrial workers, about 60 came from provincial sections of the OND and the rest were from sports societies affiliated to the OND. About 2,000 women arrived in Rome in 1937 and spent three days seeing the sights, putting on displays of different sports, including archery, and preparing for the spectacular gymnastic display, in front of Mussolini, that closed the event.[44] Nobody dared to criticise the participation of mixed groups this time.

In 1939 GIL instituted *Ludi Juveniles* (Youth Games), which, despite the possibly misleading name, were contests in culture and art, as well as in physical education and sport, for both sexes. These new games replaced the Agonali of the now defunct ONB. The *Ludi Juveniles* were initially for school students aged between 16 and 18, although older and younger competitors were admitted later on, and were held at local and provincial levels. There were plans to organise national *Ludi Juveniles* too, but there is no evidence that they were ever held. (One article reports that in 1939 about 7,000 students of both sexes were in Rome for the 'final contest',[45] but this was probably the final contest for the province of Rome.) In 1940 female members of the *Giovani Fasciste* were allowed to take part in *Ludi Juveniles* as well:[46] in that year 80,143 young women took part alongside 147,789 young men.[47] Finally, in 1941 and 1942 the GIL organised *Concorsi Nazionali Femminili di Educazione Fisica* at Montecatini Terme, involving both *Giovani Italiane* and female *Giovani Fasciste*.[48]

The GIL also involved itself in representing Italian sport abroad. In 1940 and 1941 it sent female teams to contests with the Hitler Jugend, in which the Italians had notable success in tennis and swimming, as well as to meetings in other countries that were either occupied by Italy or Germany, or allied to one or both of them. In 1942 a European Youth Association was founded to link youth organisations in these countries, and to exploit theatre, art and especially sport as means to spread the idea of a new young European community, animated by a militant anti-Communist spirit. However, because of the difficult relations between the German and Italian leaders appointed to run this association, it was wound up soon after its first and only 'European Youth Sports Championships' had been held in 1942.[49]

The activities mentioned so far must have involved large numbers of girls and young women. The official statistical data were published in the

Annuario sportivo (Sporting Yearbook), an elegant GIL publication that appeared (under slightly varying titles) every year from 1938 to 1942. It was priced at about 100 lire, or one tenth of an above-average monthly salary, but free copies were distributed to Fascist centres. It covers the most important sporting displays and results for the years 1937–41 (a final edition may have appeared, covering 1942, but it has proved impossible to trace and may not have been published at all, given the conditions of the time).[50] In each edition the text was accompanied by statistics, drawings, photographs and more or less relevant quotations from Mussolini. The *Annuario* for 1940 even has German translations of these quotations, presumably to underline the regime's view that the two dictatorships shared the same sports policy and the same bellicose ideology. The fact that there were no such German translations in the *Annuario* for 1941 (edited in 1942) may be an indication that the relationship was cooling off.

The information in the five available editions of the *Annuario sportivo* is not presented in a uniform and comparable way throughout the series, and the first few in particular lack details, especially on women's sport. For example, the *Annuario* for 1937 reports only that 23,977 *Giovani Italiane* had taken part in an unstated number of events, while 1,290,677 boys and young men had done so. The *Annuario* for 1938 gives more details: 111,415 female members of the *Giovani Italiane* and the *Giovani Fasciste* are said to have participated in 4,616 events, compared to 1,903,051 male participants, and female championships were held for track and field, gymnastics, swimming, basketball, roller-skating, fencing, winter sports, tennis and target-shooting. According to the *Annuario* for 1939 the number of female participants had increased to 168,978, whle the number of male participants had fallen a little, to 1,846,359, probably because some young sportsmen had gone off to help conquer Albania. There had been 11,746 events involving female competitors, but the number of female sports championships was exactly the same as in 1938. The *Annuario* for 1940 reports that 228,288 girls and young women competed in 12,331 displays, while 2,153,566 boys and young men did so. Finally, according to the *Annuario* for 1941 there were 253,459 female participants, compared to 1,819,753 male participants, and 10,581 female displays were held. Mountaineering had been added to the list of women's sports, and the *Annuario* claims that despite the war other disciplines, such as rowing and horse-riding, were being taken up by women and supported by the GIL.

The CONI's sporting federations were still in charge of the activities of elite sportswomen in these years. The regime exploited their activities to claim that the GIL had been successful in training large numbers of girls and young women, and in helping to select them for elite training. Their achievements included a first place at the European women's basketball championship in 1939; a number of world records in roller-skating; and, in the disciplines of track and field,[51] a world record in the 3 x 800 metre relay race, set in Turin in 1937, first place in the 200 metres at an international meeting in Paris the same year, and, at the first European women's championships in Vienna in 1938, third place in the 4 x 100 metre relay and victory in the 80 metre hurdles, equalling the world record. These achievements were, of course, enthusiastically reported in the specialist sporting press, whose writers took care to emphasise that admirable 'Fascist' results had been obtained due to these sportswomen's extraordinary courage and their love for the Fatherland.

Competitive cross-country running was abolished for both sexes in 1939, but lasted as a popular amateur activity mainly involving members of the OND. It was also in 1939 that the Italian women's athletics team gained two world records in the 80 metre hurdles, competing against Poland and Germany. By 1940 however, the Second World War had brought most national and international contests to a standstill, although some juvenile events continued until 1943.

Rhetoric and reality

The statistics presented above might lead one to think that Italians had voluntarily become a sporting people. Yet, especially at the local level, anyone who did not participate regularly was noticed by the Fascist authorities. The regime also habitually mystified and/or manipulated data about sport, as about every other subject, treating the masses as eternal children who need education and reproof, protection and little white lies. A number of examples follow.

First, in spite of the propaganda about sporting achievements, in 1930 there were only about 600,000 members enrolled in the CONI's affiliated federations, or about 0.75 per cent of the total population, and about half of them were involved exclusively in hunting.[52]

Second, although the enrolment of children and young people in the ONB and, later, the GIL was practically obligatory, and in the late 1930s membership cards were even sent to newborn babies, this was presented in propaganda as the result of the free and enthusiastic consent of the Italian people.

Third, especially in the smaller universities, students were more or less coerced by the *Gruppi Universitari Fascisti* (GUF) to train in different kinds of sport, without any previous selection. In cases where there were too few participants to form a team, or there was a shortage in some disciplines, ordinary citizens were 'warmly invited' to join university teams and were suddenly registered as university students for local contests among universities in preparation for the next national *Littoriali dello Sport*. For example, at the University of Padua two policemen were enrolled in the GUF's rugby team, and a manual worker was registered as a medical student for the javelin and the discus. This kind of cheating was officially forbidden, but there is evidence that university officials turned a blind eye to it.[53] There is also evidence that young women who had left school also participated in the national university *Littoriali*, and that their coaches supported them in an effort to increase the prestige of their home provinces (The interviews with Ondina Valla and Rina Serafini in Chapter 11 provide examples.)

Fourth, although it was proudly declared in 1937 that there were 5,000 sportswomen in Italy, the press did not report that in 1928 the number of women taking part in organised physical activities was much higher, with about 7,000 women in Lombardy and Piedmont, and smaller numbers in other regions.[54] The increasing numbers of competitors, starting from 1937, also concealed the fact that a number of all-round athletes enjoyed a number of disciplines and participated in different championships. The same names appear time and again, in athletics, basketball, swimming and so on. Finally, the number of female participants in non-elite sport was also said to be increasing year after year, but this is partly attributable to the fact that both young women aged between 18 and 21, and girls aged between eight and 14, were allowed by the GIL to take part in the Ludi Juveniles, which had previously been reserved for those aged between 14 and 18. Young women over 18 could also participate in the *Concorso Nazionale di Ginnastica*, which had originally been a contest reserved for younger girls. The sheer numbers of local contests often helped GIL organisers and coaches to inflate their reputations: they could simply count a training session as a competition, and nobody in Rome would know that they were not being efficient and enthusiastic.

In other words, although nobody could deny that women's involvement in physical activity did indeed become a nationwide phenomenon during the Fascist era, it still remained a relatively minor and marginalised affair. Even the official Fascist statistics show that in 1939, when the number of female participants in the GIL's contests rose and the number of male participants fell (as mentioned above), there were still more than ten males to every one female. Competitive women's sport was particularly poorly developed in southern Italy, where the Fascist youth organisations had to fight against, or perhaps equally often acquiesced in, deepseated prejudices about what was healthy and suitable for women. All five editions of the *Annuario sportivo* show that almost all champion sportswomen came from Rome, Florence, Milan, Turin, Venice, Trieste, Genoa and Bologna. Naples was the only southern province that produced any female champions, probably because of its longstanding tradition of encouraging women's physical education (see Chapter 2).

The differential treatment of men's sport and women's sport had consequences for Italy's sporting endeavours at the international level. While Italian sportsmen won, for example, second place overall at the Los Angeles Olympics in 1932 and third place at the Berlin Olympics in 1936, as well as the football World Cup in 1934 and 1938, Italian sportswomen's best results were victories in the 80 metre hurdles and in the first European women's basketball championship. Fascist propaganda obviously exaggerated Italian sportswomen's achievements, which were poor in comparison to those of sportswomen living in other countries, whether they were democracies or dictatorships.[55]

Fashion, aesthetics and the 'true woman'

The 'new woman' of the 1920s

In the 1920s there were no obvious differences between the prevailing aesthetics of the female body in Italy and counterparts in other countries. From the United States, Britain and France a 'sporty', tomboyish, nimble and slender stereotype of femininity had spread across the world. The Fascist regime dressed the female members of its organisations in appropriate and fashionable clothes. In the years 1926–29, for example, members of the *Piccole Italiane* and the *Giovani Italiane*, then controlled by the *Fasci Femminili*, wore short black skirts, black ties, and long, straight white blouses that made their hips and breasts look small, and their hair, cut *à la garçonne*, was held away from their eyes with coloured ribbons. Both the official Fascist organisations and the remaining women's magazines urged girls 'to disregard moonlight and feminine pallor',[1] to give up their lazy, weak, inglorious lives, and to launch themselves vigorously into dynamic activities just like men. These stereotypes were overtly linked to the mores of the most industrialised countries, and to the Futurist themes of dynamism and speed, which had become Italian national myths.

The way in which this aesthetic ideal of the 'new woman' was promoted by the Fascist regime in its early years can be illustrated by a glance at three articles published in the magazine *Lo sport fascista*. In 1929 a physician, Goffredo Barbacci, wrote a long article in favour of swimming as the most effective way in which women could make their bodies more beautiful and fashionable. Barbacci harshly criticised the Church's opposition to what it called 'nudity' in sport, and asked why embittered spinsters and seminarians, who knew nothing about family life, should decide what was moral. He exhorted women to adopt instead the modern habits of the women swimmers of northern Europe, whose harmonious and supple bodies were naturally admired by men at the beach. Barbacci thought that Italian women avoided swimming simply because they did not want to ruin their make-up or hairstyle. As a result, while the average Italian male body approached the ideal of manly aesthetics, Italian women's bodies, with their flat breasts, and their curved and flaccid hips, were ugly. American women were shapely thanks to swimming, which was the most fashionable and popular activity in their country, involving both refined ladies and movie stars. Barbacci concluded his article with this direct message to Italian women:

> You who eagerly wait for American trends in fashion, even accepting those of black people and savages, why do you not imitate American women in good things too? Swim, go to swimming pools, and you will gain beauty and health, and be shaped like statues.[2]

Later in 1929 a famous intellectual and aesthete, Anton Giulio Bragaglia wrote a piece for *Lo sport fascista* about the connection between sport and beauty. In Bragaglia's view sport was the main way to achieve physical and spiritual harmony, as exemplified by the athlete Marina Zanetti. Photographs of her slender and harmonious body showed the composed, luminous sense of beauty of the 'new woman'.[3]

Finally, in 1930 a humorist, one M. Pensuti, wrote in *Lo sport fascista* about the aesthetic reasons and especially the moral reasons why men should support modern sportswomen. Pensuti observed that female athleticisation had to be considered a revolutionary discovery, comparable to Columbus's discovery of America. Nobody could reject this phenomenon, which inevitably brought 'masculinisation' to women. He went on:

> Once Italian women were sedentary, and their small hands and feet, and big bottoms, still remain a dream for many men; but nobody can stop or control this new phenomenon, which is like a meteorological event. Who could ever tear a [steering] wheel away from a woman's hands? Although small feminine hands and feet are growing bigger nowadays, nobody could deny that, although their smaller size was the sign of true feminine grace and sweetness, our great-grandmothers could be shrewish, acerbic and gruff, even when they were in the prime of life. ... The big feet of a footballer who at the same time is a smiling and serene woman are much better than small feet that metaphorically kick at much worse things than a leather ball! Men should buy a punchball for the home, and leave their wives, daughters and mothers-in-law to give vent to their exuberance and competitive spirit. Looking at them streaming with perspiration, men should really bless sport. ... Nowadays women play tennis, cricket and golf, practise fencing, horseriding and cycling, and drive cars. They have short hair, and their bodies are not soft but hardened by physical exercise; however, let them enjoy physical exercise honestly and train peacefully, or they might even throw away their saucepans and demand the vote!'[4]

In contrast, Catholic magazines for women expressed very different opinions about what was morally good and aesthetically appropriate for women. For example, in 1921 an anonymous contributor to the magazine *Matelda* insisted that Italian women should participate only in decorous and non-competitive sports that allowed them to safeguard their Christian faith and their 'femininity', in contrast to British, American and German women, whose sporting activities were marked by 'masculinity'.[5] Eight years later, *Fiamma Viva* published an article arguing that women should definitely be banned from cycling, a disgraceful, coarse and anti-aesthetic activity for girls with good manners.[6]

The 'true woman' and her rivals in the 1930s

At the start of the 1930s the Hollywood film industry launched a new aesthetic form, embodied by its blonde female stars. They wore relatively large amounts of make-up, had beautifully slender bodies and were self-confident, but they were less tomboyish than the fashionable women of the previous decade. In Fascist Italy, however, the regime's demographic campaign and its increasingly close relationship with the Church (see Chapter 3) led it to favour a totally different, supposedly indigenous model, that of the 'true woman' with a curvaceous body who was loyal to traditional aesthetic standards, was modest and graceful, and was capable of producing numerous children. As a consequence, the members of the *Piccole Italiane* and the *Giovani Italiane* had to accept new uniforms. They now began to wear long pleated skirts and blouses that formed an ensemble in black and white, ensuring that their knees were covered and, at the same time, that their rounded hips and breasts were emphasised. The *Giovani Italiane* had to wear long ties, and all the girls in both organisations had to put on black berets, which, according to oral testimonies from former members, they generally disliked. Miniature versions of the regime's *fascio* symbol and the Italian flag were sewn onto their blouses, and insignia of rank were displayed on their sleeves. These uniforms were simple and cheap, and not far removed from 'normal' clothing for schoolgirls from the lower classes, but, apart from the symbols and the insignia of rank, they were strikingly different from the military-style uniforms worn by boys in the counterpart organisations of the *Balilla* and the *Avanguardisti*, presumably to make as clear a distinction as possible between gentle femininity and 'hard' masculinity.

Obviously, the ambivalent aesthetics of the Fascist regime did not allow room for the Hollywood-derived model of the slender 'international' woman who occasionally dared to wear trousers in public. Such women were derided as infertile, masculine and neurotic 'crisis women' in Fascist propaganda. It was said that men would dislike women who were so thin and whose 'easy ways' discouraged any serious wedding proposals. The regime joined with the Church in opening a front against 'crisis women', even in the pages of Fascist journals that normally debated serious political questions.[7] In 1930 one such journal, *Critica Fascista*, published an article by Mario Pompei in which he declared that:

10.1 *Giovane Italiana*'s uniform for physical education classes (1934–37)

10.2 *Giovane Italiana*'s uniform for athletics competitions (1934–37)

> Nowadays *chic* means to be a woman who is flat-chested, skinny and pale (the opposite of a rural woman's ruddy complexion), with an eternally adolescent body. Women cut down on their meals, swallow pernicious pills and adopt other malignant expedients in order to obey this tyrannical and arbitrary fashion.[8]

Mussolini himself led a battle in favour of 'feminine fat' and encouraged physicians to convince their women patients, especially those living in the cities and therefore more likely to be in touch with dangerous foreign fashions, that slimness was unhealthy while being comfortably heavy was a sign of good health. Gaetano Peverelli, the head of the government's press office, ordered the removal of images of 'crisis women' from newspapers and magazines, and prohibited such publications from mentioning the slimness of Hollywood film stars in the name of upholding Italian standards of health and maternity.[9] On the other hand, not all physicians agreed that being 'fat' was either aesthetically pleasing or healthy. For example, Dr Giuseppe Poggi-Longostrevi (whom we have already met in Chapter 4) declared in a book published in 1933 that the statuesque feminine beauty of ancient Greece could be attained once again through aesthetic physical activities that would help women to fight against both excessive slimness and excessive obesity, which were equally ugly and unhealthy.[10] In addition, the campaign in favour of 'feminine fat' contradicted both the aims of the regime's own youth organisations, which educated girls in keeping their bodies fit and well-toned, and the main message conveyed in specialist magazines. These continued to exhort sportswomen to try out different activities and to adhere to a sporting aesthetic that was hostile to fatness and heaviness. Thus articles in these publications celebrated famous individual sportswomen, such as the American swimmer Eleanor Holm, whose broad shoulders, slim hips, speed and tomboyishness were said to be envied by elegant women,[11] while other articles lauded the slender legs and trim bodies of German sportswomen.[12]

Another controversy of the time concerned swimming costumes for women, which could easily provoke scandalised reactions from more traditional-minded people. In 1934 female swimmers taking part in an international meeting in Turin were allowed to wear elegant costumes that were exactly the same as those worn by the male competitors,[13] but in 1935 the *Rinascente* chain stores began promoting 'decent' swimming costumes that covered women's shoulders and knees, reasserting traditional canons of 'feminine good taste' and moderation.[14]

Still more traces of the regime's campaign against slim women can be found in the popular songs, poems and humorous magazines of the mid-1930s. Undoubtedly the most prominent humorist of the time was Mussolini himself, although he was presumably trying to be perfectly serious when he declared that 'Maternity does not dim feminine beauty'. This quotation became

10.3 Sturdiness of the 'true Italian woman' at the end of the
       1930s

the subtitle of the Fascist women's magazine *Il Giornale della donna* just at
a time when discouraging photographs of flabby and prematurely faded
maternal bodies were appearing in newspapers, magazines and newsreels.

   The austere aesthetic of the 'true woman', who also had to avoid make-up
and coquetry, was predictably supported by the misogynistic Catholic Church
and many possessive Italian men; it doubtless also resonated among poorer
men who believed that their wives were spendthrift, as well as among the
more fanatical female Fascists. However, it did not by any means convince
all working women, nor did it have much appeal for the wealthy, who
continued to adhere to the more agreeable imported aesthetic. Photographs
of private gatherings at the homes of prominent Fascists clearly show that,
while the men had taken to an austere style of clothing, women's clothes
were still worldly and sophisticated: the regime's campaign in favour of the
'true woman' was not just ambivalent and only sporadically successful, it
was also hypocritical.

   This hypocrisy was even more starkly on display in the regime's campaign against foreign fashion, especially Parisian fashion. A national exhibition of fashion, sponsored by the regime and opened in Turin on 12 April 1933, included a display of modern sportswear that was intended to stress the usefulness of sporting activities in transforming female citizens into 'true women', who might be fat but could still be strong and healthy. The press dutifully gave positive coverage to the exhibition and the specialist sports magazines chimed in with articles upholding the aesthetic of the 'true woman'. For example, *Lo sport fascista* stated that:

10.4 Sport and feminine modesty

Modernity means sport, and through all kinds of sports the
Fatherland can gain healthy, robust and youthful soldiers, and
strong mothers. ... Nowadays Italian fashion creates soft and
agile lines, because the new female body should be soft and agile
as well. No corners or prominent bones any more, but harmony
of form, which is both healthy and beautiful.[15]

In 1934 women's magazines began to publish fashion plates of women's
garments without mentioning that they were foreign. In general, the Fascist
censors were not very interested in magazines for women, which were dismissed as marginal and insignificant, but in 1937 they saw to it that all pictures
of foreign fashions disappeared from these magazines.

This ruling came as part of an overhaul in Fascist cultural policy that
culminated on May 1937 in the establishment of a Ministry for Popular Culture
that was to control all mass cultural activities, from theatre and cinema to
music, from books to the press (partly, it seems, on the model of the Nazis'
Ministry for Public Enlightenment and Propaganda). The new Fascist Ministry
propagated a totalitarian 'national culture' and attempted to implement
Mussolini's policy of opposition to all foreign influences, with varying
degrees of success.[16]

In the field of women's fashion, for example, the print-run of one issue
of *Vita femminile* was confiscated in 1938, because it included a photograph
of a woman wearing a French dress, and a ban was placed on imports of
Vogue, *Harper's Bazaar* and *Marie-Claire*.[17] Yet the gap between Fascist
propaganda and reality remained as wide as before. The regime's ambivalence
was exemplified in an official booklet published in 1936 by the *Opera
Nazionale Balilla* for members of its *Piccole Italiane* affiliate: it claimed
that, far from Italian women being dominated by foreign fashion, they dominated it, by creating a national Italian style using only indigenous materials. It is not clear why the author of this booklet thought it was necessary to
tell these supposedly disciplined and austere girls, aged between eight and
14, anything at all about women's clothes, let alone tell them something that
even they could see was not true.[18]

After all, they had only to look around them. Wealthy Italian women still
dressed according to current international fashion, while magazines and novels
aimed at female readers, and above all the popular films known as *telefoni
bianchi* ('white telephones' – see Chapter 1) still depicted women who were
neither fat nor modest, but had fashionable clothes, slim bodies and easy ways.
These fictional characters, who may well have had at least as much influence on girls and young women as any Fascist propaganda had, did not submit to men at all, but were audacious protagonists of romantic, adventurous
or sporting dramas. In the mid-1930s most of the covers of the cheap magazine *La donna, la casa, il bambino* (Woman, Home, Baby), which was

mainly aimed at housewives, and ran articles on such subjects as embroidery and sewing, still showed slender women engaged in sport either on their own or together with men. Their features, their smartness and their blonde hair were similar to those of American film stars, who thus remained unrivalled aesthetic icons for most Italian women, in spite of the regime's advice.

The influence of American popular culture

Hollywood comedies in particular, with their escapist tone and their happy endings, were still very popular in Italy in the 1930s. In 1936 one of Mussolini's children, Vittorio, spoke favourably about American films, exhorting Italian cinema to follow their example,[19] and the *telefoni bianchi* originated as cheap Italian copies of Hollywood originals. Mussolini himself

10.5 Cover of *La donna, la casa, il bambino*, (March–April 1935)

enjoyed watching American films, especially musicals, and the comedies of Stan Laurel and Oliver Hardy.[20] Mussolini even allowed Charlie Chaplin's anti-authoritarian film *Modern Times* to be shown in Italy: only the scene in which Chaplin's character involuntarily consumes cocaine was cut.[21]

Italy had, of course, maintained close ties with the United States since the nineteenth century, when many Italians had emigrated there. Even during the Fascist era poverty caused 193,192 Italians to emigrate to the United States in the years 1926–30, and 114,636 more emigrants left between 1931 and 1940.[22] The emotional and financial connections between ordinary Italians and their Italian-American relatives also contributed to the popularisation of American popular culture in Italy; but most of the work was done by American films. In 1934 about 200 American films were shown in Italy and, although by 1936 the total number shown had fallen to about 40, even in the years 1939–42, 18 out of every 100 films shown came from the United States.[23] While Nazi Germany banned American films when it declared war on the United States in 1941, some were still circulating in Italy up to the end of the Second World War. The incessant anti-American propaganda of the time clearly failed to counter the impact of American music, literature and films on the Italian people. More broadly, the regime's attempts in the late 1930s to replace foreign words, such as *brioche, garage, pardon, bar, film* and *bridge*, with artificial Italian equivalents, made little headway, and the transformation of Louis Armstrong into 'Luigi Fortebraccio' was greeted with ridicule.

The independence thus demonstrated by Italian women in relation to bodily appearance and fashion was a further signal that popular support for Fascist policy was largely a formality and that the regime's propaganda had much less effect on the everyday lives of Italians than the Fascists claimed. Mussolini himself was more and more doubtful about the effectiveness of his followers' campaigns, as he indicated publicly on 3 January 1943:

> Today Italians have an historic opportunity to show their moral fibre. The problem is really serious for us. We should ask our-selves whether 20 years of Fascism have changed things only superficially, leaving them, at a deeper level, much the same.[24]

Images of women in the war years

As Fascist Italy turned increasingly to aggressive interventions abroad, starting with the attack on Ethiopia in 1935 and moving on to the subversion of the Spanish Republic from 1936 onwards, mass mobilisation was accompanied by yet another shift in official policy on women's fashion, as represented in the clothing approved for female members of the youth organisations that were brought under the control of the *Gioventù Italiana del Littorio* (GIL) in 1937 (see Chapter 5). All the little girls in the *Figli della Lupa* (Children of the She-Wolf) were now dressed in uniforms; the members of the *Piccole Italiane* and the *Giovani Italiane* had to don short military-style tunics that concealed their waists; and their older sisters in the Giovani Fasciste, young women aged between 18 and 21, had to abandon the black and white uniforms that they had worn since the organisation was founded in 1930, and put on service caps and 'Sahara' uniforms modelled on those issued to officers fighting in the Africa. Fascist women, especially those in leadership positions in these organisations, had to exchange their austere civilian clothing for military uniforms.

Even though women were much more involved in social and political life during the war years, the ideal model of the 'true woman' was not replaced, but survived alongside yet another new ideal, that of the strong sportswoman, which now became much more prominent than in previous years, partly because most sportsmen were away at the front and female celebrities were needed to take their place in the specialist press. To some extent the regime compensated for Italy's repeated failures on the battlefield with coverage of sportswomen's achievements; it also gave the media the task of pushing women towards sporting activities that would strengthen them for their new lives of even greater deprivation and uncertainty.

In response to the wartime mood, official publications and popular magazines competed with each other in prescribing which sports were the most suitable for women and in publishing articles about the aesthetic beauty of well-trained female bodies. Yet they still also pandered to traditional prejudices. For example, an article in *Lo sport fascista* on the participation of female athletes in the Berlin Olympics in 1936 stressed that, while a female politician would be a deformation and aberration of both the legislature and feminism, an athlete in her scanty costume was the perfect synthesis of the most beautiful qualities of the female sex;[25] and a booklet published by the ONB specified that Fascism wanted girls to be healthy, strong and 'curvilinear' manner, rather than slim, so that they become respected mothers who could bring up their children to practise the purest virtues.[26] On the other hand, a true sportswoman could not be too 'curvilinear'. According to former students of the *Accademia Nazionale Femminile di Educazione Fisica* in Orvieto (see Chapter 7), fat and bespectacled applicants for places at the academy were rejected, students who put on weight had their diets strictly controlled, and only tall, shapely students, generally brunettes with gracious features, were placed in the front rows in the academy's public gymnastic displays, hiding the rest of the students.[27]

The aesthetic of the ideal sportswoman also made some impact on adult women, who were advised to take part regularly in physical activities, even in the home, in order to keep fit, and avoid becoming flaccid and fat. This renewal of attention to the female body may have helped some women to become more conscious of their identity and their needs, but it had a darker side. In an article in *Lo sport fascista* Sisto Favre displayed both conscious misogyny and unintended humour. He advised busy housewives in poorer households that cleaning their basements, washing their carpets and doing the rest of their domestic duties carefully offered the best and easiest way to make their bodies beautiful. As for working women, Favre advised them to get up earlier than usual so that they could clean their homes, prepare their children for school, cook breakfast for the whole family and then go to work on foot, walking fast and with a spring in their step in order to improve their posture.[28] Favre ended his article by saying that dancing was especially to be recommended for women, citing the views of the physician Nicola Pende. Pende (whom we also met in Chapter 4) thought that dancing was much better than tonics or cosmetics because it educated women in aesthetics, gave the 'right' shape to their bodies, and enhanced their beauty and their health, thus fitting them to fulfil their highest mission: to produce numerous healthy children for the Fatherland.[29] This preference for dancing perfectly suited Pende's misogyny and his conviction that women were different from men. According to Pende and his faithful follower Favre, Italian women could not aspire to anything more than a subordinate role in society and could 'redeem' themselves only through maternity.

However, other elements in the Fascist propaganda apparatus made a positive commitment to promoting the ideal of the sportswoman during the war years, most notably in the field of 'militant art'.

In 1939 Alessandro Pavolini, an influential member of the Fascist hierarchy, founded the Cremona Prize, to be awarded to the winner of a contest for practitioners of 'militant art', a genre of art aimed at a broad popular audience, and totally at the service of Fascist ideology. The Cremona Prize encouraged the production of a large number of paintings on sporting themes, many of them depicting shapely female athletes performing in different disciplines. These 'militant' paintings were characterised by flat, pseudo-photographic representation of people, landscapes and architecture in a symbolic Fascist framework. For example, most of the paintings on sporting themes that were submitted for the Cremona Prize in 1941 have backgrounds that feature idealised Italian resorts, statues, with columns, arches and other architectural elements in a pseudo-Roman style, underlining the message that the events depicted are taking place in Italy, the sporting nation *par excellence*. All the female athletes in these pictures are slender brunettes with long hair and, while the youngest wear skirts, the older ones are dressed in shorts. Some are rather plump, with obviously muscular legs, robust arms, strong shoulders and rounded breasts. These images seem, then, to effect a compromise between the earlier Fascist ideal of the 'true woman' and the newer model of the sportswoman: they are plumper than the women who had been fashionable in the 1920s and are obviously intended to seem less sophisticated, or decadent, than the female American film stars of the 1930s, yet they are still strong and healthy. Some of them are shown competing with male athletes, but in these cases the artists were careful to give them glassy

10.6 *Artemide mussoliniana*
Picture by Bruno Amadio, Cremona Prize 1941

stares and stiff postures in an attempt to prevent anyone from having 'impure thoughts' while looking at them.

One series of portraits that conveyed the ideal of the sportswoman attracted more attention, from the regime and from the public, than any other pictures in this genre: Gino Boccasile's pictures of *signorine grandi firme*, so called because they appeared in the shortlived magazine *Le grandi firme*. Boccasile presented young women, some blonde, some brunette, with exaggerated feminine attributes, dressed in seductively light clothing. Their provocative breasts and hips, long, shapely legs, and wasp waists appealed to many of the magazine's male readers, but they also invited harsh reactions from the usual 'right-thinking' people. Mussolini himself decided that these pin-ups were too provocative[30] and they temporarily disappeared when the magazine was closed down in 1938, less than a year after it had started. Boccasile was allowed to go on providing portraits of beautiful young women for posters and magazines, but they had to be more modestly dressed and had to have dark brown hair. Once again the regime was trying to change reality by simply denying it: in fact, of course, many Italian women were, and are, naturally blonde, and even during the Fascist era many Italian brunettes had taken up the American custom of dyeing their hair blonde.

Thus, by the time the regime entered its dying phase the early Fascist model of the 'new woman', engaging in sport for the sake of health, had been brought together with the model of the old-fashioned 'true woman' that had

10.7 Mario Busini: *Mentes et corpora exercemus ad illustrandam patriam*

been revived during the 1930s, to produce the ideal of the energetic sports-woman who could also be a respectable mother and a militant Fascist. After years of debate and controversy, involving the Church, the medical profession, public opinion – which proved to be less malleable than the regime had hoped – and, of course, women's own preferences, the sporting aesthetic had become widely accepted. The paintings submitted for the Cremona Prize seem to confirm that some women at least had achieved a degree of real emancipation through sport, and were now ready to face sporting challenges and military conflicts alike, side by side with men. However, emancipation was offset by a renewed submission, for such images were also amenable to manipulation in the name of Mussolini's bellicose ideology. In theory, the women depicted by the artists competing for the Cremona Prize embodied the supreme ideal of sportswomen, but in practice only a small minority of Italian women could ever embody that ideal.

Sportswomen of the Fascist era: biographies and interviews

This chapter presents brief biographies of Ondina Valla and other prominent sportswomen of the Fascist era, along with excerpts from interviews with Valla and others. These interviews are not necessarily representative of former sportswomen in general, but are simply selected examples of the ways in which such women recall participating in the phenomenon of women's sport in the closing years of the Fascist era. The interviews include some oral testimonies collected in the region of Marche in central Italy. It has not been possible to collect information according to prearranged schemes because those interviewed, who were of course well on in years, preferred to talk about their experiences in 'semi-monologue' form. The questions were necessarily submitted in 'open form' and in a few cases the answers were a little vague. In general, by telling their own stories those interviewed predictably revealed a certain nostalgia for their early youth and promise, but also a sort of embarrassment in talking about a period that has been taboo in Italy ever since the fall of the regime. They recall singular realities that cannot be represented easily in conventional historical writing. These realities touch on private spheres, identities, emotions and silent memories, which would otherwise be irretrievably lost.[1]

Ondina Valla: biography

During the Fascist era the model of the prolific mother was officially imposed from on high as the most suitable symbol for the new Italian woman Despite this the athlete Trebisonda Valla, who came from a relatively poor background, made herself into a different symbol that inspired many Italian women.

Trebisonda Valla was born on 20 May 1916 in Bologna, her parents' last child after four sons.[2] Her family lived in a small village near the city, but soon moved to the centre of Bologna. Her father was a skilled blacksmith and her mother was a traditional housewife. Female seclusion was quite common at the time, due both to the typical Italian husband's jealousy and to the question of 'image'. Women did not like to go out carrying heavy loads, or show themselves in public when not perfectly dressed, especially in small villages where most women spent their spare time watching people in the street from their windows. Shopping, washing clothes and dishes, or cleaning shoes were all considered disgraceful work even for lower middle-class women like Valla's mother. Her obedient daughter and a part-time maid helped her take care of the five men of the household.

When Valla was only three years old she was sent out shopping for the first time and in the following years she used to walk about 500 metres to primary school on her own. She was quite a dynamic and independent little girl, and enjoyed jumping across ditches and playing various games. Her strong, tall brothers enjoyed physical activities and were particularly talented at the high jump, but after leaving school they did not continue training or competing. Their sister, however, started a brilliant career in athletics that lasted until 1943.

In 1927 Valla was trained in the high jump for about one month by a male primary school teacher, a Mr Formigini, and came first in the next scholastic

11.1 Young Ondina Valla putting the shot

championships in Bologna with a jump of 1.10 metres. In 1928 she could easily jump 1.25 metres and was enrolled in the *Bologna Sportiva* association. There she met her strongest rival, Claudia Testoni, who became one of her closest friends. Valla also met a good coach who trained female athletes about three times a week.

In 1929 Valla competed in an important athletics meeting in Bologna against women from France, Britain, Poland and Czechoslovakia. She was the youngest member of the Italian team. Although she wore old gym shoes instead of boots with spikes, she came fifth in both the high jump and the long jump. She was growing tall and strong, and started practising other sporting disciplines, such as putting the shot, the 100 metre and 80 metre hurdles, basketball, fencing, swimming, and skating.

In 1930, when Valla was only 14 years old, she attracted attention during a meeting in Naples that pitted Italian athletes against visitors from Belgium. She was once again the youngest member of the Italian team, which was then being trained by Marina Zanetti (see Chapters 4 and 9). Valla did not win the 80 metre hurdles, but the specialist press was quite impressed by the young athlete. During a boating excursion taken by the team and the press a journalist observed that the name 'Trebisonda' was too long and heavy for such an adolescent, and proposed the nickname 'Ondina'. It literally means a 'small wave' and apparently referred to the easy way she overcame hurdles as if describing a wave motion.

Valla went on to become a popular athlete both in Italy and abroad. Later in 1930, having set Italian records in the 80 metre hurdles and the high jump, she was chosen to attend the next Women's World Games, in Prague. She then had to travel by train for about 36 hours, sitting in a cheap and uncomfortable second-class carriage, and put up with poor accommodation

11.2 Ondina Valla teaching hurdling

in Prague, since first-class tickets and better accommodation were reserved only for male athletes.[3] The few female athletes who competed in the name of Italy received very little financial or practical support.[4] Competitive women's sport was both criticised and undervalued, although a number of nonconformist women were obtaining good results in more than one sport (including the pilot, skier, roller-skaters and long-distance runners profiled elsewhere in this chapter). Valla herself recalled that female athletes were given good-quality sportswear only for the duration of an event and then had to give them back (an observation made by other female athletes quoted in this chapter). At the beginning of Valla's career most of her travelling expenses were paid by her father, who, perhaps surprisingly, was her staunchest supporter along with her brothers. However, her mother insisted that Valla should give up sport as soon as possible, saying that she was not a little girl anymore. Her mother preferred to have her safe at home, waiting for a good husband. Yet Valla, who really enjoyed athletics, continued to train.

Valla and the rest of the women's athletic team could not go to Los Angeles for the Olympic Games in 1932, largely because of opposition from Pope Pius XI. However, in 1933 Valla competed internationally once again, at the World University Games in Paris, for which she was give false credentials as a university student despite having given up formal education some years before. She won the 100 metres, the 80 metre hurdles and the 4 x 100m relay in Paris and a French journalist dubbed her the 'little Italian wonder'.

In 1935 Valla and other Italian athletes began preparing for the next Olympic Games. The men's and women's teams trained together and stayed in the same hotel, in spite of the Fascist and Catholic preference for separating the sexes.[5] Valla's most celebrated victory was at the Berlin Olympics in 1936, when she came first and set a world record in the 80 metre hurdles (11″ 6). The *Führer* shook hands with her, but Valla later confessed that she had not been impressed at all: Hitler was nobody in comparison with the *Duce*, Mussolini.[6] Her gold medal was the only one awarded to any of the Italian athletes, even though the male athletic team had a very good reputation, and had long been strongly supported by the Fascist regime and the press. Valla and the six other Italian women athletes sent to Berlin also came fourth in both the 80 metre hurdles and the 4 x 100 metre relay, and at last they could see their names printed in block capitals on the pages of national newspapers and specialist sports magazines.

As soon as she arrived back from Berlin at the railway station in Bologna Valla was received like a film star by local dignitaries and excited fans. She confessed that was quite a surprise, as she was not used to such a reception, which was normally given only to Italian sportsmen. Later she was congratulated by Mussolini in Rome, together with the other members of the Italian team, and received a gold *Medaglia al Valore Atletico* (Medal for Athletic Valour) from him.[7] The success of the women's team in Berlin convinced Mussolini that a selected number of sportswomen could contribute to spreading the image of Fascist sportspeople all over the world. From then on the regime's propaganda machine worked strenuously in favour of the enrolment of girls and young women in its youth organisations. Valla, meanwhile had a special audience with Pius XI, who shook hands with her and congratulated her. The Olympic victory had suddenly opened a breach in the 'masculinist' wall erected against women's emancipation by the highest authorities in Italy, the *Duce* and the Pope.

Hundreds of letters, flowers, suitors, invitations, interviews and photographs, and even an offer of a job as a film star, changed Valla's life. Italy's first female Olympic gold medallist gained prestige, money, a good job in Bologna and a wealthy physician as her husband. Her achievement in Berlin, and her national records in the high jump (five times), the long jump, the pentathlon, the 100 metres (twice) and the 80 metre hurdles (six times), made her a heroine for many young women and contributed a little to undermining the female inferiority complex, with its deep roots both in the paternalistic tradition of the past and in the new Fascist ideology. Valla herself told the Italian press agency that she dedicated her victory in Berlin both to the Fatherland and to the achievements of Italian women's sport.

Famous Italian sportswomen of the time were still depicted by the press as examples of modesty, femininity and daughterly love, if only to reassure traditionalists and parents. Thus Angela Cressi was celebrated for being twice *Littoriali* female champion in the javelin and twice a mother, while one journalist ended an article on Valla with the lines: 'And Ondina Valla, Olympic champion, now runs off, as it is 7:45 p.m. In spite of any victory, Father Valla does not allow her to be out after 8 o'clock!'[8] However, it was also rumoured that Valla was sexually interested in women.[9] When she became a mother the news was emphasised as a demonstration that sporting competition, femininity and maternity were compatible after all. Like other famous athletes who became mothers, such as Cressi, Bruna Pizzini-Brianza, Nini Bordoni-Ray and, especially, Vittorina Vivenza, who was the happy mother of nine children, Valla was interviewed and photographed with her child to stop the gossip about her sexual proclivities.

Since Valla had, as we have seen, given up schoolwork without graduating from senior high school, she was unable either to attend the *Accademia Nazionale Femminile di Educazione Fisica* in Orvieto, or to become a teacher or official in any of the Fascist youth organisations. Instead the regime gave her a job as a secretary in the party headquarters (*Casa del Fascio*) in Bologna, where she was paid more than other employees (about 500 lire a month instead of 350 lire). However, she did not enjoy sitting for long periods typing out membership cards and after a lot of complaints she was allowed to focus on her physical training while retaining her nominal post and her special salary.

Ondina Valla: interview

On 8 May 1994 I went to Aquila to interview Ondina Valla at her home. It was a pleasure to spend a couple of hours with Valla. She was then 78 years old and had some problems with her legs, but she was still vivacious. Unfortunately, she no longer had a good memory, and sometimes forgot or confused names and data. She had not preserved much of her past, just some photographs and cuttings, and she said that her Olympic gold medal had been stolen. She did not like to speak about her belief or involvement in Fascism, but simply declared that she agreed with Mussolini – like, she claimed, most Italians between the wars – and had been honoured by the regime for her sporting achievements alone. From her omissions rather than from her words one could deduce that when the regime exploited her image and achievements it did so with her consent.

Ondina, when did you start doing physical activities?
I was 11 years old when I was recruited in Bologna by Captain Costa, who came to my primary school looking for children who were naturally talented in athletics. I was tested together with some other pupils, but was unsuccessful in the high jump. Even so, he noticed me because I was thin and agile. He asked my name and when I answered 'Valla' he said: 'Valla? Are you a sister of the two famous running and jumping Valla brothers?' My positive reply gave me the opportunity to be trained, together with a small number of other little girls, by the male teacher of the boys. This person, Mr Grimolizi, taught us to run and jump in the courtyard of the school, during the daily break.

What were the next steps you took?
Well, at school we took part in gymnastics displays and competed against other schools in Bologna, but I did not like gymnastics as much as athletics. Leandro Arpinati, then the secretary of the party, was from Bologna and, being keen on sport, he encouraged this activity among his fellow citizens. Students of both sexes were sent by bus and trained at the Littoriale Stadium.

When I became a member of the *Bologna Sportiva* sports association, which later became affiliated to the *Virtus Bologna* society, I had a good trainer from Hungary, Mr Gaspar. He used to train girls in athletic disciplines about two or three times a week, but only in the good season. Sometimes we were trained and competed on Sunday evenings, just after the football match, and crowds of football spectators came to see us as well.

When I was only 14 I was sent to Florence for the national championship. There I won both the high jump and the 80 metre hurdles against older and stronger competitors. I remember that after these victories the athletes Polacco and Martino from Trieste, and another from Venice, gave up competing.

Can you tell us the story of the nickname Ondina?
There are several stories about it, but in truth this name derives from a mistake by a journalist, who wrote 'Trebi*t*onda' instead of 'Trebisonda'. From this mistaken 'Trebi*t*onda' somebody started to call me by the nickname 'Trebi*t*ondina', and then simply 'Ondina'. From then onwards this became my name, but my parents started to call me Ondina much later, after the Berlin Olympics.

How were you able to participate in the Olympic Games in 1936?
When I was included in the national women's athletic team for the Olympics I had already set some national records and participated in international contests. That spring the team went for training to Rapallo, where the weather was warmer and more agreeable. We left Italy and arrived in Berlin one month in advance, in order to get accustomed to the different track and climate. Our trainer was Boyd Comstock from America, the official trainer of the Italian athletes. In Berlin, all the sportswomen lived in the 'Women's House', and we spent our spare time visiting the city and its fantastic shops.

Could you say something about your victorious race in Berlin?
In the semi-final of the 80 metre hurdles I was not only the winner but my time equalled the world record, so I thought I could probably win the final. On that day I had run twice in about one hour, and my right leg was painful and heavy, but on the following day the final of the 80 metre hurdles had to be run anyway. As a matter of fact, in the final my start was really slow, but after the first two hurdles I had caught up with the rest of the runners. Four of us were so close together at the wire that only a photo could sort us out and determine that I was the winner. We had to wait about half an hour for the result and two hours for the prize-giving ceremony, where only two athletes, the German and me, went up onto the podium. Unfortunately, the third, a Canadian, thinking she had only come fourth, had already left the stadium.

The prize-giving was fantastic. Among the spectators there were Princess Jolanda of Savoy and Mussolini's son. The organisers presented me with a little oak plant and wreath, while the music of the Italian royal march and the Fascist hymn *Giovinezza* (Youth) was spreading all over the very crowded stadium. And I was standing stiff in the Fascist salute!

How did you feel then, and what happened later?
At that very moment I felt an amazing sensation, as if this victory did not involve me at all. Later I was greeted by my friends in the Women's House, where maids of honour and a bottle of champagne awaited me. When I got

home my father and my brothers, together with both important and ordinary people, welcomed me. The Prefect of Bologna in person congratulated me and presented me with a bouquet of flowers, and people sent me a bagful of telegrams. During the days that followed I was told that I had to go to the railway station, where a parcel sent from Rome by the royal family was waiting for me. I was really excited trying to guess what wonderful thing might be in it, but when I opened the parcel I found just a silver frame and a photograph signed by Queen Helen. I was still young – only 20 years old at that time – and my imagination was so vivid! I delivered the little oak plant to the authorities in Bologna, who ordered it to be planted in the nearby stadium and to add a plaque with my name. Some time later somebody, I presume an anti-Fascist, tried to cut down the plant, without success, but he broke the plaque in two and it had to be joined together again.

All the athletes who had won medals at the Berlin Olympics were received by Mussolini. I was the one and only woman in the group. Everyone was trying to approach Mussolini, but the *Duce* said: 'I want Miss Valla near me!' In Rome there was also a ceremony in the *Stadio dei Marmi*, where a diploma and a medal were given to each member of the group.

Did you receive any reward for your sporting activity?
In the whole of my life I never got any money from the Italian sporting organisations, apart from 5,000 lire that I received for the Olympic victory [about half the annual salary of a high school teacher]. In addition, in Berlin the Italians received 20 lire a day. With this sum I bought a little mechanical doll for myself and a coat for my father. When I took part in national or international competitions the organisers paid only the out-of-pocket expenses, but petty expenses were paid by my father. I remember that he gave me 50 lire for national competitions and 100 lire for journeys abroad. Sometimes we also received little gifts and gadgets, collected from the shops in the host town.

Did you practise any other sport?
I enjoyed skiing, and this activity had made my arms so strong that I could compete in the classical pentathlon as well. I learned to throw the javelin and put the shot, and also won a national championship and the Italian record in this discipline. By the end of the 1930s I was ready for the Olympic Games [due to take place] in Tokyo [in 1940], but the coming of war destroyed my dreams. After the birth of my son Luigi I was still fit and I was planning to participate in the London Olympics in 1948, but I had to give up because of a number of physical problems.

Was there any disagreement over female sport?
Generally I had no problems, but once in Bologna a spectator was rude about me. I did not hear what he said, but my brother immediately struck him with

his fist and knocked him to the floor. Often my sporting society was invited to bilateral meetings in other Italian cities or abroad, and I was the only woman of the team. Of course, women had to be more careful, and dress in long shorts!

What about the Church?

After Berlin I even went to St Peter's and was received by Pope Pio XII [sic], who said: 'Well done, our compliments!' But let me remember ... Yes, the Pope was against female athleticism, because he thought that it was dangerous to women's health. In fact, in 1934 a newspaper referred to 'the dying swan of female athletics'!

Some other prominent sportswomen

Italian women involved in high-level sporting competitions were an exception during the Fascist era and offered a model of femininity that stood in contrast to the official one until very late in the regime's history (see Chapter 10). Nevertheless their presence on the national and international sporting scene was not simply tolerated but actively supported by the regime.[10]

Claudia Testoni, runner

Claudia Testoni was both Valla's closest friend and her most serious rival in athletics. They both spent most of their early years in Bologna, where Testoni was born on 19 December 1915, and were both all-round athletes. They then became involved in the same sporting adventures in Italy and abroad, travelling together, living in the same hotels and largely sharing the same emotions. Like Valla, Testoni was included in the women's athletic teams that participated in the Women's World Games in Prague in 1930 and the Berlin Olympics in 1936, but in Germany fate went against her. After the semi-final of the 80 metre hurdles she was placed fourth and therefore did not qualify, until it was discovered from the photographs that she had come third. The next day she ran in the final and apparently came second, only to be told about half an hour later that she had only come fourth. From then onwards Valla was first and Testoni second in the feelings of their fans, although both were extraordinary athletes. Testoni took her revenge in 1938, when she became European champion in the 80 metre hurdles and equalled Valla's world record (11″ 6). In addition she set the world record twice at international meetings in Milan (11″ 5) and Garmisch-Partenkirchen (11″ 3).

Testoni's brilliant career started at the beginning of the 1930s and ended at the beginning of the 1940s, in parallel with Valla's. Testoni set national records three times in the 100 metres (her best time was 12″), four times in the 200 metres (25″ 4), five times in the 80 metre hurdles (11″ 3), six times in the long jump (5.65 metres), once in the high jump (1.54 metres) and nine times in the 4 x 100 metre relay. She received one gold, two silver and five bronze *Medaglie al Valore Atletico*.

Three long-distance runners

In the years 1930–38 the best female long-distance runners in Italy were all members of the Venchi Unica sporting society in Turin: Cleo Balbo and Candida Giorda-Cecchetti, who were both natives of the city, and Leandrina Bulzacchi, who came from Cremona. The northern regions of Italy had a strong tradition in this discipline and a number of women were already taking part in it in the last years of the nineteenth century, but these three surpassed their predecessors by setting the world record in the 3 x 800 metres relay (7′ 32.1), in Turin in 1937, a feat for which all three received gold *Medaglie al Valore Atletico*.

While this was Giorda-Cecchetti's only notable achievement, Balbo and Bulzacchi remained active, and competed successfully in different races. In 1935 Balbo and Bulzacchi became joint Italian female record holders in the 3 x 800 metres, and in 1938 Balbo set a record in the 800 metres. She received four bronze *Medaglie al Valore Atletico* in addition to her gold. Bulzacchi turned out to be the most talented of the three, becoming and remaining Italian champion in the 800 metres continuously from 1930 to 1938, champion in cross-country five times and champion in the 4 x 100 relay twice. She too received four bronze *Medaglie al Valore Atletico*.

Carina Massone, pilot

There had been only a tiny number of female pilots in Italy before Carina Massone. The first was Rosina Ferrario, who gained her licence in 1913, while Tatiana Fumagalli[11] and Gaby Angelini became famous during the Fascist era. Angelini was the first Italian woman to make a tour of Europe by plane, but died young during a flight in 1932.[12] Mussolini himself did not think that this was a sport that should be chosen by women. In June 1934, having read in a daily newspaper published in Bologna that women had been invited by the local air club to take part in a course for pilots, he sent off the following telegram to the Prefect of the city:

> Please tell the head of the air club in Bologna that in Fascist Italy the most Fascist thing that women should do is to 'pilot' numerous children. Obviously they can fly for the sake of a hobby or out of necessity, but piloting is a very serious affair which should be left to men, of whom there is actually a sufficient number.[13]

This background makes Carina Massone's achievements, which have become part of the history of sporting aviation, all the more impressive.

Massone was born near Genoa on 20 June 1911. Like most of the younger women in the aristocratic milieu that she was brought up in, she enjoyed tennis, skiing, swimming, hunting and fishing. Above all, however, she loved flying, which was an expression of dynamism and modernity celebrated by both Futurism and Fascism.[14] On 5 May 1934, she took a class C seaplane up to 5,544 metres above the ground, setting a women's record for this category of plane. She received sympathy and support from Italo Balbo, the most celebrated Fascist hero of Italian aviation and an important member of the Fascist hierarchy. On his orders Massone was tested and trained by the air force just like male pilots. Her son, Vittorio Negrone, said later that when he was a child he was quite impressed by his daring mother, who used to train at the military airfield of Montecelio in Rome, wearing the same clothes as the air force pilots.[15]

On 20 June 1935 Carina Massone set off on her attempt to reclaim the women's record for class C seaplanes, which the Frenchwoman Marise Hilsz had taken from her by flying up to 11,289 metres. Massone took off from Montecelio equipped only with a rudimentary electrically heated overcoat and an oxygen bottle. Specialist physicians had recommended that Massone should not exceed 11,000 metres, given the serious shortage of oxygen and the icy temperatures at higher altitudes, but she reached 12,043 metres, setting an absolute record for women pilots. She reported that the temperature had reached minus 35°C and that she could only breathe through the oxygen bottle with difficulty. When she landed the most important air aces of the Italian air force gathered to congratulate this unique woman who had joined their ranks. She was given the gold *Medaglia al Valore Atletico* twice.

In 1954 Massone tried to set a new record in non-stop flying in an amphibious plane. She flew for about 30 hours, covering the distance of 3,000 kilometres from Brescia in Italy to Luxor in Egypt at an average speed of about 299 kilometres an hour and beat the world record set by a US flier, General Andrews, 18 years earlier. This achievement suggests that the strength and self-confidence that some women acquired young, in the general climate of enthusiasm for competition generated by the sport policies of the Fascist regime, outlasted the regime itself.

Three roller-skaters

Roller-skating was considered a typical Italian sport by the time the Fascists took power. Its roots went back to 1877, when the country's first skating rink was opened in Milan. Princess Colonna founded a skating club in Rome in 1908 and the first championship for women skaters in the province of Rome took place on 18 March 1912. A national federation for hockey and skating was founded in 1922, and from then on people of both sexes were encouraged to practise this cheap and easy discipline in gymnasiums, courts, squares and streets, and even on proper skating rinks. Skating was one of the few sports recommended for women in the programmes of the Fascist youth organisations and it was relatively easy to find talented girls for competitions. Three in particular stood out: Ada Spoto, Adriana Rianda and Liliana Sozzi-Spada.

Ada Spoto, who came from Catania in Sicily, started her brilliant career as a speed skater in 1936, when she won the women's team race at the Italian championship in Catania. For this she got her first bronze *Medaglia al Valore Atletico*. Her second bronze came in 1937, after she came first in the 8,000 metres at the Italian skating championships in Monza. Her best results were obtained at an international meeting in Catania in 1938, when she came first in the 500 metres, the 1,000 metres, the 5,000 metres and the 10,000 metres, and in Ferrara in 1939, when she set a world record in the 10,000 metres. For these victories Spoto received two gold *Medaglie al Valore Atletico*.

Adriana Rianda, from Rome, was also a specialist in speed skating. In the last three years of the 1930s she came first in the 1,000 metres, the 5,000 metres and the 10,000 metres at international meetings. She received one gold *Medaglia al Valore Atletico*.

Liliana Sozzi-Spada, also from Rome, was more eclectic than either Spoto or Rianda, since she also enjoyed artistic skating, in which she became national champion in 1935 and 1937. In speed skating she came first in the 1,000 metres, the 5,000 metres and the 10,000 metres in Italian championships (1934 and 1936), European championships (1937 and 1938), and one world championships (1938). She received one gold and three bronze *Medaglie al Valore Atletico*.

Celina Seghi, skier

By the end of the nineteenth century skiing was becoming a favoured sport among aristocratic and wealthy people, but in the following years it became more popular in Italy. The first national skiing federation was founded in 1913, joining together nine sporting societies, but in 1920 it was refounded as the Italian Federation for Winter Sports (FISI). Its success can be gauged by the fact that the number of societies affiliated to it rose from 28 in 1922 to 287 in 1932 and then 423 in 1934.[16] Following Mussolini's example, Italian men were more and more involved in skiing, both in the Alps and in the Apennines, and women were induced to practise this healthy activity as well.

Among women skiers the most celebrated was Celina Seghi. She was born in Abetone, a winter resort in Tuscany, on 8 March 1920. At the Winter Olympics in 1936, at Garmisch-Partenkirchen, she was too young and was not placed very high, but in 1937, 1939, 1941 and 1942 she reached the highest place in a number of national competitions. She was especially talented in slalom and downhill skiing, and became Italian champion 24 times. For her victories she received one gold *Medaglia al Valore Atletico* and four bronze.

Oral testimonies from five former sportswomen

The material collected here is derived from interviews with a number of women who engaged in sporting activities during the years of Fascism. All these women came from either Ancona, the capital of the region of Marche, or Pesaro, a smaller town in the same region. The names of those to be interviewed were selected chiefly by reading the press of the period.

During the Fascist era Ancona lacked certain facilities, notably swimming pools and basketball halls, but it did have tennis courts, a sailing club and an airport, all of which were mainly used by the wealthy, whether residents or tourists. Other young people trained in gymnasiums and stadiums, and swam in the Adriatic. The interviewees from Ancona whose words appear here are Lara Borghetti, a gymnast and swimmer of a high level, and Consilia Del Sordo, a basketball player, both of whom were interviewed in the winter of 1998–99 by my student Monica Ciasca.

Women in the town of Pesaro had developed a tradition of swimming long before the Fascist regime began encouraging women to take up sport. Anna Savi of Pesaro was the national champion in women's swimming from 1929 to 1931, setting a number of records in the 50 metres and the 100 metres, in both the crawl and the back stroke. The town had a limited number of sporting facilities, mainly used by men, but in 1934 some girls started practising athletics, and then basketball, systematically. They were trained by Alceo Moretti, who was in touch with Mr Comstock, the official trainer of the Italian athletics team for the Berlin Olympics. Later Moretti's work was also supported by a professional athlete from Pesaro, Amos Matteucci. The female basketball players were trained by male players and supervised by Agide Fava, a well-known local trainer. As in most towns, skating was also popular among women, while the wealthier among them enjoyed tennis and fencing. The three women from Pesaro whose memories are recorded here are Teresa Badioli, Rina Serafini and Luciana Sisa, who were all interviewed in the summer of 1999, by my student Massimiliano Pezzolesi.

These women's memories are of a very simple, provincial way of living, in the wider setting of a relatively poor country that had difficulties in providing adequate sporting facilities, organisation and general assistance for young sportspeople. This offers a striking contrast to the official image of the sporting nation *par excellence* that was presented in the media of the Fascist era, with its focus on colossal national competitions and displays.

Lara Borghetti

I was born in 1924 and started practising sport in my third year at primary school. I was on the gymnastics team, which had to show the teachers collective exercises for the annual provincial display on 24 May. Students of both sexes from the primary school and the first year of junior high school took part in this display. Gymnastic displays were compulsory then. The display on 24 May was beautiful. Each category of students had different exercises: boy's exercises were rather 'virile' (the *Avanguardisti* used muskets), while the female exercises were done without equipment and accompanied by music. I remember that this display started everywhere in Italy at the same time and [that the programme of exercises] was transmitted by radio from Rome. Mussolini regarded young people as the country's best prospects, and anyone who was talented in any sport could take part in the national *Ludi Juveniles*. The recruitment was done at school by the various federations, which selected the best students. This happened to me for gymnastics. There were national meetings for gymnastics, and we used equipment such as parallel bars, the vaulting horse, and so on, and the exercises were accompanied by music. I was good at the high jump as well, but I could not train much. Often I had to fight against my mother, because I was not good at school work.

In Ancona I attended the *Stamura* sporting club as well, and I learned the breast stroke in the sea. We were trained by expert male swimmers, even when the weather was bad. I was noticed by officials from the federation, who agreed that I could continue and compete at the national level. When I took part in competitions my travel, accommodation and meals were paid for, but I did not receive other expenses such as, for instance, the uniform, which cost my family a lot. I could wear a suitable bathing costume and sporting overalls for the contests, but then I had to give them back. I participated in the GIL's national university championships [the *Littoriali*] in Naples, Florence and Turin. I won third place in the breast stroke and was asked to commit myself to a more serious involvement, but my family opposed it.

Sport was highly regarded by the regime and at school the marks in physical education counted for a great deal in the final evaluation. The Fascist ideology was diffused at school and students agreed with it because they did not hear any alternative voices. At that time, on Sundays we had to wear a 'fez', which all of us disliked, and a black shirt. We were supported by our physical education teachers, who spent their spare time training squads of students in several disciplines, but while the male students were also trained for professional sports, the only possible way for female students to practise sport was within the educational institutions. Women were considered the 'angels of domestic life'. If they wanted to be more than this they could succeed, but it was much more difficult than it was for men.

In Ancona women's sport was only for amateurs, and the trainers were amateurs as well. There was a lack of facilities and girls could practise only a few disciplines, such as swimming, athletics, fencing, horse-riding and tennis. The last two disciplines were expensive and therefore reserved for the elite. We common girls enjoyed taking part in the mass displays for the crowd, including the dignitaries from Rome and our families, and then we felt really united and happy.

Consilia Del Sordo

I played basketball from 1935 to 1950, when I got married. Physical activities were organised at school by our physical education teacher, who selected the best students. I was one of them. We met every Saturday afternoon, wearing our uniforms, and walked in perfectly ordered squads to the monument for the fallen, where we had to sing patriotic and Fascist hymns. Once the squad had been formed we could take part in a basketball tournament, together with squads from Pesaro, Zara, Forlì and Faenza, where the best students were selected for the next national championship. The strongest team was the one from Pesaro, which won very often. Apart from basketball, the squad practised gymnastics and learned collective exercises with equipment and music. The aim was to stress individual and collective harmony. I started practising sport at school because I liked it. The first place I played basketball in was the courtyard of the town hall, then we played near the entrance to the stadium. All these activities were done at our own expense, apart from travel and accommodation. People criticised us when we showed our bare legs during training and matches. All the same, many followed our performances. The regime changed the name 'basketball' to *pallacanestro*, but apart from this it did not interfere in our sport. Although sport was propagated by the regime, in my opinion it did not invest much capital in it. In those days Italy was a society that was much poorer than it is now. Sometimes the prize was simply a pair of rubber sports shoes, but even that was an exception. We used to swim in the sea from May to September. There was no swimming pool in Ancona then, and whoever wished to swim for the rest of the year had to go to Pesaro [60 kilometres to the north]. Ancona was always second to Pesaro.

The basketball team had a notable 'bodily spirit', and used to participate in the Bellagamba tournament in Falconara [10 kilometres to the north]; this was followed by journalists, who commented on the results on the radio. The floor was horrible: it was made of asphalt. The only wooden floor I saw was the one in Forlì, but then Mussolini was born near there. At the beginning basketball players were trained by Mr Mineo, who was keen on this sport, for free; later we were enrolled in the GIL, and then the GUF. Tennis was played in Ancona as well, and I tried it, but I enjoyed basketball much more.

I don't know about female long-distance training, but I remember women's rowing competitions.

Ancona did not have a university, and the recruitment was done among students in the last year of senior high school. At the end of each school year we took part in the *Ludi Juveniles*. We had to wear the athletic uniforms bought by our families. It was necessary to be present because of the presence of the [Fascist] dignitaries. As far as I know, before Fascism sport was not important at all, but under the regime it was taken seriously. Young people were enthusiastic because of the opportunity to live together and leave the town for competitions.

Teresa Badioli

I was born in Pesaro and still live there. At school our physical education teacher suggested which discipline was suitable for each of us. In spring about eight or ten of us walked up to the stadium with the teacher, singing songs, and once we got there we tried running, jumping and throwing, depending on what we were interested in. I started to practise organised sport when I was 11 years old, but I had learned to skate much earlier. I should add that my father and my brother were true sportsmen. My father had competed successfully in target-shooting, and my brother was keen on different sports. As far as I can remember, I was as good at skating as he was. I used to skate twice a week for about three hours in a gymnasium, wearing a long heavy skirt that obstructed my movements. In summer I played tennis for free, like all the members of the ONB, but my racket was not too good in comparison to my brother's. I also tried rowing. In winter I enjoyed skiing whenever I could. At school I was the best at physical education. In athletics I was good at the javelin and the high jump. My trainer was Matteucci, and we practised athletics twice a week. I did not have special shoes for the high jump and I had to wear the same long skirt, which obstructed the jump. The underwear we wore was in a compulsory style, a kind of black Bermuda shorts.

The most important sporting contest in my life was the GIL's female athletics championship in Florence in 1940. I played tennis, which was included in the athletics programme: that was quite an exciting experience. I also took first place in the javelin in 1941, during the provincial selection for the *Ludi Juveniles*. The female athletics team went to Florence by train. On the way back we had to sleep or sit on the floor because nobody had booked seats for us. We were looked after by both male and female trainers.

My family did not obstruct my early sporting interests at all, but when I was at the University of Bologna my brother, having tested the 'moral climate' of the stadium, said: 'No, you will never go there again.'

Rina Serafini

I was born in Chicago, but my parents were from Pesaro and we soon came back home. I started competitive gymnastics when I was 14 years old. My school brought selected female students to Rome for a competition in basic gymnastics, rhythmic gymnastics and archery. I remember that we had to wear a ridiculous beret, and that our plaited, billowing shorts made us very similar to clowns. When I was 16 I started to play basketball just for fun, then I took up athletics, where I tried different disciplines on a dirt track covered with cinders. Our trainer was Moretti; we met every 'Fascist Saturday' and possibly early in the morning before school. Alceo Moretti knew the famous Comstock, who was Ondina Valla's trainer, and once he came to Pesaro just to look at us.

My debut in national competitions was in 1938, for the *Littoriali* in Rome. I came second in the 80 metres race but, being only 16 years old, I must confess I used a false name, because that competition was reserved for university students. I tried the same trick at the next *Littoriali*, in Naples, but there I was soon unmasked. I cried a lot about being still so young. Finally, in 1940, I became a university student and I had the right to participate in the next *Littoriali*, in Milan. I was there for my preferred discipline, the 80 metres, and I ran in the final. When my trainer Moretti said that I could also try a second discipline, I chose the long jump and, unexpectedly, I won. I was the youngest of the winners, and they gave me the honour of administering the solemn oath.[17] When I got back to Pesaro by train, I was received by a brass band, the most important dignitaries and, naturally, all my friends. Imagine how I felt: I was only 18 years old.

After this experience I started playing basketball and joined the female team in Pesaro, which participated with success in many competitions, including the *Littoriali* in Genoa in 1941. I was fond of tennis too, and although I played on a tennis court in bad conditions it was fun. Once I asked my younger brother to try a doubles tennis competition. We had never played together and he thought that I was completely crazy, but we won the match. I enjoyed swimming as well. At first we used to train near the harbour, and the water was oily and dirty. Anyway, this new discipline suited me as well, and after a number of victories I was asked by a member of the swimming federation to join the national team. Because of the war, however, my parents did not allow me to go and train in the distant region of Liguria. That was the end of my competitive career.

People say that I was a good sportswoman. I can only say that I was tall and thin, and every kind of sport was easy for me. But if you want to know which was my preferred sport, I would answer skiing, even though I won only a modest local competition.

In my opinion, female sport did not interest many people. Traditionalists and the middle classes looked on us with disdain, saying that we spent too much time outside our homes and mixing with boys. At that time people thought that girls should stay at home and cook, and we often went out for tennis, swimming, athletics and so on. There was some gender discrimination. Boys could do anything, but we had to learn housekeeping. My parents did not care about this and allowed me to indulge my passion, because I was a good student at school and at university. They were proud of my medals, maybe because they had lived in the United States and had a different mentality. Many of my friends had to give up athletics and basketball because of opposition from their parents. Fortunately, when female basketball became more popular in Pesaro, and the team played successfully against other towns, provinces and regions, the citizens looked at us in a new way. Although we trained and played in the same tournaments with the men, they felt proud of us. In fact, there were no problems at all, and the boys were helpful and well-educated. Our early years were a wonderful period. The day was too short for us, as we had to run from one sports facility to another.

In the Fascist era we youngsters became members of the Fascist Party from birth. A lot of adults had membership cards as well, but my parents, who were not enrolled in any Fascist organisation, had no troubles because of this. In the course of my sporting life I once met Mussolini, as a winner in the *Littoriali*. It happened in Rome, during a ceremony where the *Duce* gave the best athletes of both sexes a prize, the 'Gold M' pin. It was an exciting experience for another reason: I met many famous sportsmen of the time.

Luciana Sisa

I was born in Pesaro, but I lived and studied in Urbino. When I got married I left this region and went to the north of Italy, but in 1968 I came back to Pesaro. I do not remember when I started physical activities, but my eldest brother was keen on sports and I wanted to imitate him by following his various experiences. I was really energetic and I even enjoyed fighting boys in the street. At the start of junior high school I tried athletics in my spare time. Alceo Moretti was the trainer who opened this discipline up to me, giving me good advice on the most suitable activities, such as running and the high jump. I was trained by Agide Fava as well. I should say that officially the trainer was Moretti, but any other capable person could help out. I also did other sports just for fun, including skating, basketball and, especially, swimming, together with my brother.

Only a few girls spent time at the stadium, and then only sporadically. I don't remember if we had fixed dates for training, but I think that we voluntarily decided to go there during the week and obviously on the 'Fascist Saturday'. At that time there was no sports society, nor were there any organised activities. Nobody gave us special sportswear, and we wore our own clothes and ordinary gym shoes. When we went to the stadium I used to bring some bread and a lemon, because it had no facilities, not even running water. I remember that everything was dusty and dirty, and if you had a muscular injury you had to ask the doorkeeper for a bad-smelling oily lotion. The track was black and dusty, and for the running start we had to dig little holes in the ground with our own hands. When our coaches had enough time we were trained for competitions and tried to do our best, just for fun. Often there were no judges or spectators watching us, yet these poor attempts were regarded as authentic athletic contests.

My best results in athletics came in the high jump, but actually I was not a good athlete. Even so, I was sent to the national championship in Florence. There, in spite of the support of all my friends, I could jump only 1.25 metres. Anyway, I did not care about this because the most enjoyable thing was to be away from home with good friends. In Florence the female team from Pesaro did its best, with a lot of enthusiasm, and we even invented a little song and wore knitted hats in identical colours, to be sung and displayed in the stadium in that city. We used to eat a lot of sugar lumps to increase our energy, and we did not go to the toilet before running because it was rumoured that we would run faster. We went to Florence by train, and were looked after by trainers, assistants and the older athletes, but our parents were left out of it. We performed on the same day and at the same time together with the male athletes. I do not remember about sexual discrimination, but in fact my brother received some money, about five lire, when he went swimming, while I was not paid at all.

At home I had no problems about leaving the house for training, probably because my father had died when I was only ten years old and my mother was a physical education teacher. I should add that she never either encouraged or obstructed my passion for all kinds of physical activities. At school I enjoyed all kind of disciplines, from basic to rhythmic and artistic gymnastics, from physical exercises in the classroom or gymnasium to volleyball. Unfortunately, we had a class only once a week and we did not have any connection with organised sports outside school.

We few female athletes from Pesaro were very proud to take part in sporting activities and competitions, no matter if the results were not too good. Nothing was more important than to live through these experiences together. I remember that was a really happy period, and I regretted its passing for a long time.

Conclusion

The biographies presented above confirm that almost all of Fascist Italy's leading sportswomen were born in the north (in Turin, Genoa, Cremona or

Bologna), or in important cities in central Italy (Florence or Rome), while only one came from the South (Catania). A long-lasting paternalistic tradition, a predominantly rural economy, and the practice of 'gender apartheid' derived both from Catholic tradition and from the influence of ancient Middle Eastern cultures combined to keep southern Italian women secluded in the home. In most other provinces women's lives were not as miserable as they were in the south, but they were also much less exciting in most villages and towns in northern and central Italy than they were in the industrialised cities.

All the interviews with former athletes from Ancona and Pesaro suggest that in the second half of the 1930s most female students outside the major cities were not really interested in or pushed towards sport. In both Ancona and Pesaro life went on quietly, far from the tumultuous political events in Rome and in most of the northern cities, where modernisation and industrialisation had promoted a form of 'outer' emancipation among women (see Chapter 7). Only a small number of energetic students living in such places as Ancona and Pesaro could enjoy sports systematically, but these sports were organised in a rather crude way. As the interviewees indicate, in the 1930s and the early 1940s a number of female students voluntarily took part in sporting activities, either at school or, especially, in their spare time, with real enthusiasm. These activities were left to the goodwill of the girls themselves, who spontaneously met at the local sporting facilities, or were organised in relatively informal ways. Often their trainers were not specialists but amateurs keen on sport, although in most cases the girls were first drawn into sport by female physical education teachers at school. Generally, these sportswomen, who were more or less aware of the different treatment they received in comparison with sportsmen, belonged to families where sporting activities were already appreciated and practised.

On the occasion of the most important sporting events, such as those openly linked to the Fascist image and propaganda, things were organised better. Not only did physical education teachers and amateur trainers look out for talented girls, but also influential members of the national sporting federations visited provincial cities to recruit them, as both Borghetti and Serafini mention. Nevertheless, female athletes were initially selected at school by their teachers, who were generally good at traditional and rhythmic gymnastics but did not know much about sport. It was, after all, only between 1932 and 1943 that young women were properly trained in the teaching of sporting activities at the *Accademia Nazionale Femminile di Educazione Fisica* in Orvieto. Other female teachers of physical education had been trained, if at all, at the old-fashioned institutions that had been abolished in 1927, or had attended summer courses in later years.

As a consequence male coaches, whether professional or amateur, tended to take charge of the training of girls for sporting activities and subsequent contests. These male coaches seem to have worked enthusiastically to promote the 'athleticisation' of the girls who were most likely to become sports-women, as the gratitude expressed above by Del Sordo, Serafini and Sisa sufficiently indicates. Being keen on sport in general, these coaches did not discriminate on grounds of gender but, on the contrary, surmounted the narrow-minded attitudes inculcated in most male Italians, who considered sport a man's affair.

On the other hand, various aspects of the lives of the athletes interviewed here constituted exceptions to the generally quiet and even pattern of provincial women's lives, even before they were selected and trained. As Serafini suggests, in general the parents of schoolgirls discouraged them from getting involved in sport, believing that young women should stay at home, under the physical and moral control of their families. Even the more open-minded families of the women interviewed here were not so very permissive, given that, for example, they prohibited their daughters from playing sport at higher levels, as in the cases of Borghetti and Serafini. Most girls were not fond of sport anyway, regarding it as tiring and much too 'masculine'. Some of the women interviewed, such as Badioli and Serafini, indicate that they took up sport to imitate their brothers and/or fathers, but in addition it is striking that Serafini also considered herself different from her schoolfriends because she and her parents had lived abroad, while Sisa mentions that she was 'tomboyish'.

Del Sordo, Badioli and Serafini also complain about the technical problems arising from being compelled to wear heavy, old-fashioned sportswear for the sake of 'morality', as well as people's harsh criticisms of female athletes and their bare legs. Even Ondina Valla, the most famous woman athlete of the Fascist era, who enjoyed unprecedented success at the highest level and frequently went abroad on her own, had to maintain an appearance of blame-less behaviour in Italy by following the strict unwritten norms prescribed for daughters. Well into the second half of the twentieth century Italian women were secluded in the home at night, again for the sake of 'morality'. They were not allowed to go out after sunset, unless escorted by a male relative, especially in the more rural provinces of northern and central Italy, and of course in the south. A woman who was outside her home at night, whether on her own or with friends, was generally assumed to be dangerously easy-going, and possibly a prostitute.

12

Women's emancipation through sport under Fascism and after

The previous chapters have shown that the Fascist era saw significant changes in policies and attitudes relating to women and sport. To begin with, the 1920s saw battles for female emancipation and greater participation by women in sporting activities. The new social status achieved by working women during the First World War, together with the ideological embrace of 'modernity' by the Futurists and the early Fascists, helped some women to resist bourgeois traditionalism and Catholic misogyny, and a few of them opened up some space for themselves within the sporting world.

However, in the 1930s the Fascist regime turned to emphasising the most traditional 'womanly' values once again, partly to placate the Church and partly in pursuit of its own unsuccessful 'demographic policy', and the question was raised as to whether women should engage in competitive sport at all. The model of sportswomen in democratic countries, such as the United States or the countries of northwestern Europe, was considered too 'virile', and therefore incompatible both with traditional 'Latin' femininity and with the 'Fascist style' being consolidated in these years. A new, more austere model, the 'true woman', was promoted by the regime, which also reinforced the age-old assocation of women with maternity and domesticity. Each shift in policy was expressed through concrete efforts involving schools, universities, youth organisations and spare-time clubs for working people.

Nevertheless, a number of young girls, having been trained in physical activities within the regime's own institutions, started to compete at a higher level, supported by former female athletes of the 1920s, who had gone on to become managers and trainers in sporting federations, as well as by specialist teachers trained at the *Accademia Nazionale Femminile di Educazione Fisica* in *Orvieto* and, not to be overlooked, some professional male coaches. These sportswomen, who formed a small minority, could not be accused of seriously challenging any of the models of femininity ambivalently and inconsistently developed by the Fascist regime. Indeed, they attracted the regime's interest, as offering further chances to display to the world the image of Italy as a nation that, for all that it paid due respect to tradition, was truly modern and capable of competing with the best of its neighbours. In this context, while Mussolini incarnated the Italian sportsman, the main inspirational icon for women was the athlete Ondina Valla, the first Italian woman to become an Olympic gold medallist, although other exemplary sportswomen were admired as well. Sportswomen in particular, along with a larger minority of ordinary girls and young women, made significant progress, partly because from 1937 the *Gioventù Italiana del Littorio* (GIL) mobilised young people in an extensive programme of physical education, sporting activities and popular displays, intended to improve the Italian 'race', prepare the population for a glorious future and give these goals the widest possible visibility. Of course, as we have seen, there was a considerable gap between the GIL's plans and the realities of inadequate funding and facilities, which its massaging of statistics could not entirely conceal. Yet some of the progress made was real and had lasting effects.

Then, at the start of the 1940s, when the Second World War was consuming Italian men and resources at an alarming rate, women's sporting activities and public displays increased even further, together with their involvement in paid work and, to a strictly limited extent, in politics. Sport came to be seen as a way to strengthen women's combativeness, helping them to support the men at the front and to cope with sacrifices at home. Women's sporting displays and achievements may even have helped to distract the country from its vital problems and sorrows, even as it became clear that the future, which was to have been glorious, was frighteningly uncertain.

In reviewing the issues concerning female bodies, sport and Italian fascism, we may pose two important questions. First, did physical and sporting activity really increase among Italian women during the Fascist era? Second, did the consciousness of possessing an athletic body, well-trained within Fascist organisations, really promote the emancipation of at least some Italian women, in spite of the masculine hegemony of the time? The answers to both questions cannot but be positive. There was, of course, some mystification in the data on women's sports compiled by the regime, and the 'outer' emancipation achieved even by a small minority of women through sport was certainly not an intended result of the Fascist politics of the body. However, sportswomen and, more broadly, women involved in Fascist organisations, did experience social activities that drew them away from traditionally strict family protection, and threw themselves into a modern, dynamic way of life alongside men, although strictly in subordinate positions.

Yet if one asks whether women's achievements in Fascist Italy, which even brought a few women to the point of engaging in combat in the civil war of 1943–45, contributed to easing the way for women's emancipation after the Second World War, the answer would be doubtful. The successful engagement of women in the anti-Fascist resistance, the deprivations and sacrifices that most women suffered, and especially the diffuse sense of the need to modernise the country, combined to convince most Italians that women had the right to become all-round citizens. Soon after the dramatic defeat of Fascism and for the first time in the history of the country, 12,998,131 women used their votes, taking part in the referendum in 1946 that abolished the monarchy and established the Italian Republic. At the same time they joined in voting for a constituent assembly, which promulgated the current Constitution in 1948. This basic law does not discriminate on the grounds of gender. Thus, Article 3 states that: 'All citizens possess an equal social status and are equal before the law, without distinction as to sex …'. According to Article 37: 'Working women shall be entitled to equal rights and, for comparable jobs, equal pay with men.' Article 48 lays down that: 'All citizens, men or women, who have attained their majority shall be entitled to vote.' To take one more example, Article 51 states that: 'All citizens of either sex shall be eligible for public office and for elective positions on conditions of equality, according to the rules established by law.'

However, these and other constitutional provisions for gender equality have not been fully applied in practice, either in the fields of politics and work, or in the sporting world. Apart from the sheer weight of patriarchal and rural culture in a country that was not extensively industrialised until relatively recently, the biggest obstacles to women's emancipation were put up by women themselves. Their self-awareness was strongly affected by traditions that considered women to be inferior creatures capable only of being either sexually promiscuous 'demons' or docile domesticated 'angels'. In general Italian women have found sufficient willpower and courage to oppose male hegemony only when they have had to replace men in the emergency conditions of the First and Second World Wars. At other times they have permitted the patriarchal tradition to hamper their own progress and achievements. Their emancipation started very late, partly because of the events of 1968, when Italy felt the shock of the worldwide upheaval among the young.

In the early post-war period physical education and sport, having become associated with the hated Fascist regime, were again looked upon with suspicion, while teachers of physical education and sport, many of them typical 'children of Fascism', lost their privileged positions and found it hard to be accepted in society. The Ministry of Education resumed control of physical education in schools, but women's participation in competitive sports improved only very slowly, in line with the slow pace of their entry into workplaces and other institutions.[1] During the Fascist era many women had learned that they owned their bodies, and were strong enough to enjoy movement and to compete as men did, but they had lost the capacity to fight against the traditionalist vision of what a woman should be. From the second half of the 1940s onwards physical education at school, which remained compulsory, was strictly separated by gender. Only female teachers could give classes to girls, and those classes had to follow programmes laid down specially for them. These programmes were still influenced by the long-standing emphasis on basic, applied and rhythmic gymnastics for the sake of health, and sport had less room to develop than it had had in the later years of the Fascist era. It was only in 1990 that the physical education programmes for high schools were unified and mixed classes began to be taught by physical education teachers of either sex.

In theory, competitive sports were still open to women, but their recruitment was obstructed by a number of prejudices, as before.[2] In the late 1940s and the 1950s a few women were regularly involved in sporting activities and competed internationally, notably the athletes Amalia Piccinini and Edera Cordiale, who won silver medals at the London Olympics in 1948; the skier Giuliana Minuzzo, who won a bronze at the Winter Olympics in Oslo in 1952; and the fencer Irene Camber, who won gold at the Helsinki Olympics in the same year. However, these sportswomen belonged to the elite that had been trained for competition under Fascism. In 1959 only 0.5 per cent of female amateurs practised some motor activity and only 9.3 per cent of the people involved in sporting competitions were women.[3]

Finally, in the 1970s the international feminist movement began to change the mentalities of Italian women. Being more aware of their rights and reassured about their identities, Italian women finally started the difficult and still continuing process of emancipation, involving sport as well as other areas of life. A whole new story needs to be written on this process.

Notes

Preface

1. Mattazzi, G. (ed.), *Benito Mussolini. Breviario* (Milan, 1977), p. 138.
2. On Antonio Gramsci and his political philosophy see, for example, Caprioglio, S., and Funi, E., *Antonio Gramsci. Lettere dal carcere* (Turin, 1968); Salinari, C., and Spinella, M., *Il pensiero di Gramsci* (Rome, 1975); or Consiglio, F., and Frosini, F. (eds), *Antonio Gramsci. Filosofia e politica. Antologia dei 'Quaderni del carcere'* (Florence, 1997).
3. De Grazia, V., *Le donne nel regime Fascista*, Venice, 1993, pp. 285–95.
4. See De Felice, R., *Mussolini il rivoluzionario 1883–1920; Mussolini Il Fascista 1921–1929; Mussolini il duce 1929–1939;* and *Mussolini l'alleato 1940–1945* (Turin, 1965–90, reprinted 1996). See also De Felice, R., *Storia degli ebrei italiani sotto il Fascismo* (Turin, 1972); *Il problema dell'Alto Adige nei rapporti italo–tedeschi dall'Anschluss alla fine della seconda guerra mondiale* (Bologna, 1973); *Le interpretazioni del Fascismo* (Rome–Bari, 1995); and *Il Fascismo. Le interpretazioni dei contemporanei e degli storici* (Rome–Bari, 1998); as well as Leeden, M. A. (ed.), *De Felice. Intervista sul Fascismo* (Bari, 1977), and Chessa, P. (ed.), *Renzo De Felice. Rosso e nero* (Milan, 1995).

Chapter 1

1. It is sometimes claimed that the Russian revolution of October/November 1917 also led to the establishment of a 'secular religion'. However, its activists professed very different ideas, including, as E. Gentile has pointed out, 'atheistic materialism and anti-religious scientism, [and] the myth of internationalism'; and the regime it created 'proceeded with much less concern for the institution of a collective cult'. See Gentile, E., *Il culto del littorio. La sacralizzazione della politica nell'Italia Fascista* (Rome–Bari, 1993), p. 310. On early Fascists see, for instance, Alatri, P., *Le origini del Fascismo* (Rome, 1962); De Felice, R., *Mussolini il rivoluzionario* (Turin, 1965); Salvemini, G., *La nascita del Fascismo* (Milan, 1972); Gentile, E., *Le origini dell'ideologia Fascista* (Rome–Bari, 1975); Vivarelli, R., *Storia delle origini del Fascismo*, vol. I (Bologna, 1991); Sternhell, Z., *Nascita dell'ideologia Fascista* (Milan, 1993); Payne, S.G., *A History of Fascism, 1914–45* (London, 1995).
2. Guerri, G.B., *Fascisti. Gli italiani di Mussolini. Il regime degli italiani* (Milan, 1995), pp. 216–25.
3. Probably of Etruscan origin, the *fascis* symbolised power in ancient Rome and was carried by selected soldiers, the lictors, who served as escorts for the state's leading authorities.
4. The *Fasci di Azione Rivoluzionaria* had been founded in order to campaign for Italy to abandon the neutrality proclaimed in 1914 and enter the war, which it did in 1915.
5. The symbol of the *fascis* had returned to favour, with some variations on the ancient Roman model, during the Renaissance, at the time of the French Revolution and also during the Italian *Risorgimento* in the nineteenth century. It was its Renaissance variation that became the first symbol of the Fascist Party, while the Roman *lictorius fascis* was officially used from 1923. Following studies conducted by the archaeologist and politician Giacomo Boni, the *lictorius fascis* was adopted to reaffirm the Roman roots of the *Stirpe Italica* ('Italic Descent') and to remove any reference to ideas expressed in the intervening centuries. See Falchi, L., 'Le origini del Fascio littorio', in *Il Giornale di Roma* (12 April 1923), and Gentile, *Il culto del littorio*, pp. 84–90.

6. The *arditi* were special assault troops who had distinguished themselves during war by their bellicose spirit. The irredentists aimed at incorporating the city of Fiume and the region of Dalmatia into the fatherland. The Futurists were followers of the modernist cultural movement founded by Marinetti. The *Dannunziani* were followers of the poet D'Annunzio.

7. Giuseppe Mazzini's political mysticism was based on a coupling of God and People, in which the People were seen as a community of believers in the religious cult of the Fatherland. Besides promoting the political and moral unity of all Italians, Mazzini hoped that Rome could become the centre of a future council of European nations harmoniously fraternising through the shared religious cult of their countries. Mazzini's ideology formed the basis for a series of Italian movements that opposed the monarchy and pressed for the foundation of the 'Third Italy'. See Gentile, E., *Il mito dello Stato nuovo dall'antigiolittismo al Fascismo* (Rome–Bari, 1982), pp. 3–28, and Gentile, *Il culto del littorio* , pp. 7–12. On Mazzini's politics see Grandi, T., and Comba, A. (eds), *Scritti politici* (Turin, 1972).

8. In 1878 the Minister of Education, Francesco De Sanctis, introduced educational gymnastics in schools, with the purpose of educating the willpower of the citizens – future soldiers of the fatherland – through the training of their bodies. See Gori, G., *Educazione fisica, sport e giornalismo in Italia. Dall'unità alla prima olimpiade dell'era moderna* (Bologna, 1989), pp. 71–89. The army, which was expected to represent and defend the 'religion of the country', had the task of teaching soldiers a sense of 'national unity' and helping them to spread it to their families. See Conti, G., 'Il mito della "nazione armata"', in *Storia contemporanea* (December 1990), pp. 1149–95.

9. The year 1861, in which the Kingdom of Italy was established, saw the beginning of a kind of ethical war between the Church and the new state. In that year the Pope, Pius IX, declared his opposition to the secularism of the Italian state, which accepted 'infidels' in schools and in public offices. See Guerri, *Fascisti*, p. 6.

10. Enrico Corradini exalted the war as the occasion of the forging of heroes as the collective 'living soul of the fatherland', whose cult could form part of the celebration of the divinity of the nation. See Corradini, E., 'Una nazione', in *Il Regno* (19 June 1904). On Corradini, see also Filippi, F., *Una vita pagana. Enrico Corradini dal superomismo dannunziano a una politica di massa* (Florence, 1989).

11. See the *Foundation and Manifesto of Futurism*, as first published in *Le Figaro* of 20 February 1909. On Futurism in general see De Maria, L. (ed.), *F.T. Marinetti. Teoria e invenzione futurista* (Milan, 1990); De Felice, R. (ed.), *Futurismo, cultura e politica* (Turin, 1988).

12. On the 'sporting' enterprises of D'Annunzio, see Impiglia, M., 'Lo scudetto e il vate', in *Lo sport italiano*, 1 (1998), pp. 60–63.

13. In September 1919 D'Annunzio, leading a group of ex-servicemen – among whom there were also government officials and soldiers of the Italian army – occupied the town of Fiume in Dalmatia by means of a *coup de main*.

14. The Regency of Carnaro, a small nationalistic and revolutionary state, gave itself a constitution proclaiming the creation of a new society centred on joint representation of employers and workers. In the following year Giolitti's government negotiated a settlement with Yugoslavia, renouncing Dalmatia – with the exception of the city of Zara – and declaring Fiume an independent city state. D'Annunzio and his followers had to surrender and leave Fiume. On 27 April 1920 copies of an announcement were scattered by D'Annunzio's aviators in the sky above the main cities of Italy. The announcement declared that:

> Through the spontaneous consent of all spirits aiming at freedom, of all peoples torn by injustice and oppression, defeated and disappointed, the League of Fiume has been formed. It lifts its flag and launches its revolt against the League of Nations, a conspiracy of robbers and privileged cheats.

15. On the complex relationship between Mussolini and D'Annunzio between 1921 and 1925, see Valeri, N., *D'Annunzio davanti al Fascismo* (Florence, 1963); De Felice, R., and Mariano, E., *Carteggio D'Annunzio–Mussolini (1919–1938)* (Milan, 1971). On D'Annunzio's politics in general, see De Felice, R., *D'Annunzio politico 1918–1938* (Rome–Bari, 1978).

16. See Guerri, *Fascisti*, p. 90. The aviator Italo Balbo, who had supported Mussolini from the beginning, was given prestigious posts under the Fascist regime. On Balbo see ibid., pp. 78–83 and Rochat, I., *Italo Balbo, Lo squadrista, l'aviatore, il gerarca* (Turin, 1986).

17. On the myth of the superman see Carrouges, M., *La mystique du surhomme* (Paris, 1948); Welte, B., 'Il superuomo di Nietzsche: ambigua doppiezza', in Renzo, G. (ed.), *Friedrich Nietzsche e il destino dell'uomo* (Cittanuova, 1982), pp. 23–41.

18. Papini, G., *Maschilità* (Florence, 1915), p. 41.

19. Guerri, *Fascisti*, p. 43.

20. Mosse, G.L., 'Futurismo e culture politiche in Europa: una prospettiva globale', in De Felice, R., *Futurismo*, p. 17.

21. Marinetti said: 'We exalt patriotism and militarism; we sing of war, as the only hygiene of the world, the haughty flame of enthusiasm and generosity, the noble bath of heroism.' See Hulten, P., *Futurismo e Futurismi* (Milan, 1986), p. 18.

22. These words are taken from a piece written by Marinetti in December 1915, entitled 'Orgoglio italiano' (Italian Pride). See De Maria, *F.T. Marinetti*, p. 503.

23. Futurism was exported to Russia, where it had particular success, and to many other European countries, including Germany, Britain, Spain, and Portugal, as well as to Japan and Mexico.

24. Mussolini was an admirer of Gustave Le Bon, a scholar of mass psychology, and frequently consulted his essays *Psycologie des foules* and *Psycologie des temps noveaux*. See Moscovici, S., *L'âge des foules. Un traité historique de psycologie des masses* (Paris, 1981), p. 93. The *Duce* said that he had discovered empirically that 'the tendency of modern men to believe is absolutely unbelievable': Guerri, *Fascisti*, p. 172. On Fascist mass psychology in general, see Reich, W., *Psicologia di massa del Fascismo* (Milan, 1982).

25. Mussolini replaced May Day, which was associated with the left, with a holiday on 21 April celebrating both the foundation of ancient Rome, and Italian production and work.

26. The celebration of 20 September, commemorating the victory of the Italian state over the Church in 1870, was abolished by Mussolini. He did not want to aggravate further the problems of coexistence between two different religions: the Fascist, new and nationalistic, and the Catholic, ancient and international, the latter having its Holy See in the very heart of the Italian capital.

27. On the 'sacralisation' of Fascist ideology, see Gentile, *Il culto littorio*, pp. 63–103.

28. Cantalupo, R., *La classe dirigente* (Milan, 1928), pp. 74–75.

29. Mussolini adopted D'Annunzio's style of oratory, couched in the form of questions and answers, as used on the occasion of the Fiume adventure. On the *Duce*'s use of language see Ardau, G., *L'eloquenza mussoliniana* (Milan, 1929); Daneo, G.C., *Benito Mussolini oratore* (Genoa, 1932); Bianchi, L., *Mussolini scrittore ed oratore* (Bologna, 1937); Ellwanger, H., *Sulla lingua di Mussolini* (Milan, 1939); Saracinelli, M., and Totti, N., *L'Italia del Duce. L'informazione, la scuola, il costume* (Rimini, 1983), pp. 157–73 and Canosa, R., *La voce del Duce* (Milan, 2002).

30. On the Fascist mystics see Betri, M.L., 'Tra politica e cultura. La scuola di mistica Fascista', in *Storia contemporanea*, 1–2 (1989), pp. 377–98.

31. On biographies of Mussolini, see Passerini, L., *Mussolini immaginario. Storia di una biografia 1915–1939* (Rome–Bari, 1991), pp. 153–234.

32. Manacorda, G., *Letteratura e cultura del periodo Fascista* (Milan, 1974), p. 241. On the *veline* for the press, see ibid., pp. 232–46. On Fascist censorship in general, see, for example, Lepre, A., *L'occhio del Duce. Gli italiani e la censura di guerra 1940–43* (Milan, 1992) and Franzinelli, M., and Marino, E.V., *Il Duce Proibito* (Milan, 2003).

33. Mosse, G.L., 'Estetica Fascista e società', in Del Boca, A., Legnani, A.M., and Rossi, M.G., (eds), *Il regime Fascista. Storia e storiografia* (Rome–Bari, 1995), p. 110. See also Casini, L., *La riscoperta del corpo* (Rome, 1990).

34. Mosse, *Il regime Fascista*, p. 111.

35. On the ONMI, see Fabbri, S., *L'Opera Nazionale per la protezione della Maternità e dell'Infanzia* (Milan, 1933); Fabbri, S., *L'assistenza della maternità e dell'infanzia in Italia* (Naples, 1933); Lo Monaco-Aprile, A., *La protezione della maternità e dell'infanzia* (Rome, 1934).

36. Ferretti, L., *Il libro dello sport* (Rome–Milan), 1928, p. 189.

37. The total numbers enrolled in schools and universities doubled between 1923 and 1936. See Guerri, *Fascisti*, pp. 156–57.
38. Ibid., pp. 198–99.
39. Ibid., p. 178. On the OND, see Tannenbaum, E.R., *L'esperienza Fascista. Cultura e società in Italia dal 1922 al 1945* (Milan, 1974); De Grazia, V., *Consenso e cultura di massa nell'Italia Fascista* (Rome–Bari, 1981).
40. The popular games promoted by the OND were *bocce* (a kind of bowling), *tamburello* (the 'little drum game'), elastic-ball games, rope-pulling, volleyball, rowing, the *sfratto* ball game and chess. See Stefanelli, R., *Dopolavoro. Norme pratiche per i dirigenti* (Turin, 1940), pp. 75–90.
41. Marinetti expressed his sympathies with Italian students of physical culture by declaring that Futurism was 'the cult of progress and speed, of sport, physical strength, rash courage, heroism and danger, against the obsession with culture, classical studies, museums, literature and ruins.' Cited by De Maria, *F.T. Marinetti*, pp. 328–40.
42. Ibid., p. 370.
43. Ibid., pp. 340 and 372.
44. Marinetti, F.T., 'Alcune parti del film "Vita futurista", punto IV', in *L'Italia futurista*, 8 (1916).
45. These facilities included the monumental Littoriale in Bologna (1926), the Berta Stadium in Florence (1929), the Stadium of Marble in Rome (1932), the Mussolini Stadium in Turin (1933), the Vigorelli Velodrome in Milan (1933) and the Stadium of Victory in Bari (1934).
46. In 1928 a model *Littorio* sport track was standardised on the basis of a project by D'Albora. A track had to be built in every commune in Italy with the financial support of the state. By 1930 there were 3,280 tracks, mainly in the North of Italy. See Fabrizio, F., *Sport e Fascismo. La politica sportiva del regime 1924–1936* (Rimini–Florence, 1976), pp. 22–24.
47. These were, respectively, the Accademia Nazionale di Educazione Fisica in Rome, founded in 1928, and the Accademia Nazionale di Educazione Fisica in Orvieto, founded in 1932.
48. Comparative statistics for the years 1928–1935 (ONB), in *Lo sport Fascista*, 4 (1936), p. 10. See also Ferrara, P., *L'Italia in palestra. Storia, documenti e immagini della ginnastica dal 1833 al 1973* (Rome, 1992), p. 241.
49. In 1924 the *Federazione delle Associazioni Sportive Cattoliche* (FASCI) closed down, apparently spontaneously, and in 1927 the YMCA and the *Giovani Esploratori* (Boy Scouts) were suppressed by the authorities. Some gymnastics sections of Catholic Youth lasted until 1931, although they had to operate under numerous restrictions. See Fabrizio, F., *Storia dello sport in Italia. Dalle società ginnastiche all'associazionismo di massa* (Rimini–Florence, 1977), pp. 104–12; Ferrara, P., *L'Italia in palestra*, pp. 234–37.
50. Fabrizio, *Storia dello sport*, pp. 113–120.
51. Fabrizio, *Sport e Fascismo*, pp. 39–42.
52. On the Olympic Games of 1936, see Gori, G., 'Italy: Mussolini's Boys at Hitler's Olympics,' in Krüger, A., and Murray, W. (eds), *The Nazi Olympics. Sport, Politics and Appeasement in the 1930s* (Urbana and Chicago, 2003), pp. 113–26.
53. Among the most famous sportsmen we may mention Carnera, Bindi, Guerra, Bartali, De Pinedo, Balbo and Nuvolari.
54. Two sets of prizes, the Medaglie al Valore Atletico (Medals for Athletic Valour) and the Stelle al Merito Sportivo (Stars for Sporting Merit), were instituted in 1933. Made of gold, silver and bronze, they were awarded, respectively, to athletes and to the leaders of the sporting federations to mark victories in international and national competitions. See PNF, *Foglio d'Ordini n. 117* (20 December 1933).
55. Cited by Vaccaro, G., 'Giorgio Vaccaro illustra i modi e i fini dello sport Fascista', in *Lo sport Fascista*, 5 (1935), p. 11.
56. Banti, A., 'L'importanza dello spettacolo sportivo', in *Lo sport Fascista*, I (1936), p. 31.
57. In the 1920s the myth of Mussolini 'the great seducer' was only emphasised as a matter of potential, being in contrast with the *Duce*'s 'austerity'. In the 1930s, however, it came increasingly to be accepted as compatible with the Latin male stereotype of the good husband and good father. 'Virile' Fascist men were allowed to adopt the dictum 'many women, much honour'. See Passerini, *Mussolini immaginario*, pp. 35–36.

58. Gobetti, P., *Rivoluzione liberale*, 9 (1924), p. 34.
59. According to Mussolini, boxing was 'an exquisitely Fascist means of self-expression'. See Mack Smith, D., *Mussolini* (Milan, 1981), p. 149.
60. '[He is the] dominator and multiplier of the titanic energies of his athletic body, using methodology, enthusiasm and discipline at any and every hour of the day. [He is] the virile and generous person-ification of triumphant Italian sport.' See Ferretti, L., 'Mussolini, primo sportivo d'Italia', in *Lo sport Fascista*, 1 (1933), 3. See also Dall'Ongaro, C., *Mussolini e lo sport*, Mantova, 1928; Cotronei, A., 'Cesare gladiatore', in *Il Popolo d'Italia* (28 October 1934); Fabrizio, *Sport e Fascismo*, pp. 114–19.
61. Papa, A., and Panico, G., *Storia sociale del calcio in Italia. Dai club dei pionieri alla nazione sportiva 1887–1945* (Bologna, 1983), p. 135.
62. Mack-Smith, D., 'Vincere, vincere, vincere', in *FMR*, 26 (1984), p. 112.
63. Hoberman, J.M., *Politica e sport. Il corpo nelle ideologie politiche dell'800 e del 900* (Bologna, 1988), p. 137.
64. Preti, L., *Giovinezza, giovinezza* (Milan, 1972), pp. 109–10.
65. On the arts during the Fascist era, see Sapori, F., *L'arte e il Duce* (Milan, 1932). Among recent studies, see Manacorda, *Letteratura e cultura*; A.A. V.V., *Anni Trenta. Arte e cultura in Italia* (Milan, 1982); Alfassio-Grimaldi, U., and Addis-Saba, M., *Cultura a passo romano. Storia e strategie dei littoriali della cultura e dell'arte* (Milan, 1983); Masi, A., *Un'arte per lo Stato* (Naples, 1992); Brunetti, F., *Architetti e Fascismo* (Florence, 1993); Biondi, M., and Borsotti, A. (eds), *Cultura e Fascismo. Letteratura arti spettacolo di un Ventennio* (Florence, 1996) and Falasca-Zamponi, S., *Lo spettacolo del Fascismo* (Soveria Mannelli, 2003)).
66. Giovanni Gentile, with his idealism, his religious background and his conception of the 'Ethical State', was the philosopher of early Fascism, but in the 1930s his star progressively declined.
67. The liberal Benedetto Croce was the editor of the magazine *La Critica,* which became the rallying point for those who believed in freedom.
68. One of the most eminent Italian intellectuals of our time, Norberto Bobbio, has substantially modified the idea that Italian culture was blindly enslaved to the regime: 'Whoever looks today at the cultural panorama of those years, ... above all at literary, historical and philosophical culture ... finds it hard to realise that in Italy there had been such an earthquake that Fascism had been, or was said to be.' See Guerri, *Fascisti*, p. 154.
69. Mosse, G.L., *Il Fascismo. Verso una teoria generale* (Rome–Bari, 1996), p. 65.
70. Passerini, *Mussolini immaginario*, p. 166.
71. Malaparte, C., 'Cantata dell'ArciMussolini', in *L'Italiano*, 7–9 (1927).
72. De Maria, *F.T. Marinetti*, p. 575.
73. Manacorda, *Letteratura e cultura*, pp. 160–61.
74. 'There are thousands of portraits of the *Duce*. They will reach fabulous numbers, they will not be countable anymore.' See Sapori, *L'arte e il Duce*, p. 135.
75. A collection of portraits appears in Malvano, L., *Fascismo e politica dell'immagine* (Turin, 1988).
76. Bianchi, C., 'Il nudo eroico del Fascismo', in Bertelli, S., and Grottarelli, C. (eds), *Gli occhi di Alessandro. Potere sovrano e sacralità del corpo da Alessandro Magno a Ceausescu* (Florence, 1990), p. 162.
77. De Maria, *F.T. Marinetti*, p. 340.
78. Sironi, M., 'Manifesto della pittura murale', in *Colonna*, I (1933), p. 10.
79. Armellini, G., *Le immagini del Fascismo nelle arti figurative* (Milan, 1980), p. 165. On the Cremona Prize, which was started in 1939 thanks to an initiative by Farinacci, see ibid., pp. 175–76.
80. For example, Albino Manca carved a bust of Mussolini dressed as a Roman emperor; the painter Emilio Florio represented him completely naked, as a kind of Roman she-wolf, with the twins Romulus and Remus at his feet; and Publio Morbiducci's relief *La storia di Roma attraverso le opere edilizie* was intended as a counterpart of Trajan's Column, presenting Mussolini as a military commander hieratically erect on the stirrups of his horse.
81. For example, Giuseppe Graziosi portrayed the *Duce* in an equestrian statue that recalls both Donatello's *Gattamelata* and Verrocchio's *Colleoni*.

82. The subject of the *Duce* riding a horse, with his cloak lifted by the wind, appeared in a painting by Primo Conti and a sculpture by Cleto Tomba. Both artists imitated David's portrait of Napoleon I crossing the Alps.

83. In Montreal Mussolini was portrayed as a kind of saint in an ingenuously blasphemous fresco, on the apse of the Church of the Madonna della Difesa, painted by Guido Nincheri, who entitled it *Mussolini circondato dai Quadrumviri, dal Duca degli Abruzzi e da Marconi.*

84. The Futurist Ferruccio Vecchi, in his sculpture *L'Impero balza dalla testa del Duce*, represented Mussolini's head as giving birth to the Empire, which was sculpted as a strong, virile and athletically naked figure with the *Duce*'s features. Not only in the figurative arts but also in literature Mussolini's image was compared to mythological heroes and the most famous heroes of the past. See, for example, Ferrara, M., *Machiavelli, Nietzsche, Mussolini* (Paris, 1923); Gennaioli, G., *Mussolini e Napoleone I* (Sansepolcro, 1926); Duncan-Dalrymple, H. (*Son of Vulcano: Benito Mussolini. An Impersonation of the Superman* (Florence, n.d. [but before 1931]); Viganoni, G., *Mussolini e i Cesari* (Milan, 1933); Speciale, F., *Augusto fondatore dell'Impero romano. Il Duce fondatore dell'Impero italiano* (Treviso, 1937).

85. See Gentile, *Il culto del littorio* , pp. 213–35.

86. See Arbasino, A., 'Giovinezza giovinezza', in *FMR*, 26 (1984), pp. 96–98. On the Mussolini Forum, see Paniconi, M., 'Criteri informativi e dati sul Foro Mussolini', in *Architettura*, XII (1933); Del Debbio, E., 'Le arti figurative', in *Panorami di realizzazioni del Fascismo*, 7 (1938–42).

87. It was very soon decided to hide the penises of most of the statues by applying rudimentary fig leaves made of cement, in deference to the feelings of Catholics.

88. Cresti, C., 'Forum Beniti', in *FMR*, 26 (1984), p. 106.

89. Mack-Smith, 'Vincere', p. 118.

90. Catania, A., 'L. Freddi e il libro della solitudine', in Biondi and Borsotti, *Cultura e Fascismo*, p. 296.

91. On cinema and Fascism, see Gori, G.M., *Patria diva. La storia d'Italia nei film del ventennio* (Florence, 1988); Casadio, G.F., *Telefoni bianchi. Realtà e finzione nella società e nel cinema italiano degli anni Quaranta* (Manduria, 1991); Brunetta, G.P., *Storia del cinema italiano. Il cinema di regime, 1929–1945* (Rome, 1993); Freddi, L., *Il cinema. Il governo dell'immagine* (Rome, 1994).

92. Saracinelli and Totti, *L'Italia del Duce*, pp. 78–81.

93. Isnenghi, M., 'Il corpo del *Duce*', in Bertelli and Grottarelli, *Gli occhi di Alessandro*, p. 171.

94. Headlines in daily newspapers included, for example, 'Sulle orme del Fascismo, Hitler cancelliere del Reich guida al potere le giovani forze innovatrici delle Germania' (*Il Resto del Carlino*, 31 January 1933); and 'Hitler afferma che al glorioso esempio di Roma è dovuto il trionfo dell'idea nazionalisocialista' (*Il Popolo d'Italia*, 1 February 1933).

95. Krüger, A., 'Fasci e croci uncinate', in *Lancillotto e Nausica. Critica e storia dello sport*, I–II (1991), pp. 88–101.

96. Specifically, the Laws of 17 November 1938, 29 June 1939 and 13 May 1940.

97. The explanation included the following passage:

> The Fascist Grand Council ... reminds us that Fascism has been carrying out for ten years, and still carries out, a positive activity directed to the quantitative and qualitative improvement of the Italian race – improvement that could be heavily compromised ... by crossbreeding and degeneration. The Hebrew problem is only the metropolitan aspect of a problem of a more general character.

Mussolini affirmed that:

> The racial problem has not blown up suddenly ... Empires are conquered by weapons and they are kept by prestige ... We need a strict racial consciousness that states not only the differences, but also the very clear superiority.

See Del Boca, A., 'Le leggi razziali nell'impero di Mussolini', in Del Boca, Legnani and Rossi, *Il regime Fascista*, pp. 338–39.

98. In 1936 the Minister for the Colonies, Alessandro Lessona, issued detailed instructions forbidding any kind of fraternisation between the two races. In 1937 he summarised the Fascist racial policy as follows: '(a) clear and absolute separation between the two races; (b) collaboration without promiscuity; (c) humanity, reflecting past errors; (d) implacable severity in respect of future errors.' See ibid., pp. 336–37.

99. Mussolini's lovers included two Jewish women of great culture, Angela Balabanova and Margherita Sarfatti, who would clearly have been unacceptable partners for Hitler. See Chessa, P., *Renzo De Felice. Rosso e Nero* (Milan, 1995), p. 153. On this argument see also Spinosa, A., *Mussolini: razzista riluttante* (Rome, 1994).

100. Chessa, *Renzo De Felice*, pp. 156–57.

101. Racist announcements are cited in Manacorda, *Letteratura e cultura*, pp. 247–253. On Italian racism of the time see Muggiani, E., 'Razzismo: autarchia del pensiero', in *Il Popolo d'Italia* (21 August 1938); Orano, P., *Inchiesta sulla razza* (Rome, 1939); Tarchi, M., 'Julius Evola e il Fascismo: note su un percorso non ordinario', in Biondi and Borsotti, *Cultura e Fascismo*, pp. 123–42.

102. This substitution was made in the project for one of the sections, *Ortogenesi Fascista della Stirpe*, co-ordinated by Dr Pende, for the proposed E 42 Exhibition. See Malvano, *Fascismo e politica dell'immagine*, pp. 156 and 172.

103. Chessa, *Renzo De Felice*, pp. 149–163. On the treatment of Jews under Italian Fascism see De Felice, R., *Storia degli ebrei italiani sotto il Fascismo* (Turin, 1961).

104. Mosse, G.L., *Sessualità e Nazionalismo* (Rome–Bari, 1966), p. 199; Mosse, G.L., *The Image of Man: The Creation of Modern Masculinity* (New York, 1996).

105. Ferretti, *Il libro dello sport* , p. 217.

106. Armellini, *Le immagini del Fascismo*, pp. 159–76.

107. Silva, U., *Ideologia e arte del Fascismo* (Milan, 1973), p. 68.

108. Pivato, S., 'Sport et rapports internationaux. Le cas du Fascisme italien', in Arnaud, P., and Wahl, A. (eds), *Sports et relations internationales* (Metz, 1994), pp. 64–72.

109. Hoberman, *Politica e sport*, p. 146. On mutual influences between the fascist regimes of Italy, Germany and Spain, see Krüger, A., 'Strength through Joy: The Culture of Consent under Fascism, Nazism and Francoism',. in Riordan, J., and Krüger, A. (eds), *The International Politics of Sport in the Twentieth Century* (London, 1999), pp. 67–99.

Chapter 2

1. Obermann, who was a citizen of Switzerland, based his methodology on the schemes developed by the German *Turnen* movement and on Spiess's pedagogical gymnastics.

2. Enlightenment ideals also inspired Italian intellectuals. Under the influence of Locke and Rousseau, some of them considered bodily culture as an essential part of education. Gaetano Filangieri, for example, wrote about physical culture in Chapter IV, 'Delle leggi che riguardano l'Educazione, i Costumi, e l'Istruzione Pubblica', of his *Scienza della legislazione* (Milan, 1786), while Antonio Genovesi, in his essay *Lezioni di commercio, o sia d'economia civile* (Bassano, 1788) recommended that educationists pay close attention to Jacques Ballexerd's *Dissertazione sull' educazione fisica de' fanciulli* (Naples, 1763).

3. On the history of the Italian Gymnastics Federation see Ballerini, F., *La Federazione ginnastica italiana e le sue origini* (Rome, 1931); Riva, A. (ed.), *Cento anni di vita della Federazione Ginnastica d'Italia* (Rome, 1969); Ferrara, P., *L'Italia in palestra. Storia, documenti e immagini della ginnastica dal 1833 al 1973* (Rome, 1992); Gori, G., *L'atleta e la nazione. Saggi di storia dello sport* (Rimini, 1996).

4. Specialised national sports federations were founded as follows: the *Unione delle Società Veliche Italiane* (sailing) in 1879; the *Unione Velocipedistica Italiana* (cycling) in 1885; the *Federazione Italiana Canottaggio* (rowing) in 1888; the *Federazione Italiana Tennis* in 1895; the *Federazione Italiana Gioco Calcio* (football) in 1898; and the *Unione Pedestre Italiana* (running) in 1899. The Genoa Cricket and Football Society, the first Italian football association, had been founded in 1893 by British residents of Genoa.

5. On the game *pallone al bracciale* see Pivato, S., *I terzini della borghesia. Il gioco del pallone nell'Italia dell'Ottocento* (Milan, 1990).

6. See Gori, G., 'Sports Festivals in Italy between the 19th and 20th Centuries: A Kind of National Olympic Games?', in Naul, R. (ed.), *Contemporary Studies in the National Olympic Games Movement*, Vol. 2 (Frankfurt am Main, 1997), pp. 19–52.

7. See the introduction to the well-documented volume by Bonetta, G., *Corpo e nazione. L'educazione ginnastica, igienica e sessuale nell'Italia liberale* (Milan, 1990), pp. 11–69.

8. These laws included Casat's Law of 1859 and De Sanctis's Law of 1878, both discussed below.

9. This shift towards militarism culminated in the occupation of Libya in 1912.

10. Pope Leo XIII reinforced these views with his encyclical *Arcanum* (1880), in which maternity and the role of women within the family are exalted.

11. Article 134 of the Pisanelli Code.

12. On the Italian feminist movement in general see Pieroni-Bortolotti, F., *Alle origini del movimento femminile in Italia, 1848–1892* (Turin, 1963).

13. Eugenio Young not only propagated the practice of gymnastics within the military College of Milan, which he headed, but also published both translations and original texts on gymnastics, inspired by the ideas of Clias, Guts Muths and Amoros y Odeana.

14. See Sancipriano, M., and Macchietti, S.S. (eds), *F. Aporti, Scritti pedagogici e lettere* (Brescia, 1976).

15. Obermann, R., 'Della ginnastica. VII. Dei Ginnasticanti', in *Letture di famiglia*, 26 (1845), pp. 207–08.

16. See Di Ferdinando, D., 'Contro le bugie del cosmetico. Alle origini della ginnastica femminile', in *Lancillotto e Nausica. Critica e storia dello sport*, 7 (1990), p. 42.

17. Ceci, G., *Reali educandati femminili in Napoli* (Naples, 1900), pp. 96–97. See also Article 12 of the 'Statuto dei Reali educandati femminili,' in *Gazzetta Ufficiale* (4 December 1861).

18. 'Statistica delle scuole di ginnastica del Regno d'Italia. Anno 1863–64', in *Monografia della società ginnastica di Torino e Statistica generale delle scuole di ginnastica in Italia* (Turin, 1873), pp. 60–61.

19. Gallo, P., *VI Relazione annua per Pietro Gallo direttore della ginnastica* (Venice, 1872), p. 6.

20. Ferrara, *L'Italia in palestra*, p. 59.

21. Baumann, E., *Progetto di una Scuola magistrale di Ginnastica compilato dal direttore della palestra Dott. cav. Emilio Baumann, Bologna, 1877*, in ACS, Ministero della Pubblica Istruzione, Segreteria Affari Generali, *Ginnastica*, b 50.

22. Anonymous, *Lettera del Segretario Generale ai provveditori agli studi, ai sindaci e agli Ispettori Scolastici del Regno in data 9-6-1884*, in ACS, Ministero della Pubblica Istruzione, Segreteria Affari Generali, *Ginnastica*, b 3.

23. See Gori, G., *Educazione fisica, sport e giornalismo in Italia. Dall'unità alla prima olimpiade dell'era moderna* (Bologna, 1989), pp. 73–99.

24. Cammarota, G., *Lettera del R. Provveditore agli studi di Firenze al ministro della Pubblica Istruzione, 2 Aprile 1879*, in ACS, Ministero della Pubblica Istruzione, Segreteria Affari Generali, *Ginnastica*, b 50.

25. See Gallo, P., *Discorso pronunciato dal direttore della Ginnastica Pietro Gallo in occasione del saggio dato dagli alunni delle scuole comunali il 13.7.1871* (Venice, 1871), p. 4.

26. Valletti, F., 'La ginnastica come mezzo di educazione civile e militare negli stati d'Europa', in *Bollettino ufficiale del Ministero dell'Istruzione* (6 July 1887), p. 47.

27. *Il Ginnasiarca*, 3 (1887), p. 20. From 1878 onwards a number of letters denouncing the discrimination that gymnastics teachers had to face – evidenced by their relatively low wages and status – were sent to the Ministry of Education. See Ferrara, *L'Italia in palestra*, pp. 134–39.

28. De Amicis, E., 'Non si sgomentino le signore ...', in Ferraro-Bertolotto, M. C., *Prospettiva storica dell'educazione fisica nel trentennio successivo all'unità* (Genoa, 1984), pp. 91–135.

29. De Amicis, E., *Amore e ginnastica* (Turin, 1971), p. 88. See also Salina-Borello, R., 'Raccontare lo sport', in Di Donna-Prencipe, C. (ed.), *Letteratura e sport* (Bologna, 1986), pp. 69–73.

30. ISTAT (ed.), *Sommario di statistiche storiche dell'Italia. 1861–1985* (Rome, 1987).

31. Mosso, A., 'La riforma della ginnastica', in *Nuova Antologia* (1892), p. 263; Mosso, A., *L'educazione fisica della gioventù* (Milan, 1894), pp. 76–77.

32. See Mosso, A., *L'educazione fisica della donna* (Milan, 1892). In 1892, during a meeting organised in Rome by the Female Society of Education, Mosso stated that female gymnastics with apparatus was not practised sufficiently because most young women regarded it as a practice suitable only for little girls. See De Giorgio, M., *Le italiane dall'Unità a oggi. Modelli culturali e comportamenti sociali* (Rome–Bari), 1993, pp. 242–43. On Mosso's activity, see also Gori, G., 'The apostle of Italian Sport: Angelo Mosso and English athleticism in Italy' in Mangan, J.A. (ed.), *Reformers, Sport, Modernizers Middle-Class Revolutionaries* (London and Portland, OR, 2002) pp. 230–52.

33. Gamba, A., 'La riforma della ginnastica. Note ed osservazioni', in *Gazzetta medica*, 30 (1892), p. 400.

34. These programmes were prepared by a commission led by the most important Italian scholars of the time, including Mosso, Baumann, Gamba and Abbondati from Naples.

35. In 1893 it was reported that 'the commission traced back the Italian traditions still in use in various villages, and collected and briefly described typical Italian games that it proposed for the new programmes of physical education. Primary school teachers were given the capacity to add any other games that may have been in use in different regions.' The report has been republished in Gori, *Educazione fisica*, pp. 100–10. On 'gymnastic games' see Jacomuzzi, S., *Gli sport*, Vol. II (Turin, 1965), pp. 648–52.

36. Anonymous, Lettera al Presidente della Commissione Sua Eccellenza Il Ministro, in *Bollettino ufficiale del Ministero dell'Istruzione*, Vol. 2 (1893), p. 4105.

37. Mosso, A., 'I giuochi olimpici a Roma?', in *Nuova Antologia* (1905), p. 422.

38. Martini, M., *Correre per essere. Origini dello sport femminile in Italia* (Rome, 1996) pp. 42–43.

39. Anonymous, 'Arona', in *Bollettino della Società Ginnastica Milanese Forza e Coraggio* (October 1889), pp. 2–3.

40. See Giuntini, S., 'La donna e lo sport in Lombardia durante il fascismo', paper presented at the Congress on Donna Lombarda (The Woman of Lombardy) 1860–1945 (Milan, 1989).

41. On Giulia De Luca see Martini, M., *Correre per essere. Origini dello sport femminile* (Rome, 1996), pp. 43–46.

42. Ibid., p. 43.

43. Ibid., pp. 40–41.

44. Candela, S., *I Florio* (Palermo, 1986), p. 329.

45. De Giorgio, *Le italiane*, p. 246.

46. Jacomuzzi, S., *Gli Sport*, Vol. 3 (Turin, 1965), p.208.

47. See De Giorgio, *Le italiane*, p. 246, and *La Bicicletta* (September 1895).

48. See Martini, *Correre per essere*, pp. 32–33.

49. On this and other 'sporting' performances at La Scala see Macchi, G., 'Lo Sport alla Scala', in *Lo sport fascista*, 2 (1929), pp. 73–78.

50. ISTAT (ed.), *Sommario di statistiche storiche dell'Italia 1861–1975* (Rome, 1976), pp.10–14.

51. Ballerini, F., *La Federazione ginnastica italiana e le sue origini* (Rome, 1931), p. 214.

52. Ibid., p. 92.

53. Giacometti-Ferrari, D., *Relazione del Comitato Centrale Femminile al XVI Consiglio Federale* (Rome, 16 March 1903).

54. Ballerini, *La Federazione ginnastica*, p. 232.

55. Giuntini, S., 'Sport e storia. La nascita della ginnastica femminile', in *Ricerche storiche*, 3 (1989), p. 705. Data about Turin are in Caimi, N.G., 'Mens sana in corpore sano', in *La Donna*, 19 (1907), pp. 24–25.

56. Valle, G., 'Echi del Concorso di Milano', in *Il Ginnasta*, 9 (1902).

57. There is a detailed report on the contest in Florence in 1904 in *Il Ginnasta*, 12 (1906).

58. On the contest in Vercelli see Ballerini, *La Federazione ginnastica*, pp. 211–212; on the contest in Venice see *Il Ginnasta*, 6 (1907).

59. Conditions in the South of Italy were denounced in Guerra, R., 'L'indirizzo della ginnastica sociale in Italia', in *Il Ginnasta*, 9 (1906).

60. Di Ferdinando, 'Contro le bugie del cosmetico', pp. 48–49. On the contest in Turin see *La Gazzetta del Popolo* (14 May 1911), which contains a dramatic description of the race.

61. On Rosetta Gagliardi see Martini, *Correre per essere*, pp. 67–68.

62. Giuntini, S., *Società ginnastica milanese Forza e Coraggio. Alle origini dello sport a Milano* (Milan, 1994), p. 98.

63. Giuntini, 'La donna e lo sport', pp. 2–3.
64. On Rosina Ferrario see 'La prima aviatrice italiana', in *Margherita*, 3 (1913), p. 46; on Vittorina Sambri see Martini, M., 'Sesso debole? Un secolo di smentite', in *Lo Sport Italiano*, 8–9 (1994), pp. 40–41.
65. See Martini, 'Sesso debole?', p. 41, and Martini, *Correre per essere*, pp. 67–69.
66. Martini, *Correre per essere*, pp. 72–74.
67. Ibid., p. 72. On early mountaineering see De Giorgio, *Le italiane*, p. 248.
68. On the hygienic conditions of Italian schools and gymnasiums at the beginning of the twentieth century see Ferrara, *L'Italia in palestra*, pp. 188–194.
69. Italian versions of their books, Moebius's *Inferiorità mentale delle donna* and Weininger's *Sesso e carattere*, were published in Turin in 1904 and 1912 respectively.
70. Sighele, S., *La donna e l'amore* (Milan, 1913), p. 28.
71. See Papini, G., *Maschilità* (Florence, 1915).
72. Most of D'Annunzio's writings present negative images of women as vamps.
73. See *Programma politico futurista* (1913).
74. See Marinetti's manifesto *In questo anno futurista* (29 November 1914).
75. Marinetti's manifesto *Simultaneità nello sport*, published in the 1930s, includes a long list of bizarre 'simultaneous sports', sometimes involving spectators, such as boxing and wrestling during foot races; cycling at the lowest possible speed while spectators throw fruit, eggs or water at the cyclists; and playing golf while spectators shoot at the ball. See Gori, G., 'Supermanism and culture of the body in Italy. The case of Futurism,' in *The International Journal of the History of Sport, 1* (1999) pp. 160–61.
76. All the 'air dances' performed by Giannina Censi were aimed at offering the same sensations that pilots felt in flight. *Fisicofollia* was a theatrical way of freely expressing Futurist values by means of the body. On Futurist ballets see Marinetti's manifesto *La danza futurista* (1917); Bentivoglio, L., *La danza moderna. Da Isadora Dancan a Maurice Béjart* (Milan, 1977); Lista, G., *Lo spettacolo futurista* (Florence, 1989); Bonfanti, E., *Il corpo intelligente – Giannina Censi* (Turin, 1995).
77. See Marinetti's manifesto *Contro l'amore e il parlamentarismo* (1910).
78. Vianello, A., 'Donne: a voi!', in *Roma futurista*, 1–2 (1919), p. 2.
79. The Futurists favoured divorce and sex outside marriage, including sex with prostitutes, as is clearly demonstrated in such texts as Tavolato, I., 'Elogio della prostituzione', in *Lacerba* (1 May 1924). D'Annunzio political proclamations are collected in D'Annunzio, G., *Per la più grande Italia* (Rome, 1939). On D'Annunzio see Ledeen, M.A., 'Gabriele D'Annunzio: l'avventura fiumana e la politica del Novecento', and Nolte, E., 'L'impresa di Fiume e lo scenario europeo', in *Nuova Storia Contemporanea*, 5 (1999), pp. 15–21 and pp. 23–30 respectively.
80. On women's movements before the First World War see De Grazia, V., *Le donne nel regime fascista* (Venice, 1993), pp. 42–54.
81. Laura Casartelli, one of the pioneers of the Italian women's movement, wrote a long article stigmatising the lack of participation by women in political parties, with the exception of some Catholic and socialist women: see *Almanacco della Donna Italiana*, 1 (Florence, 1920).
82. D'Annunzio, G., *Per la più grande Italia*, p. 183. See also De Felice, R., *La carta del Carnaro nei testi di Alceste De Ambris e di Gabriele D'Annunzio* (Bologna, 1973).
83. See Mondello, E., *La nuova italiana. La donna nella stampa e nella cultura del Ventennio* (Rome, 1987), p. 166.

Chapter 3

1. Matilde Serao, one of the most famous women writers in Italy, supported this ideology in her *Parla una donna. Diario femminile di guerra, maggio 1915–marzo 1916* (Milan, 1916). On the peculiarities of Italian feminism see, for example, Parla, G., *L'avventurosa storia del femminismo* (Milan, 1976) and De Giorgio, M., *Le italiane dall'Unità ad oggi* (Rome–Bari, 1993), pp. 508–11.
2 On the *Arditi* see note 6 to Chapter 1 of this volume.

3. De Grazia, V., *Le donne nel regime fascista* (Venice, 1993), pp. 9 and 57–58. On Regina Terruzzi see Detragiache, D., 'Du socialisme au fascisme naissant: formation et itinéraire de Regina Terruzzi', in Thälmann, R. (ed.), *Femmes et fascismes* (Paris, 1986), pp. 41–66.

4. See Lazzero, R., *Il Partito Nazionale Fascista* (Milan, 1985). On the early years of the Fascist women's movement see Detragiache, D., 'Il fascismo femminile da San Sepolcro all'affare Matteotti, 1919–1924', in *Storia contemporanea*, 2 (1983), pp. 211–51.

5. RADA (pseudonym), 'Una pagina d'italianità sportiva', in *Lo sport fascista*, 1 (1931), pp. 39–40.

6. On the assault in Verona see Bertoldi, S., *Camicia nera* (Milan, 1994), pp. 111–12; on the assault near Udine see Macciocchi, M.A., *La donna 'nera'. 'Consenso' femminile e fascismo* (Milan, 1976), pp. 16–17.

7. Margherita Sarfatti and Elisa Majer Rizzioli were fascinated by Mussolini's personality, and remained loyal to him even when they fell into disfavour in later years. See De Grazia, *Le donne nel regime fascista*, pp. 57–61.

8. During a Fascist celebration in the Piazza San Lorenzo in Rome opponents started shooting into the crowd from their hiding places, but these women reportedly did not panic and helped the wounded: see Garibaldi, L., *Le soldatesse di Mussolini* (Milan, 1997), p. 34.

9. Ibid., pp. 34–35.

10. Mattazzi, G. (ed.), *Benito Mussolini. Breviario* (Milan, 1997), p. 148.

11. See *La Provincia di Padova* (1–2 June 1923).

12. Mattazzi, *Benito Mussolini. Breviario*, p. 150–51.

13. Montesi-Festa, I., 'La Donna italiana', in *La Donna italiana*, 1 (1924), p. 6.

14. On anti-Fascism see: *Enciclopedia dell'antifascismo e della Resistenza* (Milan, 1968–89); Colombo. F., and Feltri, V., *Fascismo, antifascismo* (Milan, 1994); De Luna, G., *Donne in oggetto. L'antifascismo nella società italiana (1922–1939)* (Turin, 1995).

15. There is a brief profile of the powerful intellectual Margherita Sarfatti in De Grazia, *Le donne nel regime fascista*, pp. 305–08. See also Sarfatti's biographical book *Acqua passata* (Bologna, 1955).

16. Scaramuzza, E., 'Professioni intellettuali e fascismo. L'ambivalenza dell'Alleanza muliebre culturale italiana', in *Italia contemporanea*, 151 (1983), p. 121.

17. Mussolini, B., *My Autobiography* [ghostwritten by Arnaldo Mussolini and edited by Richard Washburn Child] (New York, 1928). On the relationship between Mussolini and his mother see also Passerini, L., *Mussolini immaginario. Storia di una biografia 1915–1939* (Rome–Bari, 1991), pp. 90–93.

18. In 1928 about 1.5 million of the most prolific Italian families became the object of an investigation by a group of researchers. The report on this research, which was co-ordinated by Corrado Gini of the Central Institute of Statistics, claimed that it showed that 'inelegant' (!) and short women with broad hips were the most prolific: De Grazia, *Le donne nel regime fascista*, p. 79.

19. On this speech see Fusco, G.C., *Le rose del ventennio* (Milan, 1974), p. 29.

20. See Mussolini, B., *Opera Omnia*, edited by Susmell, E. and D., vol. 22 (Florence, 1951–80), p. 360.

21. On women's employment and specific laws see De Grazia, *Le donne nel regime fascista*, pp. 229–71.

22. Ibid., p. 125.

23. Ibid., pp. 107–11.

24. *Critica Fascista* (1933), pp. 303–04.

25. Gianfranceschi, L., 'Un'italiana fra i semidei ariani', in Panathlon International Club Valdarno Inferiore (ed.), *Proceedings of the National Prize 'L'atleta nella Storia' 1988 Ondina Valla, Montecatini Terme, 22 October 1989* (Montecatini, 1989), p. 29.

26. SVIMEZ (ed.), *Un secolo di statistiche italiane Nord e Sud, 1861–1961* (Rome, 1961), p. 79.

27. On the numbers of children in different social classes under Fascism see Livi-Bacci, M., *A History of Italian Fertility during the Last Two Centuries* (Princeton, NJ, 1972), pp. 176–273.

28. See *Il Popolo d'Italia* (30 May 1934).

29. Part of an interview with Mussolini by the journalist Bodil Borge Ciccarella in Rome, November 1934, now in Mattazzi, *Benito Mussolini. Breviario*, p. 149.

30. Ibid.

31. Momigliano, E. (ed.), *Tutte le encicliche dei Sommi Pontefici* (Milan, 1973), p. 932; English version from the Catholic Truth Society's edition of *Quadragesimo Anno* (London, 1932).

32. Pende, N., *Bonifica umana razionale e biologia politica* (Bologna, 1933), p. 102.

33. Parla, G., *L'avventurosa storia del femminismo* (Milan, 1976), p. 96.

34. Scaramuzza, 'Professioni intellettuali e fascismo', pp.121–23.

35. Meldini, P., *Sposa e madre esemplare. Ideologia e politica della donna e della famiglia durante il fascismo* (Rimini–Florence, 1975), p. 266.

36. See Mondello, E., *La nuova italiana. La donna nella stampa e nella cultura del Ventennio* (Rome, 1987), pp. 58–59.

37. Ibid., p. 189.

38. Ceserani, G.P., *Vetrina del Ventennio 1923–1943* (Rome–Bari, 1981), p. 132. On Fascist propaganda disseminated through the mass media see Cannistrato, P.V., *La fabbrica del consenso. Fascismo e mass-media* (Rome–Bari, 1975); Castronovo, V., and Tranfaglia, N., *La stampa italiana nell'età fascista* (Rome–Bari, 1980); Saracinelli, M., and Totti, N., *L'Italia del Duce: l'informazione, la scuola, il costume* (Rimini, 1983).

39. Mondello, *La nuova italiana*, p. 83.

40. Mattazzi, *Benito Mussolini. Breviario*, pp. 152–153.

41. On the militarisation of women in the colonies see Salvatici, S., 'Modelli femminili e immagine della donna attraverso la fotografia della stampa fascista', in *AFT–Rivista di Storia e Fotografia*, 18 (1993), p. 51; there are data on the mobilisation of women in Italy in ISTAT (ed.), *Compendio statistico* (Rome, 1938), p. 16.

42. De Grazia, *Le donne nel regime fascista*, pp. 351–52.

43. In Mussolini, B., *Opera Omnia*, Vol. 28, pp. 204–05.

44. Loffredo, F., 'Politica della famiglia e della razza', in *La difesa della razza*, 2 (1939), p. 31.

45. Loffredo, F., *Politica della famiglia* (Milan, 1938), pp. 361 and 370. On Loffredo's anti-feminist theories see Macciocchi, *La donna 'nera'*, pp. 107–14.

46. Macciocchi, *La donna 'nera'*, pp. 91–93.

47. See De Felice, R., *Mussolini il Duce*, Vol. 2 (Turin, 1981), pp. 73–82; De Grazia, *Le donne nel regime fascista*, p. 351; Mondello, *La nuova italiana*, p. 61.

48. See Castellani, M., 'La nazione armata. Donne professioniste e laureate ausiliarie civili', in *Almanacco della donna italiana* (1936), pp. 52–54.

49. There is a vivid description of this parade in De Grazia, *Le donne nel regime fascista*, pp. 300–01; the official documents are in ACS, Presidenza del Consiglio dei Ministri, 1937–1939, dossier 1.7.7493.

50. SVIMEZ, *Un secolo di statistiche*, p. 79.

51. Mattazzi, *Benito Mussolini. Breviario*, p. 155.

52. De Grazia, *Le donne nel regime fascista*, p. 147.

53. Gozzini, L., 'La donna nel quadro del Regime', in *Almanacco della donna italiana*, 20 (1939), pp. 39–45.

54. See Macciocchi, *La donna 'nera'*, p. 102, and Mondello, *La nuova italiana*, p. 111.

55. See Mattazzi, *Benito Mussolini. Breviario*, p. 152.

56. ACS, Presidenza del Consiglio dei Ministri, 1940–41, dossiers 582 and 586.

57. On the Civil Code see Ungari, P., *Storia del diritto di famiglia in Italia* (Bologna, 1974), pp. 217–43; Bessone, M., Alpa, G., D'Angelo, A., Ferrando, G., and Spallarossa, M.R., *La famiglia nel nuovo diritto. Principi costituzionali, riforme legislative, orientamenti della giurisprudenza* (Bologna, 1995), pp. 8–15.

58. The young man in question was one Oberdan Freddosio, who won the *Littoriali* of Culture in 1940. The quotation is from Freddosio, O., *Il regime per la razza* (Rome, 1941), p. 87.

59. Macciocchi, *La donna 'nera'*, pp. 87–88.

60. De Grazia, *Le donne nel regime fascista*, p. 375.

61. Parla, *L'avventurosa storia del femminismo*, pp. 100–02.

62. De Grazia, *Le donne nel regime fascista*, p. 368.

63. Garibaldi, *Le soldatesse di Mussolini*, p. 105.

64. Ibid., pp. 31–89.

65. On women fighters for the RSI and the auxiliary groups see Giuliani, F., *Donne d'Italia. Le ausiliarie della RSI* (Rome, 1952); Lazzero, R., *Le Brigate Nere* (Milan, 1963); Scarpellini, A., *La Repubblica Sociale Italiana nelle lettere dei suoi caduti* (Rome, 1963); Pisanò, G., *Storia delle Forze Armate della RSI* (Milan, 1967); Fraddosio, M., 'La mobilitazione femminile: i gruppi Fascisti repubblicani femminili e il SAF', in *Annali della Fondazione Luigi Micheletti*, 2 (1986); Garibaldi, *Le soldatesse di Mussolini*. On partisan women see, for example, Banfi-Malaguzzi, D., *A Milano nella resistenza* (Rome, 1964); Battaglia, R., *Storia della Resistenza italiana* (Turin, 1964); Bilenchi, R., *Cronache degli anni neri* (Rome, 1984).

Chapter 4

1. For a general view of the history of the FIMS under Fascism see Barbieri, F., *Evoluzione storica della federazione medico sportiva italiana. Cinquant'anni di attività della FIMS* (Siena, 1979), pp. 5–36.

2. Poggi-Longostrevi, G., *Cultura fisica della donna ed estetica femminile* (Milan, 1933), p. 241.

3. A long list of the foreign works that influenced Italian sports medicine can be found in Chiurco, G.C., *L'Educazione fisica nello stato fascista. Fisiologia e patologia chirurgica dello* sport (Siena, 1935), pp. 59–61.

4. Ibid., pp. 78–84.

5. Some of these scientists presented their research at FIMS congresses, for example, Davì, M., 'Bevande eccitanti e sport', in FIMS (ed.), *Atti del I Congresso Nazionale di Medicina dello Sport, Roma 19-20-21 Aprile 1932* (Rome, 1932), and Cassinis, U., 'Caffè, caffeina, cloruro di sodio nel rendimento lavorativo', in FIMS (ed.), *Atti del Congresso Internazionale di Medicina dello Sport, Torino–Roma, Settembre 1933* (Rome, 1934).

6. See FIMS (ed.), *Atti del Congresso Internazionale di Medicina dello Sport, Torino–Roma, Settembre 1933* (Rome, 1934).

7. Cassinis, U., 'Può la donna fare lo sport?', in FIMS (ed.), *Atti del I Congresso Nazionale di Medicina dello Sport, Roma 19-20-21 Aprile 1932* (Rome, 1932), pp. 5–13.

8. Viziano, A., 'Prime indagini sull'influenza dello sport femminile sul periodo mestruale e considerazioni generali', in FIMS (ed.), *Atti del I Congresso Nazionale di Medicina dello Sport, Roma 19-20-21 Aprile 1932* (Rome, 1932), pp. 15–33.

9. Giaccone, A., 'Può la donna fare dello sport durante il periodo mestruale?', in FIMS (ed.), *Atti del I Congresso Nazionale di Medicina dello Sport, Roma 19-20-21 Aprile 1932* (Rome, 1932), p. 43.

10. Viziano, 'Prime indagini', p. 33.

11. Zanetti, M., 'Deve la donna praticare lo sport?', in FIMS (ed.), *Atti del I Congresso Nazionale di Medicina dello Sport, Roma 19-20-21 Aprile 1932* (Rome, 1932), p. 37.

12. Ibid., p. 38.

13. Lugnani, 'L'educazione fisica della donna col metodo Mensendick', in FIMS (ed.), *Atti del I Congresso Nazionale di Medicina dello Sport, Roma 19-20-21 Aprile 1932* (Rome, 1932), pp. 47–52.

14. Baglioni, S., 'Donna e sport', in FIMS (ed.), *Atti del I Congresso Nazionale di Medicina dello Sport, Roma 19-20-21 Aprile 1932* (Rome, 1932), pp. 53–58.

15. Rabino, A., 'Rapporti tra mestruazione e fatica sportiva', in *Atti del Congresso Internazionale di Medicina dello Sport, Torino-Roma Settembre 1933* (Rome, 1934), pp. 453–54.

16. Lentini, S., 'L'educazione fisica e sportiva per l'avvenire della razza', in FIMS (ed.), *Atti del II Congresso Nazionale di Medicina dello Sport, Bologna 24-26 Ottobre 1935* (Bologna, 1936), p. 65.

17. Ibid., p. 67.

18. Tranquilli-Leali, E., 'Casistica sui traumatismi sportivi', in FIMS (ed.), *Atti del II Congresso Nazionale di Medicina dello Sport, Bologna 24-26 Ottobre 1935* (Bologna), 1936, pp. 20–21.

19. Montanari-Reggiani, M., 'L'assistenza sanitaria e medico-sportiva nei G.U.F', in FIMS (ed.), *Atti del III Congresso Nazionale di Medicina dello Sport, Genova 12-14 Novembre 1938* (Rome, n. d.), pp. 405–09.

20. Pende, N., 'La sorveglianza medica per gli esercizi ginnici sportivi nei campeggi e nelle colonie', in ONB (ed.), *Atti ufficiali del I Convegno Nazionale dei Medici dell'ONB, Roma 2-4 Febbraio*

1930 (Rome, 1932). Among the most influential of Pende's writings were *Bonifica umana razionale e biologia politica* (Bologna, 1933) and *Trattato di biotipologia umana individuale e sociale* (Milan, 1939).

21. Poggi-Longostrevi, G., 'La donna e lo sport. La università dello sport femminile: l'atletica leggera', in *La Gazzetta dello Sport* (8 October 1930).
22. Poggi-Longostrevi, G., 'I lavori del Gran Consiglio Fascista. La delicata questione dello sport femminile affrontata: la donna non deve essere distolta dalla sua missione fondamentale', in *La Gazzetta dello Sport* (18–19 October 1930).
23. Poggi-Longostrevi, *Cultura fisica della donna*, pp. 232–41.
24. Chiurco, *L'Educazione fisica nello stato fascista*, pp. 69–70.
25. Loffredo, F., *Politica della famiglia* (Milan, 1936).
26. Poggi-Longostrevi, G., *Medicina sportiva* (Milan, 1940), pp. 99–113.
27. Ibid., p. 102.
28. Chiurco, *L'Educazione fisica nello stato fascista*, pp. 52–53.
29. Pius XI, 'Lettera al Cardinale Vicario', in *Civiltà Cattolica*, 2 (1928), pp. 367–72.
30. The Holy Office issued its denunciation of eugenic and sexual education on 21 March 1931.
31. 'B.P.', 'La donna e l'atletismo', in *L'Osservatore Romano* (16 May 1934).
32. De Grazia, V., *Le donne nel regime fascista* (Venice, 1993), p. 293.
33. The athlete Ondina Valla has described how she was noticed and recruited at her primary school in Bologna, and discussed her coaches, in Artom, S., and Calabrò, A.R., *Sorelle d'Italia. Quattordici Grandi Signore raccontano la loro (e la nostra) storia* (Milan, 1989), pp. 273–79.
34. ONB (ed.), *Norme programmatiche e regolamentari per le organizzazioni delle 'piccole e giovani italiane'* (Rome, n. d.), p. 6.
35. See also Gori, G., 'Sports Medicine and Female Athleticism in the Years of the Fascist Regime', in Terret, T. (ed.), *Sport and Health in History: Proceedings of the Fourth ISHPES Congress, Lyon 16–22 July 1997* (Sankt Augustin, 1999), pp. 192–201.

Chapter 5

1. Motti, L., and Rossi-Caponeri, M., *Accademiste a Orvieto. Donne ed educazione fisica nell'Italia fascista 1932–1943* (Ponte San Giovanni, 1996), pp. 45–46.
2. Mussolini, B., 'Discorso agli universitari fascisti', in *La Nuova Scuola Italiana*, 1 (25 December 1923).
3. See, for example, Bonetta, G., *Storia della scuola e delle istituzioni educative* (Florence, 1997); Bonetta, G., 'Genesi e formazione della concezione scolastica gentiliana', in Spadafora, G. (ed.), *Giovanni Gentile. La pedagogia. La scuola* (Rome, 1997); Genovesi, G., *Storia della scuola in Italia dal Settecento a oggi* (Rome–Bari, 1998).
4. Gentile, G., *Il problema scolastico del dopoguerra* (Naples, 1919), p. 8.
5. Genovesi, *Storia della scuola in Italia*, p. 227.
6. Ibid.; see also De Grazia, V., *Le donne nel regime fascista* (Venice, 1993), pp. 213–214.
7. De Grazia, *Le donne nel regime fascista*, p. 214
8. Ibid., pp. 211–12.
9. De Felice, F., *Mussolini il Duce. Gli anni del consenso 1929–1936* (Turin, 1974), p. 189.
10. Bottai, G., *La Carta della Scuola* (Milan, 1939); Gentili, R., *Bottai e la riforma fascista della scuola* (Florence, 1979); Charnitzky, J., *Fascismo e scuola. La politica scolastica del regime (1922–1943)* (Florence, 1996). On Bottai see Guerri, G.B., *Giuseppe Bottai, fascista* (Milan, 1996). On Jewish students see Ostenc, M., *L'éducation en Italie pendant le fascisme* (Paris, 1980), pp. 356–61.
11. Bottai, *La Carta della Scuola*, pp. 209–10; see also Rossi, G., *Educazione fascista* (Milan, 1942), p. 191.
12. In Bertone, G., *'I figli d'Italia si chiaman balilla.' Come e cosa insegnava la scuola fascista* (Rimini–Florence), 1975, pp. 161–76. This volume contains many similar examples of compositions written by schoolchildren during the Fascist era.
13. Ferretti, L., *Il libro dello sport* (Rome–Milan), 1927, p. 84.

14. Salvatorelli, L., and Mira, G., *Storia d'Italia nel periodo fascista*, Vol. I (Milan, 1972), pp. 523–29.
15. See Sica, M., *Storia dello Scoutismo in Italia* (Florence, 1987).
16. On FASCI see Fabrizio, F., *Storia dello sport in Italia. Dalle società ginnastiche all'associazionismo di massa* (Rimini–Florence, 1977), pp. 40–49.
17. Ferretti, *Il libro dello sport*, p. 171.
18. See *Annali dell'Italia Cattolica 1925* (Milan, 1926), pp. 216–19.
19. ONB (ed.), *Opera nazionale Balilla per l'Assistenza e l'Educazione Fisica e Morale della gioventù. Norme legislative e regolamentari* (Rome, 1927), p. 38.
20. Motti and Rossi-Caponeri, *Accademiste a Orvieto*, p. 24.
21. *Rassegna Femminile Italiana*, 1 (1925), p. 3.
22. Betti, C., *L'Opera Nazionale Balilla e l'educazione fascista* (Florence, 1983), p. 160. See also PNF (ed.), *Il Partito fascista e le sue opere 'I fasci femminili'* (Milan, 1929), pp. 13–26.
23. Pomba, G.L. (ed.), *La civiltà fascista illustrata nella dottrina e nelle opere*, Vol. 8 (Turin, 1928), p. 604.
24. Majer-Rizzioli, E., 'I fasci femminili italiani', in *Almanacco della donna italiana 1926* (1927), p. 279. See also Diby (pseudonym), 'La donna nel partito fascista', in *La Scuola Fascista*, 17 (1929).
25. PNF (ed.), *Il Gran Consiglio del Fascismo nei primi quindici anni di vita* (Bologna, 1938), p. 354.
26. ONB (ed.), *Bollettino dell'Opera Nazionale Balilla* (1 January 1930), p. 3; ONB (ed.), *Bollettino dell'Opera Nazionale Balilla* (1 November 1932), p. 12.
27. Mondello, E., *La nuova italiana. La donna nella stampa e nella cultura del Ventennio* (Rome, 1987), pp. 121–22. On Catholic women's associations see the ample bibliography in Di Cori, P., 'Storia, sentimenti, solidarietà nelle organizzazioni femminili cattoliche dall'età giolittiana al fascismo', in *Nuova DWF*, 10–11 (1979), p. 84.
28. On the problematic relations among Ricci, Mussolini and other leading members of the PNF see Ferrara, P., *L'Italia in palestra. Storia, documenti e immagini della ginnastica dal 1833 al 1973* (Rome, 1992), pp. 228–40. See also Teja, A., 'Le fascisme entre éducation physique et sport', in Krüger, A. and Trangbaek, E. (eds), *The History of Physical Education and Sport from European Perspectives* (Copenhagen, 1999), pp. 249–66.
29. ONB–Comitato Provinciale di Vicenza (ed.), *Norme e programmi dell'O. N. Balilla* (Vicenza, 1930), pp. 58–59.
30. Camera dei Deputati (ed.), *La legislazione fascista 1929–1934* (Rome, 1934), p. 1444.
31. Ibid.
32. ACS, Segreteria Particolare del *Duce*, Carteggio riservato, 1922–1943, b. 31, f. 242/R; *Starace*, 1.
33. See Finocchiaro, S., 'Il Foro Mussolini', unpublished paper presented at the fourth CESH Congress on the History of Sport in Europe, Florence, 2–5 December 1999. Comparative research suggests that the programmes of physical education and sport in schools in Italy and France were very similar: see Terret, T., and Vescovi, R., 'L'éducation physique à l'école primaire dans l'entre-deux guerres. Une comparaison des systèmes français et italiens', in Kruger, A., and Trangbaek, E. (eds), *The History of Physical Education and Sport from European Perspectives* (Copenhagen, 1999), pp. 269–83.
34. Paulin, E., *La ginnastica del lattante* (Trieste, 1935).
35. On the Italian Fascist influence on Nazi organisations see Krüger, A., 'Fasci e croci uncinate', in *Lancillotto e Nausica. Critica e storia dello sport*, 1–2 (1991), pp. 88–101.
36. On Baden-Powell and the ONB see Sica, *Storia dello Scoutismo*, p. 191, and Betti, *L'Opera Nazionale Balilla*, p. 169.
37. ONB (ed.), *La capo-squadra piccola italiana* (Milan, 1935), p. 8.
38. The pamphlet was ONB (ed.), *Norme regolamentari per le piccole e giovani italiane* (Rome 1931); the second edition was ONB (ed.), *Norme programmatiche e regolamentari per le organizzazioni delle 'Piccole e Giovani Italiane'* (Rome, n.d.).See also Ostenc, *L'éducation en Italie pendant le fascisme*, pp. 254–61.
39. In the same year there were 65,000 men filling equivalent posts in the ONB's affiliates for boys and young men. See Campagnuolo, E., *L'Opera Balilla e l'educazione fisica* (Portici, 1937), p. 42.

40. See ONB (ed.), *Programmi d'insegnamento e d'esame di educazione fisica per alunni ed alunne delle scuole elementari e medie pubbliche e private e per i privatisti in genere* (Rome, n. d.).
41. Ibid., pp. 7–8 and 13.
42. Ibid., pp. 8–9 and 13–14.
43. Ibid., pp. 9–11.
44. Ibid., pp. 14–15.
45. Ibid., pp. 11–12.
46. Ibid., pp. 15–16.
47. Ferrara, *L'Italia in palestra*, p. 254.
48. Betti, *L'Opera Nazionale Balilla*, pp. 162–79.
49. On the *Sabato Fascista* see Del Buono, O. (ed.), *Eja, eja, eja, alalà* (Milan, 1971), p. 64; Salvatorelli, L., and Mira, G., *Storia d'Italia nel periodo fascista*, Vol. 2 (Milan, 1972), p. 318.
50. Ferrara, *L'Italia in palestra*, p. 246
51. PNF (ed.), *Foglio di disposizioni n. 905* (15 November 1938); Rossi, *Educazione fascista*, p. 184.
52. PNF (ed.), *Foglio di disposizioni n. 1,377* (3 August 1939).
53. See Betti, *L'Opera Nazionale Balilla*, pp. 176–79; and Ostenc, *L'éducation en Italie pendant le fascisme*, pp. 381–84.
54. Guerri, G.B., (ed.), *Rapporto al Duce* (Milan, 1978), p. 5.
55. Del Boca, A., Legnani, M., and Rossi, M.G., *Il regime fascista. Storia e storiografia* (Rome–Bari, 1995), pp. 11–12.
56. PNF (ed.), *Foglio di disposizioni n. 38* (26 December 1939).
57. *Il Ginnasta*, 10 (1921); and Fabrizio, *Storia dello sport in Italia*, p. 114.
58. Fabrizio, F., *Sport e fascismo. La politica sportiva del regime 1924–1936* (Rimini–Florence, 1976), pp. 35–36.
59. Ferretti, *Il libro dello sport*, p. 110.
60. Ibid.
61. Ibid., pp. 111–12. See also Impiglia, M., and Lange, P., 'Goliardi in gara. I Giochi mondiali universitari prima delle Universiadi', in *Lancillotto e Nausica. Critica e storia dello sport*, 1 (1997), pp. 8–39.
62. The Charter is given in full in Fabrizio, *Sport e fascismo*, pp.39–43.
63. ACS, Segreteria particolare del *Duce*, Carteggio riservato, 1922–1943, b. 31, f. 242/R; *Riunione del Direttorio del 3/6/1931*; and Acquarone, A., *L'organizzazione dello Stato totalitario* (Turin, 1965), p. 180.
64. ACS, Segreteria particolare del *Duce*, Carteggio riservato, 1922–1943, b. 31, f. 242/R, 1, *Relazione 11/7/1931*.
65. Ibid. See also Betti, *L'Opera Nazionale Balilla*, pp. 164–65.
66. Fabrizio, *Sport e fascismo*, p. 97.
67. See Gori, G., *L'atleta e la nazione. Saggi di storia dello sport* (Rimini, 1996), pp. 97–139.
68. Caporilli, P., *L'educazione giovanile nello stato fascista* (Rome, 1930), pp. 159–60.
69. De Betta, G., 'L'evoluzione dei littoriali', in *Lo sport fascista*, 4 (1936), pp. 43–45.
70. Ibid., p. 45
71. Ferrara, *L'Italia in palestra*, p. 44.
72. De Grazia, *Le donne nel regime fascista*, pp. 222–24.
73. ISTAT (ed.), *Compendio statistico italiano, 1947–48*, Vol. 2 (Rome, 1948), p. 168.
74. Ibid.
75. Ibid.
76. Benedettini-Alferazzi, P., 'La donna in regime fascista: l'assistenza e i fasci femminili', in *Almanacco della donna italiana 1933* (1934), pp. 137–54.

Chapter 6

1. Anonymous, *Colonie alpine per i fanciulli poveri, Relazione morale, fisiologica ed economica del 2° esperimento 1873* (Turin, 1895), pp. 6–7 and 16; Anonymous, *Colonie alpine per i fanciulli*

poveri, Relazione e rendiconto della stagione estiva 1875 (Turin, 1896), p. 6. These are referred to respectively as *Relazione 1873* and *Relazione 1875* in later notes.

2. Jocteau, G.C., *Ai monti e al mare. Cento anni di colonie per l'infanzia XIX, XX* (Milan, 1990), p. 22.

3. *Relazione 1873*, p. 9, and *Relazione 1875*, p. 14.

4. For example, the Turin co-operative alliance, founded in 1902, created numerous children's health resorts for its affiliated organisations; by 1927, under the control of Fascism, it was providing places for about 600 children every summer: see Jocteau, *Ai monti e al mare*, pp. 38–9.

5. ISTAT (ed.), *Annuario* (Rome, 1916–22).

6. Sanjust, F., 'Un problema ricorrente – le colonie estive', in *Assistenza d'oggi*, 1 (1950), p. 6.

7. Ibid.

8. Lo Monaco-Aprile, A., *La protezione della maternità e dell'infanzia* (Rome, 1934), p. 7.

9. De Grazia, V., *Le donne nel regime fascista* (Venice, 1993), pp. 55–67.

10. Parini, P., *I figli degli Italiani all'Estero in patria nell'anno XII* (1934), p. 8.

11. Jocteau, *Ai monti e al mare*, p. 45.

12. Ibid. See also Deganutti, V., *L'alimentazione nelle colonie estive* (Padua, 1939); Roatta, G.B., *La leggenda del sole, del mare e della montagna, ossia del clima qualunque* (Bologna, 1940); Pignatari, M., 'Colonie estive della GIL. Identità di criteri direttivi', in *Gioventù del Littorio*, 8 (1941); PNF (ed.), *Ginnastica nelle colonie climatiche* (Rome, 1942); Monterisi, F., 'Le colonie marine e montane', in *Quaderni Italiani*, 5 (1943); ONB (ed.), 'Guida per le direttrici e vigilatrici delle colonie climatiche', in *Posta da campo*, 711 (1944).

13. Betti, C., *L'Opera Nazionale Balilla e l'educazione fascista* (Florence, 1984), p. 127.

14. PNF (ed.), *Il Partito Fascista e le sue opere 'I fasci femminili'* (Milan, 1929), pp. 28–29.

15. PNF (ed.), *Colonie Fasciste della provincia di Pavia. Come sorsero – come funzionano* (Pavia, 1930), p. 12.

16. Anonymous, 'Primo anno di vita della colonia *Duce*', in *Il Popolo di Romagna* (22 December 1930).

17. PNF (ed.), *Il Partito Fascista e le sue opere 'I fasci femminili'*, pp. 29–30.

18. PNF (ed.), *Bollettino del Comando Generale* (2 July 1934), p. 52.

19. PNF (ed.), *Bollettino del Comando Generale* (26 July 1933), pp. 40–46.

20. *Circolare n. 100-3/13* (24 February 1938).

21. GIL (ed.), *Bollettino quindicinale della GIL*, 10 (1938), p. 6.

22. PNF (ed.), *Il Partito Fascista e le sue opere 'I fasci femminili'*, pp. 30–31.

23. Ilvento, A., 'Colonie estive', in *Maternità ed Infanzia*, 5 (1927), p. 4; Anonymous, 'La vita in colonia', in *Maternità ed Infanzia*, 4 (1927), p. 79.

24. PNF (ed.), *Il Partito Fascista e le sue opere 'I fasci femminili'*, pp. 33–34 and 38.

25. Diaz, G., 'Che cosa si chiede ad una direttrice di colonia per bambini', in *Bollettino della Croce Rossa Italiana*, 1 (1921); see also Anonymous, 'La vita in colonia', pp. 78–84.

26. Collina, P., 'Donde è nata e come funziona una colonia marina', in *Argento vivo: campeggio dei fasci giovanili bolognesi di combattimento, Rimini 10–20 Agosto, anno 10* (Bologna, 1932), p. 27.

27. PNF (ed.), *Norme per il funzionamento delle colonie climatiche temporanee e diurne* (Rome, 1932), pp. 11–18.

28. PNF (ed.), *Bollettino del Comando Generale* (13 April 1933), p. 228.

29. Collina, 'Donde è nata e come funziona una colonia marina', p. 26.

30. PNF (ed.), *Regolamento per la ginnastica nelle colonie climatiche, anno XIX* (Rome, 1941), pp. 4–5.

31. See photographs in Jocteau, *Ai monti e al mare*, pp. 24–25, 70–71, 93 and 147.

32. PNF (ed.), *Regolamento per la ginnastica nelle colonie climatiche*, pp. 6–9.

33. Ibid., p. 6.

34. Ibid., pp. 9–11.

35. Ibid., pp. 16–17.

Chapter 7

1. De Puppi, R., *La funzione educativa dell'Opera Nazionale Balilla. Conferenza tenuta dal co. dott. R. de Puppi, presidente del Comitato Provinciale dell'Opera Nazionale Balilla, nell'aula Magna del R.. Istituto Tecnico di Udine li 5 febbraio 1929 – VII* (Udine, 1929), p. 25.
2. Ferretti, L., *Il libro dello sport* (Rome–Milan, 1928), pp. 94–95.
3. ONB (ed.), *Leggi–Regolamenti–Decreti* (Brescia, 1931), p. 50.
4. ONB (ed.), *Bollettino dell'Opera Nazionale Balilla* (1 May 1930), p. 2.
5. Ibid.; see also Betti, C., *L'Opera Nazionale Balilla e l'educazione fascista* (Florence, 1983), pp. 154–155.
6. Motti, L., and Rossi-Caponeri, M. (eds), *Accademiste a Orvieto. Donne ed educazione fisica nell'Italia fascista 1932–1943* (Ponte San Giovanni, 1996), p. 24.
7. Under Decree no. 1227, dated 28 August 1931.
8. Di Donato, M., *Indirizzi fondamentali dell'educazione fisica moderna* (Rome, 1962), p. 182.
9. See the 29 written and 31 oral testimonies of former students in Motti and Rossi-Caponeri, *Accademiste a Orvieto*, pp. 75–148 and 149–176.
10. *Bollettino Ufficiale dell'ONB* (15 May 1933).
11. Motti and Rossi-Caponeri, *Accademiste a Orvieto*, p. 109.
12. Benetti-Brunelli, V., 'Una visita all'istituto superiore femminile fascista di educazione fisica in Orvieto', in *Rivista pedagogica*, 3 (1932), p. 447.
13. Arcamone, G., 'L'Accademia Femminile Fascista di educazione fisica', in *Rivista dell'istruzione elementare*, 3 (1932), pp. 68–74.
14. Motti and Rossi-Caponeri, *Accademiste a Orvieto*, pp. 94–97.
15. Ibid., p. 98.
16. Cammarata, A., 'Fucine della Rivoluzione: le accademie dell'ONB', in *Lo sport fascista*, 5 (1936), pp. 13–15.
17. Ibid., p. 15.
18. In 1936 there were 496 female physical education teachers. If one compares this figure to its equivalent for 1921 – 386 teachers –the increase may seem unimpressive. However, it should be recalled that there was no institution for the training of new female teachers of the subject from 1923 to 1932, and that many female teachers left the profession, whether to get married or for other reasons.
19. Motti and Rossi-Caponeri, *Accademiste a Orvieto*, p. 148, note 195; PNF–GIL General Command (ed.), *Accademie e Collegi della GIL, ammissioni anno XX–XXI* (Rome, 1942), pp. 8–9.
20. See Lombardi, E., *Quand'ero piccola* (Dronero–Rome, 1991–92), and … *Da grande* (self-published 1993).
21. Motti and Rossi-Caponeri, *Accademiste a Orvieto*, pp. 111–16.
22. Ibid., pp. 75–176.
23. Ibid., p. 192.
24. Lombardi, … *Da grande*, p. 26; ACS, Segreteria particolare del *Duce*, Carteggio ordinario, dossier 540.186, '*Orvieto, Accademia femminile della GIL*'.
25. ASO, *Archivio Lombardi*, b. 2 and 4.
27. Ibid., dossier B.
28. Bargellini, P., *L'Accademia femminile di Orvieto* (Rome, n.d.), pp. 12–13.
26. See *FILMLEXICON degli autori e delle opere*, Vol. I (Rome, 1959).
29. Motti and Rossi-Caponeri, *Accademiste a Orvieto*, pp. 218–19.
30. Trangbaek, E., 'Purity of Heart and Strength of Will' – The Role of Female Teachers in the Modern Sports Movement', in Trangbaek, E., and Krüger, A. (eds), *Gender and Sport from European Perspectives* (Copenhagen, 1999), pp. 45 and 61–62. See also Trangbaek, E., 'Gender in Modern Society: Femininity, Gymnastics and Sport', *International Journal of the History of Sport*, 3 (1997), pp. 136–56; Müller, A., 'Women in Sport and Society', in Riordan, J., and Krüger, A. (eds), *The International Politics of Sport in the Twentieth Century* (London, 1999), pp. 121–49.

Chapter 8

1. On the OND in general see Tannenbaum, E.R., *L'esperienza fascista: Cultura e società in Italia dal 1922 al 1945* (Milan, 1974); De Grazia, V., *Consenso e cultura di massa nell'Italia fascista. L'organizzazione del Dopolavoro* (Rome–Bari, 1981); Cannistraro, P. V., *La fabbrica del consenso. Fascismo e mass-media* (Rome–Bari, 1975).
2. Ferretti, L., *Il libro dello sport* (Rome–Milan, 1928), p. 141–42.
3. Guerri, G.B., *Fascisti. Gli italiani di Mussolini. Il regime degli italiani* (Milan, 1995), p. 178.
4. Stefanelli, R., *Dopolavoro. Norme pratiche per i dirigenti* (Turin, 1940), p. 12.
5. Ferretti, *Il libro dello sport*, p. 133.
6. Guerri, *Fascisti*, p. 178; see also De Grazia, *Consenso e cultura di massa*, p. 64.
7. Stefanelli, R., *Dopolavoro*, p. 40.
8. Ibid., pp. 70–72.
9. Ibid., p. 39.
10. De Grazia, *Consenso e cultura di massa*, pp. 178–184.
11. Stefanelli, *Dopolavoro*, pp. 75–87.
12. On *volata* see Starace, A., *L'opera nazionale Dopolavoro* (Milan, 1933), p. 49; De Grazia, *Consenso e cultura di massa*, pp. 201–02; Pivato, S., *I terzini della borghesia. Il gioco del pallone nell'Italia dell'Ottocento* (Milan, 1990), pp. 9–10; Impiglia, M., 'The Volata Game: When Fascism Forbade Italians to Play Football', in Krüger, A., and Teja, A, *La comune eredità dello sport in Europa. Atti del I Seminario Europeo di Storia dello Sport, Roma 29 November–1 December 1996* (Rome, 1997), pp. 420–26.
13. Ferretti, *Il libro dello sport*, pp. 132–42 and 241–43.
14. Fabrizio, F., *Storia dello sport in Italia. Dalle società ginnastiche all'associazionismo di massa* (Rimini–Florence, 1997), p. 119.
15. De Grazia, *Consenso e cultura di massa*, p. 206.
16. De Felice, R., *Mussolini il duce. Gli anni del consenso 1929–1936* (Turin, 1974), p. 219.
17. De Grazia, *Consenso e cultura di massa*, p. 206.
18. OND (ed.), *Annuario* (1937), p. 43.
19. Cuesta, U., *Il libro del Dopolavoro* (Rome, 1937), p. 123.
20. De Grazia, *Consenso e cultura di massa*, p. 196.
21. OND, *Annuario* (1937), p. 45.
22. De Grazia, *Consenso e cultura di massa*, pp. 202–03.
23. On Italian participation in the 1936 Winter Olympics see Gori, G., *L'atleta e la nazione. Saggi di storia dello sport* (Rimini, 1996), pp. 105–12.
24. PNF, *Foglio di Disposizioni No. 93* (29 February 1940).
25. De Grazia, V., *Le donne nel regime fascista* (Venice, 1993), pp. 281–82.
26. See Giuntini, S., 'La donna e lo sport in Lombardia durante il fascismo', in Torcellan, N., and Gigli-Marchetti, A. (eds), *Donna lombarda 1860–1945* (Milan, 1992), p. 601.
27. *Bollettino del lavoro e della previdenza sociale* (31 July to 31 December 1930), p. 61.
28. De Grazia, *Consenso e cultura di massa*, p. 141.
29. De Grazia, *Le donne nel regime fascista*, p. 242.
30. De Grazia, *Consenso e cultura di massa*, p. 91.
31. Ibid., p. 51.
32. *Civiltà Cattolica*, 3 (1938), p. 230.
33. De Grazia, *Consenso e cultura di massa*, p. 203.
34. Much of the information in this section is from Tonelli, A., *E ballando ballando. La storia d'Italia a passi di danza (1815–1996)* (Milan, 1998).
35. Anonymous, 'Ancora sui balli e il Dopolavoro', in *Diario Cattolico* (18 July 1936).
36. De Rensis, R., *Mussolini musicista* (Mantua, 1927), pp. 14–15.
37. Anonymous, 'Sobrietà', in *Il Popolo di Romagna* (4 July 1926).
38. Anonymous, 'Crisi di costume?', in *Critica fascista* (1 July 1931), p. 249.
39. See, for example *Critica fascista* (15 February 1930), p. 69; (1 January 1933), pp. 18–19; (15 April 1938), p. 190.

40. See, for example, Anonymous, 'Italia e americanismo', in *Critica fascista* (15 April 1928); Anonymous, 'Ordini del giorno', in *Il Popolo d'Italia* (23 July 1935); Anonymous, 'La radio. Musica da ballo', in *Il Popolo d'Italia* (14 August 1938).
41. De Grazia, *Consenso e cultura di massa*, pp. 238–48.

Chapter 9

1. See, for example, *La Gazzetta dello Sport* and *Lo sport fascista*.
2. Anonymous, 'La principessa sportiva', in *Lo sport fascista*, 4 (1929), pp. 19–22.
3. Boin, V., 'La bella coppia sportiva', in *Lo sport fascista*, 12 (1929), pp. 6–9; Petacco, A., *Regina. La vita e i segreti di Maria José* (Milan, 1997), pp. 96–9.
4. Gerbi, G., 'Successi italiani nel "golf"', in *Lo sport fascista*, 9 (1930), pp. 75–76; Crivelli-Massazza I., 'Sport e Maternità', in *Lo sport fascista*, 7 (1929), p. 73.
5. Set (pseudonym), 'Le emule italiane della "diva Suzanne"', in *Lo sport fascista*, 3 (1929), pp. 80–83.
6. Nadi, N., 'La scherma femminile', in *Lo sport fascista*, 11 (1929), pp. 41–43. See also Ferralasco-Nadi, R., *Nedo Nadi l'alfiere dello sport delle tre armi nel mondo* (Genoa, 1969).
7. Anonymous, 'Scherma femminile a Firenze', in *Lo sport fascista*, 6 (1931), p. 70.
8. On the *Mille Miglia* see Gori, G., 'The Classic *Mille Miglia* Motor-Race (1927–1938): Tourism and Propaganda in the Years of the Fascist Regime', in Krüger, A., Teja, A. and Trangbaek, E. (eds.) *Europäische perspektiven zur geschitchte von sport, kultur und tourismus* (Berlin 2000), pp. 77–86.
9. On Avanzo see Martini, M., *Correre per essere. Origini dello sport femminile in Italia* (Rome, 1996), p. 90, and the item cited in note 10.
10. Avanzo, M.A., 'La donna al volante', in *Lo sport fascista*, 1, (1928), p. 65.
11. See Simri, U., *A Concise World History of Women's Sports* (Netanya, 1983), pp. 47–48.
12. *La Gazzetta dello Sport* (27 March 1921). See also Anonymous, 'L'Olimpiade della Grazia tra le palme e i fiori della Costa Azzurra', in *Lo sport Illustrato* (3 April 1921) and Brambilla, A., Donne nello Sport a Busto Arsizio (Busto Arsizio, 1999).
13. Simri, *Concise World History of Women's Sports*, p. 52. Most information on female athleticism has been taken from Martini, M., *Storia dell'atletica italiana femminile*, an unfinished work divided into seven booklets that were enclosed in issues of the specialist magazine *Atletica*, published by the FIDAL, in 1995, 1996 and 1997. See also Giuntini, S., *Società ginnastica milanese Forza e Coraggio. Alle origini dello sport a Milano* (Milan, 1994), pp. 97–109.
14. See *Il Giornale d'Italia* (8 May 1923) and Roffarè, L., 'Atletesse', in *La cultura fisica*, 7 (1952), p. 1.
15. On Andreina Sacco see Teja, A., *Educazione fisica al femminile. dai primi corsi di Torino di ginnastica educativa per le maestre (1867) alla ginnastica moderna di Andreina Gotta-Sacco (1904–1988)* (Rome, 1995), pp. 67–120.
16. On Marina Zanetti's involvement in sports medicine see the section 'The FIMS and female athleticism' in Chapter 4 of the present volume.
17. Martini, *Storia dell'atletica*, p. 54; De Giorgio, M., *Le italiane dall'Unità a oggi* (Rome–Bari, 1993), p. 252.
18. Bononcini, T., 'Atletica leggera', in *Lo sport fascista*, 3 (1928), pp. 32–33; Tifi, C., 'Le "Piccole Italiane" in maglia azzurra', in ibid., pp. 58–60.
19. Simri, *Concise World History of Women's Sports*, p. 51.
20. Martini, *Correre per essere*, pp. 58–60.
21. *Il Ginnasta*, 6–7 (1922), pp. 11–18.
22. Sacco, A., 'Come abbiamo vinto a Dinard', in *Lo sport fascista*, 8 (1929), pp. 98–99.
23. Lazotti, U., 'Le giovani italiane', in *Lo sport fascista*, 6 (1928), pp. 49–52.
24. Pius XI, 'Lettera al Cardinale Vicario', in *Civiltà Cattolica*, 2 (1928), pp. 367–72; Anonymous, 'Contro l'atletismo femminile. Lettera di Pio XI al Cardinale Vicario di Roma', in *Lancillotto e Nausica. Critica e storia dello sport*, 3 (1988), pp. 79–81.
25. De Grazia, V., *Le donne nel regime fascista* (Venice, 1993), p. 293.

26. See Gori, G., 'Supermanism and the Culture of the Body in Italy: The Case of Futurism', in *International Journal of the History of Sport*, 1 (1999), pp. 159–65.

27. See *Azione Muliebre*, 6 (1926), p. 358.

28. Anonymous, 'Collaborazione delle Abbonate. Che pensate degli sports femminili', in *Azione Muliebre*, 6 (1931), pp. 368–76.

29. *Almanacco della donna italiana 1934* (1934), p. 255.

30. Giuntini, S., 'La donna e lo sport in Lombardia durante il fascismo', in Torcellan, N., and Gigli-Marchetti, A. (eds), *Donna lombarda 1860–1945* (Milan, 1992), pp. 597 and 600.

31. Ibid., p. 598; Isidori Frasca, R., ... *E il duce le volle sportive* (Bologna, 1983), pp. 98–102. On the uncomfortably 'chaste' sportswear for women, see the interviews in Chapter 11.

32. Martini, *Storia dell'atletica*, p. 56.

33. Cassinis, U., 'Denatalità e sport femminile', in *Il Ginnasta*, 5 (1937), pp. 11–14.

34. Ibid., p. 12.

35. Martini, *Storia dell'atletica*, pp. 60–95.

36. On the university *Agonali* see the section 'Physical education and sport in universities' in Chapter 5.

37. ONB (ed.), *Gli Agonali dell'Opera Balilla* (1936), pp. 3–29.

38. Zanetti, M., 'Ragazze del Littorio', in *Lo sport fascista*, 8 (1937), pp. 12–14.

39. Banti, A., 'L'importanza dello spettacolo sportivo', in *Lo sport fascista*, 1 (1936), p. 31.

40. Ferrauto, E., 'L'educazione fisica giovanile', in *Lo sport fascista*, 4 (1936), p. 10.

41. PNF (ed.), *Annuario sportivo dei Giovani Fascisti e delle Giovani Fasciste – A. XV* (Varese, 1938). The next volumes in the series were PNF–GIL (eds), *Annuario generale sportivo della GIL dell'anno XVII* (Varese, 1940); PNF–GIL (eds), *Annuario sportivo generale della GIL – A. XVIII* (no place of publication stated, 1941); PNF–GIL (eds), *Annuario sportivo generale – A. XIX* (Bergamo, n.d. but probably in 1942).

42. Anonymous, *Piccolo prontuario magistrale 1940–41* (Rome, 1940), p. 31.

43. ONB (ed.), *IV concorso per giovani italiane. Programma–regolamento* (Milan, n.d.), pp. 1–22.

44. Pizzi, E., 'La donna al Concorso Ginnico del Dopolavoro', in *Lo sport fascista*, 8 (1937), pp. 11–13; Pizzi, E., 'La G.I.L. e l'O.N.D.', in *Lo sport fascista*, 1 (1938), pp. 15–17.

45. Favre, S., 'Ludi Juveniles e Littoriali, vaglio delle promesse della stirpe', in *Lo sport fascista*, 6 (1939), pp. 13–15.

46. Anonymous, *Piccolo prontuario*, p. 5.

47. PNF (ed.), *Annuario sportivo generale della GIL–a. XVIII* (Rome, 1941), p. 10.

48. PNF–Comando Generale GIL–Servizio Educazione Fisica (eds), *Concorsi Nazionali di Educazione Fisica A. XX. Programma–Regolamento* (Rome, 1942).

49. Ölrich, H., '"Whoever has Youth has a Future": Youth Sports Activities of the Berlin–Rome Axis from 1940 to the Foundation of the European Youth Association in 1942', in Krüger, A. and Teja, A. (eds), *La comune eredità dello sport in Europa: Proceedings of the 1st European Seminar for the History of Sport, Rome 29 November to 1 December 1996* (Rome, 1997), pp. 427–39.

50. Some information on 1942 can be found in Tedeschi, L.L., 'Il VII raduno dello sport femminile a Torino', in *Lo sport della GIL*, 4 (1942), p. 5.

51. Martini, *Storia dell'atletica*, pp. 96–112; GIL (ed.), *Annuario sportivo 1937–41* (as detailed in note 41 above); AMOVA. (ed.), *Medaglie d'oro al valore atletico 1934–1985* (Rome, 1987).

52. Cataldo, G., 'Gli sportivi col ma', in *Il Littoriale* (29 April 1930).

53. Fabbri, A.M., *Giovinezza, giovinezza ...* (Milan, 1964), pp. 18–25.

54. Bassetti, R., *Storia e storie dello sport in Italia. Dall'Unità a oggi* (Venice, 1999), p. 110.

55. Simri, *Concise World History of Women's Sports*, pp. 67–88.

Chapter 10

1. Pierazzi, R.M., 'Piccola posta', in *Cordelia*, 14 (1923), p. 669.

2. Barbacci, G., 'Per voi, donne italiane, che non nuotate ...', in *Lo sport fascista*, 4 (1929), pp. 32–37.

3. Bragaglia, A. G., 'Sport e bellezza;', in *Lo sport fascista*, 11 (1929), pp. 55–57.

4. Pensuti, M., 'La donna e lo sport', in *Lo sport fascista*, 4 (1930), pp. 99–101.

5. Anonymous, 'La gioventù femminile e lo sport', in *Matelda*, 13 (1921), pp. 227–28.
6. Patrizi, M., 'Un pò di galateo. Giuochi e sport', in *Fiamma Viva*, 12 (1929), p. 722.
7. Mondello, E., *La nuova italiana. La donna nella stampa e nella cultura del Ventennio* (Rome, 1987), pp. 111–12.
8. Guerri, G.B., *Fascisti. Gli italiani di Mussolini. Il regime degli italiani* (Milan, 1995), pp. 187–88.
9. De Grazia, V., *Le donne nel regime fascista* (Venice, 1993), p. 287; Tonelli, A., *E ballando ballando. La storia d'Italia a passi di danza (1815–1996)* (Milan, 1998), p. 211.
10. Poggi-Longostrevi, G., *Cultura fisica della donna ed estetica femminile* (Milan, 1933), p. 214.
11. She (pseudonym), 'Ondine americane', in *Lo sport fascista*, 3 (1933), pp. 66–68.
12. See, for example, Anonymous, 'Donne sportive in Germania', in *Lo sport fascista*, 4 (1933), pp. 58–60.
13. De Giorgi, M., *Le italiane dall'Unità a oggi. Modelli culturali e comportamenti sociali* (Rome–Bari), 1992, p. 264.
14. These received favourable comment in, for example, an anonymous article in *Fiamma Viva*, 6 (1935), pp. 210–11.
15. Livia (pseudonym), 'La moda di noi sportivi', in *Lo sport fascista*, 6 (1933), pp. 52–56.
16. On the Ministry's activities see De Felice, R., *Mussolini il duce. Lo stato totalitario 1936–1940* (Turin, 1981), pp.109–12, and Cannistrato, P.V., *La fabbrica del consenso* (Rome–Bari, 1975), pp. 101–73.
17. Saracinelli, M., and Totti, N., *L'Italia del Duce. L'informazione, la scuola, il costume* (Rimini, 1983), p. 137; Mondello, *La nuova italiana*, p. 115. On Italian fashion and its relationship with international fashion, see Gnecchi-Ruscone, A., 'La moda italiana dalla crisi alla guerra', in AAVV (eds), *Anni trenta. Arte e cultura in Italia* (Milan, 1983); Giordani-Aragno, B., 'La moda italiana fra le due guerre', in Comune di Roma–Ipsoa (eds), *L'economia italiana tra le due guerre* (Rome 1984).
18. ONB (ed.), *La capo-squadra piccola italiana* (Rome, 1936), pp. 57–58.
19. Mussolini, V., 'Emancipazione del cinema italiano', in *Cinema*, 9 (1936); see also De Felice, R., *Mussolini il duce. Lo Stato totalitario 1936–1940*, pp. 107–08.
20. Biondi, M., and Borsotti, A., *Cultura e fascismo. Letteratura, arti e spettacolo di un ventennio* (Florence, 1996), p. 388.
21. Ibid., pp. 393–94. On Fascism and films in general see also Argentieri, M., *L'occhio del regime. Informazione e propaganda nel cinema del fascismo* (Florence, 1979); Redi, R. (ed.), *Cinema italiano sotto il fascismo* (Venice, 1979); Brunetta, G. P., *Storia del cinema italiano. Il cinema del regime 1929–1945* (Rome, 1993).
22. ISTAT (ed.), *Sommario di statistiche storiche 1926–1985* (Tivoli, 1986), p. 59.
23. *Annuario del cinema italiano 1939–1942* (Rome, 1943).
24. Mattazzi, G., *Benito Mussolini. Breviario* (Milan, 1997), p. 243.
25. Favre, S., 'Venti ragazze hanno provato a Rapallo il costume azzurro. A chi l'onore di indossarlo a Berlino?', in *Lo sport fascista*, 3 (1936), p. 35.
26. Campagnuolo, E., *L'opera balilla e l'educazione fisica* (Portici, 1937), p. 44.
27. Motti, L., and Rossi Caponeri, M. (ed.), *Accademiste a Orvieto. Donne ed educazione fisica nell'Italia fascista 1932–1943* (Ponte San Giovanni, 1996), pp. 203–04.
28. Favre, S., 'Sport e ginnastica per la salute e la bellezza della donna', in *Lo sport fascista*, 6 (1939), pp. 55–58.
29. Ibid., p. 59.
30. See Boccasile, G., *La signorina grandi firme* (Milan, 1981).

Chapter 11

1. On women's oral history in Italy more generally see Marcuzzo, C., and Rossi-Doria, A. (eds), *La ricerca delle donne. Studi femministi in Italia* (Turin, 1987); Società Italiana delle Storiche (ed.), *Discutendo di storia. Soggettività, ricerca, biografia* (Turin, 1990); Passerini, L., *Storie di donne e femministe* (Turin, 1991).

2. Information on Valla is mainly from Giovannini, A., 'La gara di Ondina Valla campione olimpionica vista e raccontata da lei', in *Lo sport fascista*, 9 (1936), pp. 17–19; Anonymous, 'Primato olimpionico delle atlete azzurre', in *Tutti gli Sports*, 33 (1936), p. 5; Dotti, R., 'La quercia di Ondina Valla', in *Stadio* (24 October 1958); Artom, S., and Calabrò, A.R., *Sorelle d'Italia. Quattordici Signore raccontano la loro (e nostra) Storia* (Milan, 1989), pp. 271–85; Dominici, F., 'Gli intramontabili – Ondina Valla. Oro a Berlino negli 80 ostacoli primatista nel lungo e nell'alto. La regina con le ali', in *Corriere dello Sport – Stadio* (1 April 1989); Panathlon International Club Valdarno Inferiore (ed.), *Proceedings of the National Prize 'L'atleta nella Storia' 1988 Ondina Valla, Montecatini Terme, 22 October 1989* (Montecatini, 1989), pp.1–32; Valla, O., 'Ondina Valla', in *Ternisport* (Terni, n.d.), p. 5.
3. De Grazia, V., *Le donne nel regime fascista* (Venice, 1993), p. 293.
4. Artom and Calabrò, *Sorelle d'Italia*, p. 275.
5. Ibid., p. 279.
6. Ibid., p. 280.
7. AMOVA (ed.), *Medaglie d'oro al valore atletico 1934–1985* (Rome, 1987), p. 1061. AMOVA is an association for holders of gold *Medaglie al Valore Atletico* (Medals for Atheltic Valour, the 'O' standing for 'd'Oro', '[in] gold'. On these and other medals see note 54 to Chapter 1 of the present volume.
8. Colonnelli, I.C., 'La donna italiana e lo sport', in *Lo sport fascista*, 9 (1940), p. 29; Giovannini, 'La gara di Ondina Valla', p. 19.
9. Artom and Calabrò, *Sorelle d'Italia*, p. 279.
10. Most of the information in this section is from Martini, M., *Correre per correre. Origini dello sport femminile* (Rome, 1996), and AMOVA, *Medaglie d'oro*.
11. See Castellini, R., 'Tatiana Fumagalli prima aviatrice italiana', in *Lo sport fascista*, 1 (1931), pp. 6–7.
12. See Mura (pseudonym), 'Ritorno di Gaby', in *Lo sport fascista*, 1 (1933), pp. 21–22.
13. De Giorgio, M., *La italiane dall'Unità a oggi. Modelli culturali e comportamenti sociali* (Rome–Bari, 1992), p. 259.
14. Gori, G., 'Supermanism and the Culture of the Body in Italy: the Case of Futurism', in *International Journal of the History of Sport*, 1 (1999), pp. 159–65.
15. Some of the information on Massone is taken from a leaflet published to accompany a section about her within the exhibition *Futurismo. I Grandi Temi 1909–1944* in Genoa a few years ago.
16. Enrile, E. (ed.), *Enciclopedia dello sport* (Rome, 1977), p. 1082.
17. See Colonnelli, G.C., 'I Littoriali femminili', in *Lo sport fascista*, 6 (1939), p. 39.

Chapter 12

1. Gori, G., 'Woman and Sport in Italy', in Christensen, K., Guttmann, A., and Pfister, G., *International Encyclopedia of Woman and Sport* (New York, 2001), pp. 597–601.
2. On women's sport in Italy since 1945 see, for example, Andreoli, P., *La donna e lo sport nella società industriale* (Rome, 1974); Salvini, A., *Identità femminile e sport* (Florence, 1982), pp. 33–48.
3. CONI (ed.), *I numeri dello sport. Atlante della pratica sportiva in Italia* (Florence, n.d.), p. 31.

INDEX

Page references for illustrations are in *italics*; those for notes are followed by n